THE AUDIENCE,
THE MESSAGE,
THE SPEAKER

THE AUDIENCE, THE MESSAGE, THE SPEAKER

SIXTH EDITION

JOHN HASLING
Professor Emeritus
Foothill College

Boston, Massachusetts   Burr Ridge, Illinois   Dubuque, Iowa
Madison, Wisconsin   New York, New York   San Francisco, California   St. Louis, Missouri

McGraw-Hill

A Division of The McGraw·Hill Companies

THE AUDIENCE, THE MESSAGE, THE SPEAKER

This book is printed on acid-free paper.

1 2 3 4 5 6 7 8 9 0 DOC DOC 9 0 9 8 7

ISBN 0-07-027027-9

This book was set in Palatino by Graphic World, Inc.
The editors were Marjorie Byers and Gwyneth Meeks;
the production supervisor was Richard A. Ausburn.
The cover was designed by Edward Butler.
Project Supervision was done by The Total Book.
The photo editor was Debra Hershkowitz.
R. R. Donnelley & Sons was printer and binder.

Cover photo by Rod Rolle/Gamma-Liaison

Library of Congress Cataloging-in-Publication Data

Hasling, John.
    The audience, the message, the speaker / John Hasling. -- 6th ed.
        p.   cm.
    ISBN 0-07-027027-9
    1. Public speaking.   I. Title.
PN4121.H267   1997
808.5′1--dc21   97-10840

http://www.mhhe.com

ABOUT THE AUTHOR

John (Jack) Hasling has retired after teaching speech communication for 27 years at Foothill College in Los Altos Hills, California. As Professor Emeritus he continues to be involved in campus activities and teaches a course occasionally. His recent interest is in children's literature, and this year his first collection of stories was published. He travels and lectures on a theme stressing the importance of reading out loud to children.

Jack Hasling received his M.A. from Sacramento State University in 1963, where he later became a lecturer in speech and coach of the debate team. In 1966 he accepted a position at Foothill College and taught there until his retirement. His primary area of expertise has always been public address, but he has also taught courses in group discussion, interpersonal communication, and radio broadcasting. In his earlier years he worked as an announcer and engineer at several Northern California radio stations. In 1980 he published a book with McGraw-Hill entitled *Fundamentals of Radio Broadcasting*.

In addition to teaching, Jack Hasling has been actively involved in faculty affairs at the state and local levels. He served as chairperson of the Foothill College Improvement of Instruction Committee, and later as president of the Academic Senate. He is a former member of the Commission on Instruction for the California Association of Community Colleges and is a charter member of the Bay Area Speech Teachers Association. He has also served as parliamentarian at several conventions of the California State Academic Senate.

PHOTO CREDITS

CONTENTS

PART TWO
THE MESSAGE   67

CHAPTER 12
SPEAKING WITH VISUALS   **180**

CHAPTER 13
MEETING ETHICAL STANDARDS   **197**

PREFACE

When I wrote the first edition of this textbook in 1971, my tools were a manual portable typewriter, scissors, paste, and white-out. I did not have access to duplicating equipment, so I sent my only copy of the manuscript to McGraw-Hill through the mail. I shudder when I think of how primitive our facilities were in those days, and I wonder how we ever got along without the word processor, copy machine, fax, e-mail, and the Internet. I reflect upon this bit of nostalgia because my intent is to have the 6th edition of *The Audience, The Message, The Speaker* be a vehicle for transporting the classical concepts of rhetoric into the twenty-first century.

Technology is not all that has changed in the past 27 years. We have significantly expanded our awareness of social behavior in a pluralistic society, and we have a greater understanding and appreciation for the role the listener plays in the communication process. This new edition, therefore, brings the textbook up to speed in three areas of consideration: computerized access to information in databases and on the World Wide Web, challenges and opportunities in relating to a culturally diverse audience, and the responsibility of listeners to fill their share of gaps in communication.

Computer Access to Information

One of the first things I had to learn when I began writing the 6th edition was how to footnote information acquired on the Internet. Actually, there was a good deal of catching up that I had to do in matters pertaining to computer access of information, and the process of doing that helped me to empathize with the struggles and frustrations that I knew students would be experiencing. There is a wealth of data that comes to us on a cathode ray tube, but learning the procedure is slow, crashes are frequent, downtime is lengthy, and computer availability is limited. For these reasons I did not drop from the new edition the methods of using the *Reader's Guide to Periodical Literature* and the other bound indexes and reference books.

Certainly the World Wide Web is a useful tool for research, and I want to encourage students to use it. But at the same time I want them to be discerning about the *quality* of the information they find. In Chapter 5 I express my concern that much of the data, interpretations, and viewpoints that are put on the Web may not have gone through the kind of editing process that is required for articles to appear in professional journals. Students who are serious about their education, their ethical standards, and their personal credibility should be aware of this limitation and not let their confidence in electronic wizardry short-circuit their critical judgment.

What has not changed in this edition is the emphasis placed on the need for the content of a speech to be substantive. Whether information is displayed on a computer screen or on a printed page, the student must be able to recognize specific facts and know how to employ them in supporting a thesis.

Relating to a Pluralistic Audience

A new feature of this edition of the textbook is a chapter on the audience in a pluralistic society. The subject has been mentioned before in previous editions under the heading of "audience analysis," but it has never received the thorough treatment that I believe it should have. Frankly it has been pretty much of a "hot potato" that many of us in the field of communication have been reluctant to touch. We know that cultural differences can profoundly affect the way an audience may react to a speech, but we have hesitated to say anything about it for fear of offending someone. Furthermore, we may not really be sure what to recommend, or how to advise a student to deal with a situation that involves addressing an audience when ethnic background might affect the reception of the message. Consequently, mistakes that could be avoided are made inadvertently by speakers.

The position I have taken comes from Aristotle's teachings that "the central task for the speaker is to find or make common ground with the audience." That may have been less difficult at a time when the audience consisted of 500 Greek citizens rather than a television audience of millions of people from hundreds of different cultures. Nevertheless, I believe that Aristotle would stick by that principle even in this time and place. To find the common ground is to find that which is reasonable. To exacerbate differences by exploiting the human weaknesses of hate, revenge, envy, and greed is to follow the path of demagoguery. By seeking the common ground of reason, it is possible for the speaker to gain respect, if not agreement, from everyone in the audience regardless of race, sex, religion, or cultural origin.

Of course, it is much easier to make generalizations than to be specific. There are some questions that do not have clear answers. For example, how do you find common ground with people whose perspective on racism—based upon their own personal experiences—is fundamentally different from your own? Is it likely that what you say in your speech is going to affect their thinking? I suggest that in such a case making forceful assertions from the podium may not be the best approach. To increase the rhetorical pressure when the opposition is rooted in emotional conviction can only make matters worse. The issue might be addressed more productively in small groups on an interpersonal basis, and not from the stance of what Teddy Roosevelt used to call "the bully pulpit."

Listening and Reacting

In previous editions of this text, emphasis has been placed on the efforts a speaker can make to overcome the careless listening habits of people in the audience. That emphasis is still there, but a chapter has been added in the 6th edition that calls attention to the responsibilities of the receiver of the message. What I have attempted to do is expand the scope of the text so that the whole issue of oral communication in a public setting is examined. Making the point that listening is active behavior is very much a part of public address as well as of interpersonal communication. We know that unfortunate social consequences can result when people who need to act on the information they hear "tune out" when they should be focused on the subject at hand. One clear example is that of a court trial when the life and property of a defendant rests on the attentiveness of the jury. My hope is that Chapter 4 will prepare students, who may never have the opportunity to give a speech, to serve the democratic process as quiet but competent decision makers.

Chapter 4 has been given the title "Listening and Reacting" for the specific reason that effective listening is not passive behavior. Receivers must regard themselves as active participants in the communication process. Good listening doesn't happen accidentally; an effort is required and skills need to be employed. Furthermore, the reaction of the listener has a very real effect on the sender of the message. It's important for people in the audience to recognize the extent to which their verbal and nonverbal responses influence the speaker.

McGraw-Hill and I would like to thank the following reviewers for their thoughtful insights: Martha Einerson, University of Idaho; Dayle Hardy-Short, Northern Arizona University; Vanessa Thompson, College of West Virginia; and Mike Ingram, Whitworth College.

This new edition of *The Audience, The Message, The Speaker* is as small as ever. The size has always worked well for me, and apparently it has for other instructors, too. As a group, those of us who teach public speaking tend to lean toward the loquacious side of the continuum, and we don't want a textbook that covers the whole field. It's better to have a little ball that we can pick up and run with. That has been my game plan for the past 27 years.

John Hasling

THE AUDIENCE,
THE MESSAGE,
THE SPEAKER

THE AUDIENCE

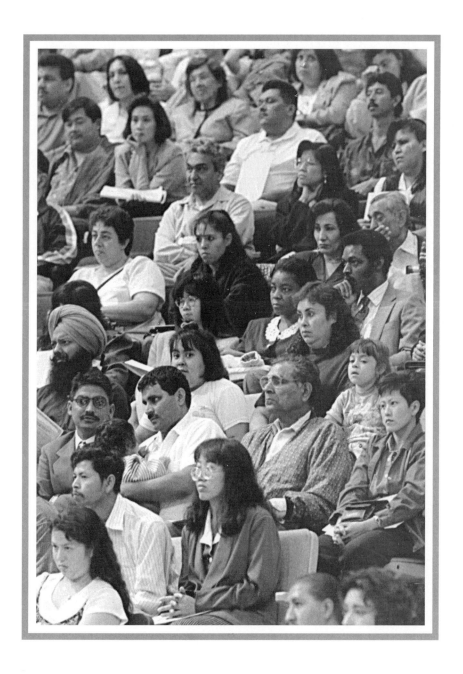

THE COMMUNICATION PROCESS

**AFTER READING THIS CHAPTER, YOU SHOULD
BE ABLE TO DO THE FOLLOWING:**

Understand the contributions Aristotle made to the art of rhetoric;
recognize the names of orators whose speeches have
influenced world history.

Explain how oral communication works and what forces affect the
transmission and reception of meaning.

Put together the components of communication and understand the
relationship between the speaker and the audience.

Start the process of preparing a speech by recognizing
the criteria for evaluation.

Our Constitution guarantees our rights to freedom of speech. This is a privilege that we are inclined to take for granted in the United States because it seems reasonably certain that the First Amendment will not be repealed. Indeed, the greatest danger to our freedom is more likely to be public apathy than government intervention. We could lose our right to free speech in a very real sense by not exercising it. If we become content to have others speak for us and to allow the positions and interests of the few to dominate public policy and law, we might just as well not have it at all. An important dimension of the First Amendment is that we also have the right to *listen*, if we will, and to evaluate what we hear. What *free speech* means is that we will be exposed to all kinds of viewpoints. We will hear false information as well as truth, and we must learn to separate one from the other. That is not always easy and requires that we keep informed on significant issues. Truth is never self-evident; if it were, there would be no need for us to study the art of persuasion. Our Constitution can guarantee that we have the right to speak our minds, but it cannot guarantee that anyone will listen. Although what we say may be true, there is no assurance that it will be accepted and believed. If we want to have influence over other people, our government officials, and those who control our institutions, we must be able to make our perception of the truth sound plausible. The capability for this comes more easily to some than to others, but the opportunity is available to all, regardless of sex, religion, nationality, or economic status. It is denied only to those who choose to remain silent.

We have been speaking and listening our whole lives. How effectively we have been doing these things may depend to some extent on our natural ability and inclinations, but it has a lot to do with the speaking and listening skills that we acquire.

In this text we will explore the fundamentals of the art of public speaking. We begin in this chapter with a brief look at the history of public speaking before moving into a study of the communication process. Next, the chapter presents an overview of the three essential elements of public speaking: the audience, the message, and the speaker. These three topics form the basic framework of the text. The chapter concludes with "Getting Started"—a checklist for effective public speaking.

THE HISTORICAL PERSPECTIVE

As far back as 2080 B.C. an aging pharaoh gave some advice to his son, Merykare, who would succeed him: "Be a craftsman in speech (so that) you mayest be strong. . . . The tongue is a sword . . . and speech is more valorous than fighting."[1]

The words had little practical application for the lives of his subjects, however, since the pharaoh was not a man who tolerated members of the general

---

[1] "Elba, Splendor of an Unknown Empire," *National Geographic,* December 1978, p. 750.

population's making speeches in the public square. It was, in fact, another 1,600 years before there appeared a social climate conducive to the study of public speaking. The first noteworthy scholar of the art was the Greek philosopher Corax, who began writing and teaching in about 480 B.C. At that time the Greek city-states were experimenting with a democratic form of government—a concept that was completely unheard of before then. There was a legal procedure that permitted people who were charged with a crime to defend themselves in court. The defendants, however, were not allowed to have an attorney; they had to plead the case themselves. This system created a need for instruction. Those who lacked communication skills sought the services of Corax and others like him to receive coaching in the art of public speaking. Corax originated some of the basic principles that we teach today. He laid the groundwork for the Greek scholars who were to follow—Socrates, Plato, and the most important contributor, Aristotle.

Aristotle and the Art of Rhetoric

Traditionally the speaker's art is referred to as *rhetoric*, and it was Aristotle who provided us with the best definition. He said, "Let rhetoric be defined as an ability, in each particular case to see the *available means of persuasion*. . . . This is the function of no other art, for each of the others is instructive and persuasive about its own subject. . . ."[2] In other words, the study of *how* to explain and persuade has subject matter of its own that is separate from the body of knowledge that is central to any particular discipline. It is for this reason that public speaking is taught as an individual subject.

The "available means of persuasion" refers primarily to the power of words to create mental images, to provide explanations, to introduce concepts, to organize ideas, and to offer supporting evidence. In the context of public speaking, the "available means of persuasion" also refers to vocal inflection, gesticulation, and every other aspect of oral delivery. Because there are so many variables, the best way to study rhetoric is to observe those who apply the art in an effective manner and to analyze what they are doing. This is precisely what Aristotle did in 320 B.C. and, subsequently, what other scholars have done in studying the art of rhetoric.

Aristotle's definition suggests that rhetoric is an applied art. It can add a practical dimension to your academic pursuits because it will help you to use the information you learn in other subject areas. In applying the art of rhetoric, you have an opportunity to pull together the principles inherent in the arts, humanities, and sciences so that you can see their interrelationships and how the ideas are interconnected. In the process of learning how to express what you know and how to influence other people, you will find that your education will begin to take on new significance.

[2]Aristotle, *On Rhetoric*, trans. George A. Kennedy, Oxford University Press, New York, 1991, pp. 36–37.

THE LEGACY OF PUBLIC ADDRESS

Much of the history of the world can be told in the words of the orators who spawned or guided significant social, political, and religious movements. The causes that were advocated have not always been beneficial to humanity or civilization; nevertheless, we have all been profoundly influenced by them:

431 B.C.: *Pericles,* presiding over Greece during the "golden age," delivered his eulogy called the "Funeral Oration" for the men who had died in battle during the Peloponnesian War. Under his leadership the Greek culture became the inspiration for Western civilization.

399 B.C.: *Socrates* defended his principles and answered charges of "corrupting the youth" before the Council of Five Hundred in his speech of defense called "The Apology." Though he was critical of the Sophists, who taught the art of persuasion, he himself spoke eloquently.

44 B.C.: *Marc Antony* faced a hostile audience after the assassination of Julius Caesar, but he reversed the sentiments of the people with oratory that "raised the stones of Rome" as he called for mutiny against Brutus.

1521: *Martin Luther,* after a series of disputes with the pope, appeared before Charles V at Worms and said, "Here I stand; I can do no other." His defiance of the Catholic Church resulted in the Reformation and the rise of the Protestant movement.

The first woman prime minister of India, Indira Gandhi, campaigned on the platform of abolishing poverty.

THE LEGACY OF PUBLIC ADDRESS

1775: *Patrick Henry* delivered his fiery address at St. John's Church in Richmond, Virginia, during the Revolutionary convention. His words rallied the colonial militia to confront the British forces at Lexington and Concord, signaling the start of the American Revolution.

1863: *Abraham Lincoln* spoke only briefly at the dedication ceremony in Gettysburg, Pennsylvania, but his words brought hope to a nation in the midst of a devastating Civil War. As Pericles had done, he honored the soldiers who had fallen on both sides during the battle.

1925: *Clarence Darrow* achieved his reputation for courtroom speaking with his defense of union organizer Eugene Debs. In a later trial he debated the famous orator and prosecuting attorney Williams Jennings Bryan when charges were brought against John Scopes for teaching the theory of evolution in public schools. Darrow lost the case but won the cause.

1932: *Adoph Hitler* used the beer halls of Munich as his forum and projected the Nazi party into power with his tirades against the Jews and the Bolsheviks. His flamboyant oratorical style is credited with the success of the movement.

1933: *Franklin Delano Roosevelt* reassured the nation by saying that "The only thing we have to fear is fear itself," during the great depression of the 1930s. His "fireside chats" brought him into the living rooms of homes all over the country and gave a boost to the infant industry of broadcasting.

1940: *Winston Churchill* gave hope and inspiration to the British people after the retreat from Dunkirk and assured them that they would achieve victory over the German war machine, even though he could offer nothing more than "blood, toil, sweat, and tears."

1961: *John F. Kennedy* challenged the American people by having them ask what they could do for their country. He kept Soviet missiles out of Cuba, prevented the fall of Berlin, launched the Apollo space program, and gave impetus to the cause of civil rights.

1963: *Martin Luther King* spoke of his dream from the steps of the Lincoln Memorial to a crowd of over 200,000 people. He raised the consciousness of the nation for the cause of racial equality and set the wheels in motion for civil rights legislation and freedom from discrimination.

1966: *Indira Nehru Gandhi* became the first woman prime minister of India, campaigning on the platform *Garibi Hatao*—"to abolish poverty." She reformed the banks and the constitution in her country.

1982: *Margaret Thatcher* served as Great Britain's prime minister for eleven years. Her speech to Parliament, "My Country Right or Left," established her reputation for toughness by standing firm in maintaining possession of the Falkland Islands.

To this list of orators, we could add many others from this century alone. From the United States, we could add the names of Susan B. Anthony, Oliver Wendell Holmes, Eleanor Roosevelt, George C. Marshall, and Adlai Stevenson— all of whom used the spoken word to influence thought and effect social changes. As students of public address we can learn about the practice of the art by studying the work of those who have applied it; however, we can also learn by examining the theory and principles.

THE FUNDAMENTALS OF COMMUNICATION

A writer, a book, and a reader provide a communication model. It is a basic and fairly simple model, but it is one that is useful to examine. It consists of a sender, a message, and a receiver—the three elements that are essential for human communication to take place. As the writer of the message, I am the sender. Your task as the receiver is to interpret what I write. The model is a simple one because I am not getting any immediate response from you. If we were in the same room, there would be another dimension, because messages would be flowing in both directions. Even if you were not saying anything, I would be getting feedback that would tell me something about the way you were reacting.

When people relate to one another face-to-face, we say that the communication is *transactional* (Figure 1-1): That means there are messages flowing in both directions simultaneously; you and the other person are both senders and receivers.[3] The term *transactional* does not mean that each person is *talking* at the same time; messages do not have to be *verbal*. A great deal of the meaning that we convey to other people is in the form of *nonverbal* messages. When you smile and nod your head you are saying, "I hear you, and I like what you say," just as clearly as you would be if you were to speak the words. Often, we forget that when we are in the presence of another person we are sending messages, whether we intend to or not; in fact, it is impossible for us *not* to communicate. Communication models can give you a picture of the process in which you participate every day of your life, whether you are aware of it or not, and they can show you how components vary from one situation to another. When you understand the nature of communication, you will have a better chance of knowing how to be intentional in what you do and say.

Making Ourselves Understood

If I speak or write to you without being able to hear you or see you, I have no way of knowing whether or not my message is being received. You might be reading the words on this page right now and understanding everything I

[3]Sylvia Moss and Stewart L. Tubbs, *Human Communication,* 6th ed., McGraw-Hill, New York, 1991, pp. 6–7.

FIGURE 1–1. A sender, a message, and a receiver. Communication is transactional when the receiver gives feedback.

mean; on the other hand, you could be staring at the words, with your thoughts a million miles away. In communication theory, anything that is causing you to be distracted from the message is called *noise.*

Noise

The interference we call *noise* can be of a physical nature or a psychological nature. If it's physical, in a private situation it might be something such as a smoky room that is causing you discomfort or a television program that you can see out of the corner of your eye while you are trying to read. In a public speaking situation it might be distractions caused by members of the audience who are rattling chairs, or a faulty sound system that squeals when the volume is turned up. Noise can also be of a psychological nature. For example, you may resent the fact that you have been assigned to read this chapter when there are other things you would much rather be doing, or there may be references in the book that remind you of experiences that are difficult for you to put out of your mind. Psychological noise could be any emotional feeling that competes with the cognitive reception of the message. Both the sender and the receiver could be aware of physical noise, but only the receiver would be affected by psychological noise.

Feedback

If I were in the same room with you and were trying to explain what I mean, we would have *two-way communication.* I would be able to observe physical noise distractions that might be interfering with your reception of the message, and I would be able to receive your verbal and nonverbal feedback. You might just nod your head as I talk, or you could respond verbally and say, "I know what you mean." If you had any difficulty in comprehending, you could say, "I don't understand that." Feedback is a very important part of the communication process because it enables the sender to correct for error or to clarify the message.

Meaning

When I write I use words to convey my meaning, and my assumption is that you as the reader will have an understanding of those words. But even if we both speak the same language I can never be sure that we attach the same meaning to the words. For example, I may talk about the *folklore* of the Hollywood movie industry, meaning the popular stories that describe its development and the people who played the principal roles. The dictionary says that *folklore* is "a body of widely accepted but *specious* notions about a place, a group, or an institution." We look up the word *specious*, and we find that the definition is "seemingly fair, attractive, sound, or true, but actually not so." My intention is to say that we can learn to understand an institution by studying its folklore; however, you might perceive the message to be that folklore obscures the reality of what actually happened, because the stories are untrue. Observations of this kind remind us that words can mean different things to different people. In other words, one meaning is contained in the mind of the person who initiates the message, but a different meaning may reside in the mind of the receiver. In "The Walrus and the Carpenter," Lewis Carroll relates how the self-centered Humpty-Dumpty says, "When I use a word, it means just what I choose it to mean—neither more nor less." What we (and the foolish egg) need to understand is that our attempts to communicate would be pointless if we did not consider the way the message is received.

Communication Models

The two-person model is fairly easy to understand, but models become complex when we add more people and vary the structure and purpose of the communication. When we do that, we are changing the *dynamics* of the event. That term could refer to the way people relate to one another, their communication skills, their attitude toward the topic, the intensity of their emotions, the physical environment, or anything else that influences what they say and do. Again, we can look at models to help us in our analysis.

Conversation Model

In an ordinary conversation, we say that the communication is *unstructured*—there are no formalized requirements placed upon any of the individuals to conform to any particular style, topic, or sequence of expressed thought. The only rules or guidelines imposed on people in a conversational model are those that social convention and common courtesy require, and the interaction is often more important than the content of the message (Figure 1-2). The dynamics become more complex, of course, as we introduce more people to the circle. In the case of a larger group, there may be one person to whom you relate differently, and that variation may affect the way the others relate to you. From your own experience in groups you are probably aware that what others do and what they say have a strong influence on your own behavior. If you perceive that people are interested and are listening to your ideas, you may elaborate more fully; if you believe they are bored or are disapproving, you might

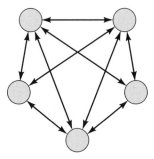

FIGURE 1–2. In unstructured communication personal contact may be more important than message retention.

hold back some ideas or even say nothing at all. Probably the best conversations you have are those in which the participants regard each other as equals. When one person attempts to introduce structure to the conversation by leading or directing the flow of communication, the dynamics change and the model begins to take a different shape.

Group Discussion Model

The model changes when people get together for a specific task. A group with an identified purpose might be called a *committee* or a *task force*, and it probably would have an *agenda* so that members stick to the topic that they are supposed to be addressing. An agenda puts limitations on the subject matter and gives focus and direction to the discussion (Figure 1-3). At such gatherings there is usually a specified time for the meeting to start and end, goals that the group is expected to accomplish, and probably a summary statement to review the decisions that have been made. Participants might make some preparation for a discussion of this kind, but they speak in an *impromptu* fashion—that is, they do not plan their remarks in advance, and they do not expect to speak in any particular order.

FIGURE 1–3. An agenda gives focus to a group discussion.

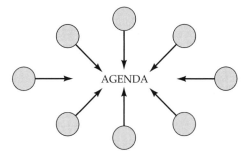

Public Speaking Model

We have a much different kind of model when one person has the attention of many people for an extended period of time. This is the one we call the *public speaking* model. There are a number of characteristics that distinguish this model from the others we have mentioned.

First is *structure*. This means the speaker has some sort of organizational framework in mind and has given thought to how the message will start, how the ideas will be developed, and what conclusion will be drawn at the end. The speaker will make an effort to focus on a central theme and not drift off onto tangents. Also, there is probably an expectation that audience members will hear the message all the way through to the end before asking questions or making their own remarks. These are characteristics that would not be appropriate in a social conversation or group discussion.

Second is *purpose*. Speakers need to maintain consistency in the main idea they express. If they are advocating a particular point of view, they should defend that position even if they get objections from members of the audience. It is inappropriate for a speaker to make structural modifications of a thesis while standing on the podium. Qualifications that need to be made in a speaker's main purpose should be thought of before the speech begins, rather than after.

Third is *posture*. In public speaking we *stand* when we speak. Assuming this posture may be the very thing you dislike most when you have to make a presentation, but there is a very good reason for doing so: When you address an audience you want to be the focus of attention. Standing is a nonverbal message that means, "I have the floor and I want you to listen until I am finished." Sitting down is an invitation for others to speak. There is an expectation on the part of the audience that the person who is standing wants to be heard and has something to say that is worthy of attention (Figure 1-4).

Fourth is *motivation*. This is one of the most important differences between public speaking and conversation. You converse with your friends because you enjoy the experience. You are not doing it for *their* benefit; you are doing for your own. When you make a presentation you may still be enjoying the

FIGURE 1–4. In the public speaking model, receivers allow the sender to "have the floor."

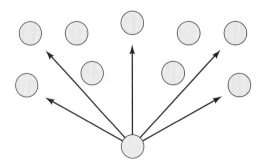

experience (certainly you want your audience to believe that you are), but it's the *audience's* interest that you serve more than your own. You don't stand up in front of a group of people because you have a burning desire to give a speech. You do it because you believe you have information that will be useful to those who hear it. That may be an important notion for you to keep in mind on those occasions when you really don't want to subject yourself to the anxiety of addressing an audience.

PUTTING IT TOGETHER

The elements of communication are interconnected. We'll be looking at each one individually, but we must keep in mind that they are all essential parts of a complete package. The principles of Aristotle provide the basis for just about everything that has been written on the subject of rhetoric since his time, and a great many textbooks, including this one, borrow heavily from his fundamental model of the audience, the message, and the speaker.

The Audience

The communication process does not begin until you have an audience—someone to receive the message that you send. You probably would not bother to talk in an empty room unless you were practicing your delivery. Only when someone else is present do we have the *potential* for communication, and even then we know that it might not occur unless the person is listening and has some capacity for understanding. Often speakers believe that what they mean to say is replicated in the listener's mind, but that is not always the case, as we noted earlier. You need to be realistic about your ability to communicate and understand that *the message* is *the message received.* What you intend your message to be is the way it is for you, but the message *received* is the way it is for the listener.

The Message

When people take courses in public speaking, they often feel that the most difficult part will be (1) conquering their fears of facing an audience and (2) learning the skills of delivery. While those two elements may initially be the significant concerns of students, the most important consideration in speechmaking is the quality of the message. As students begin to understand what public address is all about, they learn that the most fundamental and most difficult part is gathering the information and putting it together in a well-organized fashion.

   Content. In classical rhetoric the process of developing the content of speech is called the *inventio.* In contemporary language you could say it's *preparing the substance.* This is the time when you examine your resources to discover what information you want to include in the message. What you say should be something that you, yourself, have found to be interesting and significant, but, most important, it must be a message that will be useful in some way to the audience. The best source of material for a speech is the information that is already in your head, but that should be substantiated with ideas and evidence that you gather from your research. Take as much time as you need in the planning stage. Don't be motivated by what is the easiest thing to say; instead, think in terms of what will be of the greatest value to the audience.

Structure. As noted earlier, public speaking is a *structured* form of communication—the progression of thought forms a pattern and the ideas move in a logical sequence from the beginning to the end. These characteristics may not be prevalent in other forms of oral communication. In ordinary conversation, for example, we may ramble, go off on tangents, and perhaps never reach any kind of conclusion because we don't prepare for conversations as we prepare for speeches. Consequently, conversations may contain a limited amount of factual information, cumbersome expression of ideas, and many digressions to trivialities. The advantage in prepared and structured communication is that it is a faster and more comprehensible means of transmitting the message to the listener. Conversation can be fun and is often informative, but it is very time-consuming. Class discussion can also be stimulating and enjoyable, but, in terms of efficiency, a professor can cover more material in a shorter period of time by delivering a well-prepared lecture.

The Speaker

Seeking opportunities to speak in public may not be something that occupies a great deal of your time. However, even without looking for them, you will find that such occasions occur frequently, and they present you with a chance to give expression to beliefs or experiences you would like to share. Some occasions at which you could speak might be a graduation ceremony, a business meeting, a memorial service, or a town-hall gathering. The setting could be in a school, a church, a home, a conference room, or an auditorium. One excellent opportunity for developing proficiency in public speaking is to become a member of Toastmasters International. You probably will be able to find a local chapter by looking in your telephone directory.

But why would a person volunteer to give a speech in the first place? Sitting in the audience is much more comfortable than standing on a speaker's platform. What is it that causes people to accept the risk of criticism and rejection for the sake of expressing their ideas in a public forum? Do these people suffer less from speech fright than most people do? Not necessarily. They probably have the same anxieties as everyone else. Are they people who are smarter or better informed than others? Maybe, but maybe not. You might know just as much as they do. The difference is that they are *willing* to do it.

Willingness is an important factor in the process of developing public speaking skills. In order to make any progress at all, you must be able to set aside negative attitudes you might have and convince yourself that there is real value in the effort you will be called upon to expend. Your willingness to speak may develop as a result of your perception that something needs to be said; however, that might not be sufficient motivation for you if you perceive the task to be greater than the reward. What do you have to gain by exposing your ideas to the scrutiny of an audience?

1. You have a chance to clarify your thinking and gain a firmer grasp on what you believe by organizing your ideas in a way that makes them understandable to you and your audience and useful to others.
2. You may succeed in motivating other people to support a cause that is important to you.
3. You demonstrate leadership capabilities and show others that you are able and willing to take responsibility.
4. You build your self-confidence and raise your self-esteem by learning to defend the positions you take on controversial issues.
5. You enrich your life with new relationships by attracting people who share your interests and points of view.

There is, perhaps, one more personal value connected to the study of public speaking skills, and that is an appreciation for rational thought. The student who takes the art seriously becomes part of a tradition that goes back thousands of years. Aristotle said, "It is absurd to hold that a man ought to be ashamed of being unable to defend himself with his limbs, but not of being unable to defend himself with speech and reason, when the use of rational speech is more distinctive of a human being than the use of his limbs."[4]

In a society that seems to value physical prowess over effective articulation, we may wonder how much impact Aristotle's assertion has had. It is unlikely that a debate tournament will ever draw as many spectators as a football game will. Yet, it is certainly true that in a civilized culture, we rely more heavily on our verbal abilities than on our physical strength to defend our lives, our property, and our principles.

The Speaker-Audience Relationship

Public address is not an *adversarial* relationship between the speaker and the audience; it is a *cooperative* arrangement. Just as there are responsibilities on the part of the person at the podium, so are there common courtesies that should be observed by the people in the audience. The speaker should be able to anticipate that those addressed will be attentive and not obstruct delivery of the message. While we study public speaking, we should also be developing our listening skills, because we know that, as members of the audience, we can either enhance or jeopardize the success of the speech. Nothing productive is

[4]Ibid.

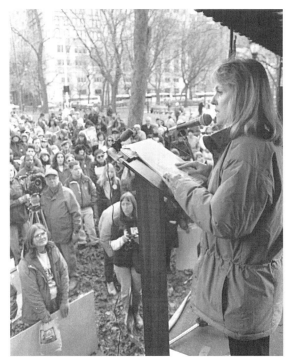

The speaker should be able to expect the audience to
observe common courtesies.

ever accomplished by heckling a speaker. I know there are some who will say
that heckling has been refined to an artform at Hyde Park in London, and that
encouraging it is regarded as an acceptable strategy of debate in the Oxford
Union. It is also quite common in the British Parliament; nevertheless, it is a
practice that impedes reasoned discourse. If you disagree with what a speaker
is saying, wait for your turn before you advance your refutation. Heckling is a
form of censorship, and all too frequently it silences the views of those who are
less aggressive and suppresses ideas that may need to be heard.

The question period that comes after a presentation is a time when the
speaker-audience relationship is clearly illustrated. When you are the one on
the podium, you hope that there will be questions; that's the way you find out
whether the audience has been interested and whether your words have been
understood. As a member of the audience, you will want to take advantage of
the opportunity to add your own thoughts and concerns to the dialogue. You
may be required to stand when you ask your question, which means that you
will have to employ the rhetorical skills of a speaker. Be sure to use enough volume so that the whole audience can hear you. As a general rule, you want to
keep your question short; it is a discourtesy to begin making a speech of your
own from the floor.

Your job as a speaker is to make your message clear even if you know that what you have to say is controversial and may draw criticism from the audience. If you use language that is intentionally obscure, and you jeopardize the relatonship of trust that a speaker must have with the audience, you violate your ethical contract. Sometimes we use the term *hidden agenda* to refer to a covert motive that a speaker may have. For example, let's say an accountant of a business firm is speaking to a group of its investors. The company has had a series of financial setbacks and is on the verge of bankruptcy; the management does not want the investors to know that. Therefore, instead of making a clearly articulated presentation, the accountant deliberately speaks in abstract language, using technical jargon that no one in the audience understands. The hidden agenda in this case is to go through the motions of providing an explanation but to conceal the real information from the listeners. As another example, political figures sometimes find themselves in "hot water" when a story breaks that suggests their involvement in an indiscretion or scandal of some kind. At such times a spokesperson who is skillful at handling the press may be brought in to minimize the criticism and keep the story from doing too much damage to the politician's image or cause. This procedure is called *damage control.* The term refers to the practice of answering questions in such a way as to give as little information as possible and to justify the role that the politician played in the incident.

GETTING STARTED

good list

There is much to learn about the preparation and delivery of a good speech. As you proceed in the reading of this text you will get some insight into the basic theory, and as you begin to give speeches in class you will discover that experience is the best teacher. Here is a brief checklist of what you need to know to get started:

1. *Content.* Your first step is to pick a topic that meets the requirements of the assignment you are given. Choose one that interests you and contains examples that the audience will find significant and relevant. Start by thinking of topics about which you already have some knowledge or with which you are somewhat familiar.
2. *Organization.* The information must be arranged in some sort of logical sequence, so plan on making an outline. Give thought to your organizational structure, and stick to that pattern when you present the material. Make sure you have a statement of purpose, clearly phrased main contentions, specific information that is relevant to your main ideas, and a conclusion to reinforce what you have said.
3. *Language.* Don't write the speech out word for word; plan on delivering it extemporaneously from your outline. When you speak, choose language that effectively communicates your meaning. Pronounce words correctly, and use proper and appropriate grammar.

4. *Voice.* Use enough volume so that you can be heard by everyone in the room, and enunciate your words and syllables clearly. Employ vocal inflection to place emphasis on key words and phrases.
5. *Timing and Pacing.* Be sure to start and end the speech on time. Speak fast enough to keep your audience alert and to ensure that you have time to cover all your material, but not so rapidly that you run words together.
6. *Attitude.* Before you begin to give the speech, develop a positive attitude toward the subject matter and toward the audience. Convey a sense of interest and enthusiasm for what you are saying, and let the audience know that you think it's important for them to listen.
7. *Appearance.* Project an air of confidence to the audience; stand up straight and maintain eye contact with your listeners. Your posture, gestures, and facial expressions should reinforce the message. Be sure to dress appropriately for the occasion.
8. *Integrity.* Honesty and sincerity are the hallmarks of effective public speaking. Never attempt to deceive your listeners or exploit them in any way. Maintain a high ethical standard for your own sake, as well as for theirs.

These are the criteria that will probably be used for evaluation when you give your speeches in class. Your fellow students in the audience may make observations about what they saw and heard, and, of course, your instructor will give you a grade. But rather than relying entirely on the feedback you get from other people, learn to be your own critic. Keep these criteria in mind as you prepare your speech and as you deliver it, and afterward make your own evaluation of how well you did. Try to discover for yourself what worked and what didn't work, and never let a public speaking opportunity go by without learning something from the experience.

EXERCISE

In the box entitled "The Legacy of Public Address" there are names of several famous people who affected the world in a powerful way through the application of their oratorical skills. Select one name, read about what the person did, and make a brief report to the class. Use the following framework as your organizational structure.

- Start by telling the person's name, title, nationality, and period in history.
- Describe briefly the significant social conditions that prevailed in his or her time.
- Relate the point of view expressed in one or more of the person's speeches.
- Quote at least one line of what the person said.
- Conclude with the results that were achieved by the person's oratorical efforts.

QUESTIONS FOR REVIEW

1. What might be a greater danger to free speech than government intervention?
2. How far back can we trace the study of public speaking?
3. What Greek philosopher made the most important contribution to the study of rhetoric? How did he define the art?
4. What are the three essential elements of any model of communication?
5. What do we mean when we say communication is *transactional?*
6. In communication theory, what is meant by the term *noise?* How does physical noise differ from psychological noise?
7. What is the difference between "structured" and "unstructured" communication?
8. How does communication in a committee or a task force differ from ordinary conversation?
9. What is meant by *impromptu* speaking?
10. What are the features that distinguish the public speaking model of communication from those that are less structured?
11. What do we mean when we say the speaker-audience relationship is cooperative rather than adversarial?
12. What is meant by *hidden agenda?*
13. What are the eight criteria that can be used as a checklist for preparing and delivering a speech?

PREPARING TO MEET THE AUDIENCE

**AFTER READING THIS CHAPTER, YOU SHOULD
BE ABLE TO DO THE FOLLOWING:**

Know what to do when you receive an invitation to speak; understand
the importance of logistics and demographics.

Adapt your speech topic to the interests of the people in the
audience; allow for differences in culture, attitudes,
political perspectives, and religion.

Recognize the gaps in your own listening behavior; understand the
obstacles to listening that you will have to overcome when
you are speaking to an audience.

Apply public speaking techniques that are designed to
ease the difficulties that people have in receiving
and retaining messages.

Have respect and appreciation for the rights of the audience
and the rights of the speaker.

The more you know about the people to whom you are speaking, the better prepared you will be to adapt your presentation to their needs. When your audience is a group of your friends or members of an organization with which you are affiliated, the task of planning what you need to say is somewhat simplified. You would already have some understanding of how much they already know about the topic and how much technical detail you could include. You would also have a certain amount of insight into their feelings and attitudes toward the subject matter that you plan to cover. If some part of your presentation is controversial, you would know when and where you might encounter opposition. But when you are speaking to a group of strangers, your task is more difficult. Suppose you receive an invitation from the program chairperson of a local service club to speak at its weekly luncheon meeting— what do you do?

RECEIVING AN INVITATION TO SPEAK

Before you do anything in the way of preparing a speech, *listen* to what is being said by the people who have invited you. They have picked you as a speaker because they believe you can tell them something that they need to know. The message you present must accommodate that need in some way. You'll have to make a quick assessment of your own background to see if you can give them what they want and if you have the time to prepare.

Logistics

First, make sure you are clear about the *logistics* of the speaking occasion—that means the date and the time, the size of the group, the location, and the physical arrangements. Certainly, you want to know how long you are expected to speak and if there is to be a question period afterward. You should also know if there are going to be other speakers on the program, and if so, what their topics will be. If you plan to use visual aids, find out what facilities are available. You may need an easel for charts, a chalkboard, or perhaps a projector and screen. These things are not generally provided unless you request them—even if you are a prominent person. When Queen Elizabeth II was invited to speak at the White House, for example, she may have assumed that all provisions would be made for her. Unfortunately, no one thought about her need to stand on a raised platform. She gave what may have been an excellent speech, but all that anyone was able to see of her over the lectern was the top of her hat. So try to anticipate what your particular needs might be.

Demographics

Next, find out from the person who invited you as much as you can about the *demographics* of the audience—the members' average age, sex (in the case of a same-sex group), vocations, socioeconomic levels, education, ethnic backgrounds, and anything else that might affect their beliefs, attitudes, and perceptions. That information does not have to be scientifically gathered; it can be based simply on casual observations made by someone who is familiar with the group you will be addressing. Knowing just a few specific characteristics about your listeners will help you plan a speech that is relevant to their needs and interests. The people who serve as program directors for large organizations that invite speakers on a regular basis often distribute questionnaires to their audiences to collect demographic information that they can use for planning purposes. Be sure to ask if such a survey has been taken and if the results would be available to you.

Read your daily newspaper. There is much you can learn on a day-to-day basis about the population trends in the vicinity where you live. Is employment up or down? Is traffic becoming congested? Is there a shortage of housing or rental units? Are more children starting school, and are they coming from other countries of the world? Do the schools offer courses in English as a second language? Are local merchants stocking more ethnic foods than before? Knowing the answer to some of these questions will start you thinking about the kind of audience you might face if you are invited to speak.

ADAPTING YOUR SPEECH TO THE AUDIENCE

Let's say, for example, that you have been invited to speak to the Junior Chamber of Commerce in your community. You can probably expect an audience of men and women in their late twenties and early thirties who are college-educated and career-oriented. Their affiliation with the Junior Chamber tells you that they probably have a concern for social issues, particularly those that affect the local economy. Knowing this about them makes it possible for you to select examples that are within their frame of reference.

Particular Interests

Suppose you have been asked to speak because of your association with the local college or university. That gives you some idea of what interests the audience has, but the subject area is still pretty broad. You want to address the concerns of your audience, so you need still more information about them. It may be that you have been invited so that a particular group of high school students could hear you. In this case you might orient your remarks to those who are considering enrollment in the college. You could talk about the courses that are offered; scholarships and financial aid; and the social activities, athletics, and other aspects of college life that would be of interest to incoming students. What if you were addressing the business executives of the community—the ones who pay the taxes that support the college? Here your approach would be quite different. You might discuss the funding of programs, the financial health of the institution, the research that is being done by the college that will benefit business and industry, and the cultural offerings. If your audience were made up of graduate students and prospective teachers, you might talk about academic freedom in the classroom, the quality of education, the opportunity for tenure, or the role that faculty plays in the governance of the college. These are just some examples of entirely different speeches in the same subject area, each designed for the interest of a specific audience.

In terms of the subject matter itself, I believe you can adapt just about any topic to suit the interest and the understanding of the audience. The people in the Junior Chamber of Commerce, for example, would probably be just as concerned about Social Security as would be members of the American Association of Retired People (AARP). The difference might be that the younger people would want to know about new taxation laws and the AARP members would be more interested in benefits. But that's just a difference in your emphasis. One word of caution: Be very careful about making generalized assumptions based on conventional stereotypes. Older people are not always conservative, and young folks are not necessarily progressive; a great many women have an interest in science, and there are a lot of men who enjoy cooking. Avoid the mistake of allowing people in the audience to believe that you have classified them into restricted categories.

Possible Opposition

Try to understand the particular orientation of the audience you plan to address and make an informed guess as to the members' willingness to agree with you. This advice does not imply that you must always try to appease your

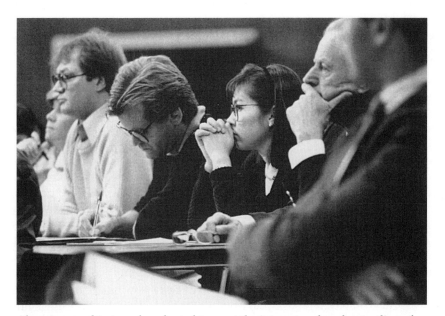

Almost any subject can be adapted to meet the interest and understanding of the specific audience.

listeners; there will be times when you may have to say things that they don't want to hear. A good example of this occurred on the first day of the 1996 Republican convention when Colin Powell faced a largely conservative audience and said, "You all know that I believe in a woman's right to choose, and I strongly support affirmative action." There was a murmur of "boo's" from the crowd, as Powell had known there would be, but he regained the listeners' goodwill by adding, ". . . we are a big enough party—and a big enough people— to disagree on individual issues and still work together for our common goal." Powell was not trying to change anyone's mind on the issues of abortion and civil rights; his objective was to make his own position clear and commend the party for its willingness to accept differences.

Public Opinion Polls

Trying to analyze how listeners might react to your position on a complex issue is not an easy task. Even if you ask people what they believe, you can't always count on their answers being an accurate reflection of their thinking. For example, polltakers might pose the question, "Do you favor the continuation of affirmative action in hiring policies?" It's impossible to give an intelligent yes or no answer to a question like that. A considered response might be something like this: "I favor having companies make every effort they can to seek out qualified minorities to fill job vacancies, but I don't think preference should be given solely on the basis of race." So, does that mean "yes" or "no"? The point is that complex issues are never entirely true or false even though polltakers will try to make you think that they are. If a lot of yes or no answers are given to questions such as that one, public opinion might appear to be very different from what it really is.

Another factor that makes analysis difficult is that public opinion is never firmly fixed. This can be illustrated by the changes that occur every month in the responses people make to questions pertaining to the President's performance. Apparently, thousands of people change their minds periodically about how well the President is doing his job. Presidential advisers are kept guessing as to what particular event caused the shift in opinion.

Descriptive Labels

Analyzing expected audience reaction is uncertain even when you have access to demographic information, because over the years labels that were used to describe political inclinations have become blurred. You might be able to make broad generalizations about groups that are said to be "conservative" or "liberal," but these categories are unreliable when it comes to making predictions regarding the way individual audience members will respond. Contrary to what you might think, there are conservatives who favor the legalization of marijuana and liberals who vote to put restrictions on welfare payments. Given this, how can you as a speaker predict audience reaction even when you know that, say, your listeners as a group are Republican (or Democrat), or that they favor a liberal (or conservative) point of view? The answer is that regardless of who your audience may be, the presentation you make must be reasonable and supportable. If it is, even those who disagree will be obliged to respect you. When you are speaking on a controversial issue, you never want to assume that you will have 100 percent approval. And conversely, it's not a good idea to expect complete disapproval, either; if you do, you may find yourself sounding defensive.

Cultural Differences

Failure to communicate effectively from the podium may occur when the audience believes that the speaker does not understand or does not appreciate the values and the attitudes of those who are being addressed. Cultural differences may sometimes interfere with your ability to gain the respect of the audience— for example, if you are perceived as a person whose perspective on life is significantly different from the listeners. If you were reared in a middle-class neighborhood it may be difficult for you to relate to the experience of people who were brought up in a ghetto. There is much to be gained in a college classroom when there is some measure of cultural diversity—particularly in a speech class where students have the opportunity to share their experiences and talk about their beliefs, attitudes, values, and feelings. One subject area that is frequently discussed in the classroom is that which involves social welfare. Opposition to such programs as subsidized housing generally comes from people who have spent their entire lives in middle-class, suburban neighborhoods, and have never known anyone who was living on welfare. For the most part, attitudes are formed by mental pictures of welfare recipients as being lazy, irresponsible, and probably dishonest. It can be beneficial to have someone in the class who is able to dispel the image by revealing that he or she was reared in a subsidized housing unit by a parent receiving welfare. The effect is better still when the person who has had that experience is intelligent and articulate and can testify to the critical support that social welfare programs can provide. One of the important contributions to education afforded by the study of public speaking is that it fosters the development of a broad perspective on life. People who are the most effective speakers are those who are able to recognize that the point of view they are expressing is not the only one that exists. Speakers who do not learn this are going to be confronted by questions they did not anticipate, coming out of attitudes they never considered.

Attitudes and Beliefs

Factors that affect changes in attitudes and beliefs have been examined extensively. One study conducted at Ohio State University concluded that personal relevance, argumentative strength, and source credibility were the three most important elements in determining whether or not a belief structure could be modified by oral persuasion.[1] When an issue has a *high personal relevance factor*

---

[1]Richard Petty and John Cacioppo, *Attitudes and Persuasion: Classic and Contemporary Approaches,* Wm. C. Brown, Dubuque, Iowa, 1981.

it means that a concerned individual has a lot to gain or lose if a particular course of action is followed. For example, someone in the audience who is employed in the tobacco industry, which depends on government crop supports, will probably be very much opposed to an increase in tobacco tax or to having those subsidies cut. You, on the other hand, may believe it is immoral to sell a product that jeopardizes the public's health, particularly when the victims are often young people. The person employed in the tobacco industry is going to be very difficult to convince and may not be moved by arguments based on moral concepts. Studies showing that smoking is hazardous to health may be very convincing to you, the speaker, but the recipient of the message will be thinking about the possibility of being laid off, and how he or she is going to pay the bills and support the family if there is no income.

When the personal relevance factor is high, strong argumentation is needed that will satisfy the concerns of the message receivers. You would have to be able to convince tobacco workers that new and perhaps better employment could be found if the tobacco industry were to be eliminated. On the other hand, when the personal relevance factor is low, specifically tailored argumentation may not be necessary. For example, for an audience composed of non-smokers who have secure jobs not related to the tobacco industry, there is no risk. Under those circumstances the listeners may be willing to take what the researchers at Ohio State University called the *peripheral route* and accept what you say solely on the basis of source credibility. In other words, if their lives are not going to be severely affected, and if they like you and believe you can be trusted, they may come over to your side without requiring that you give a lot of supporting evidence.

Political Perspectives

A good way to get experience in audience analysis is to work as a volunteer for a political candidate. You will develop an understanding of the extent to which politicians will go in order to discover the best approaches for gaining the voters' attention and favor. Large political organizations at the national level try to hone their campaign techniques to a science by compiling massive amounts of data that reveal which particular issues are of concern to every demographic profile in each section of the country. Speeches that are given by politicians and their supporters can then be tailored to fit a specific audience.

In recent years it has become increasingly difficult to predict the voting patterns of the American people. For one reason, there are a great many independent voters who do not align themselves with any particular political party. And even those who do choose a party often do not feel a sense of loyalty to it. There was a time when you could be fairly certain which side of a controversial issue would be taken by people who described themselves as Democrats or Republicans, and you could discover what they believed by reading the platforms that were drawn up by the party leaders. But election analysts have a much more difficult time now because candidates themselves do not always agree with the planks written into their own party's platform. Also, there are a great many people who have become *single-issue voters*—people who will vote for a candidate only if he or she has taken the "correct" stand on one particular issue. It may have to do with capital punishment, gun control, abortion, or taxes—but whatever it is, the single-issue voter will disregard all other matters or personal characteristics and focus only on that one item.

If you are giving a speech in support of a political candidate, your best strategy would be to describe the accomplishments and the qualifications of the person rather than attempt to interpret his or her policies. Surveys have indicated that people often decide to vote for someone on the basis of personal characteristics that they like, even though they disagree with the candidate on policy matters. Ronald Reagan became one of the country's most popular presidents because he was regarded as a great communicator, even though the people who voted for him often disagreed with the stands he took on specific issues. If it seems that candidates are putting a lot of emphasis on "image," it's because they know that the persona they project may have more to do with their getting elected than their foreign or domestic policies will have.

Religious Influences

A Gallup poll taken in 1968 reported that 53 percent of the population said that churches should stay out of politics. But according to a study made by an independent research company in Washington, D.C., in 1996, there has been a significant change of attitude in this country concerning religion and politics.[2] A majority of Americans now believe that it's all right for churches to express political opinions. The strongest support for this point of view came from white evangelical Protestants, a group that now accounts for about one-quarter of the U.S. electorate. The survey also relied on supplemental information taken from phone interviews in 1994 and 1995 reporting that 65 percent of the population placed themselves into one of three categories: 23 percent white evangelical Protestant; 22 percent white mainline Protestant; 20 percent white Catholic. Of the remaining 35 percent, 9 percent were black Christians; 4 percent were Jews and Mormons; and 9 percent made up the smaller affiliations. Only 11 percent said they had no religious tradition at all. No religious group has the power to carry a national election, but churches in general have become a force to be reckoned with by U.S. politicians.

Certainly religious groups have an influence on politics, but it is hard to say if the bias is to the left or to the right. Students often regard churches as being morally or politically conservative. The fact is that church people are represented on both sides of issues such as abortion, capital punishment, and homosexuality, and a great many clergy from all denominations have played a leading role in social reform movements of this century. If you are asked to speak at a church function, you will probably find the same kind of diversity as you would in any other group of concerned citizens.

---

[2]"The Diminishing Divide: American Churches, American Politics," Pew Research Center for the People and the Press, Washington, D.C., reported by the *New York Times,* June 24, 1996.

STEPPING INTO THE LISTENER'S SHOES

Some studies say that 70 percent of our waking hours are spent in some form of verbal communication, and almost half of that time is spent in listening. With all that practice, you might think that the receptive skills of an audience would be highly developed, but don't count on it. Even though listening is an extremely important skill, not much instruction on it is given in our public schools, because it is very difficult to teach. We know how to teach people to speak—we can provide them with methods and guidelines, let them try it, observe their behavior, and critique their performance. Speaking is an observable art, but listening is not. We can't know for sure if people are listening just by watching their reactions. We can make some guesses based on their facial expressions and eye contact, but nonverbal feedback often proves to be inaccurate. In a classroom, of course, the instructor can give students a quiz to test their comprehension of a lecture, but you do not have that opportunity in an average speaking situation. The fact is that an audience may stop listening without your ever knowing it.

You can get some insight into the listening habits of the average audience by reflecting on your own listening behavior patterns. You may regard yourself as someone who is able to pay attention to a speaker most of the time, but chances are that you have the same obstacles to overcome as everyone else. Let's say, for example, that you've had plenty of sleep, the time is mid-morning, the environment is comfortable and attractive, and the topic is one that interests you. Even under those ideal circumstances, are you going to be able to hear and retain everything?

- Do you normally start listening from the very beginning of the speech?
- Are you generally able to construct a clear picture of the speaker's main idea?
- Are you able to recognize all the points that are really important, and can you grasp new information as well as that which you have heard before?
- Can you connect the specific information to the generalizations?
- Do you make a practice of giving the speaker your undivided attention without allowing your thoughts to drift away to other matters that concern you?
- Are you able to sustain your attention when a speaker is tedious, hard to hear, or has mannerisms that annoy you?
- Do you never allow prejudices based on age, race, sex, or ethnic origin to get in the way of your hearing a speaker's message?
- Do you listen all the way through to the end to hear how the speaker's conclusion reinforces the main idea of the approach?

If you can answer "yes" to all of those questions, you are truly remarkable. But if your listening habits fall short of being perfect, you can understand that the average person is going to have difficulties as well.

SPEAKING SO THAT PEOPLE WILL LISTEN

Public speaking would be a lot easier if we could select for our audience only those people who are skilled and highly motivated listeners. But, alas, we can't do that. We have to take whatever audience we get, and do what we can to gain and hold the audience members' attention. The challenge of the speaker is to ease the task of the listeners and overcome whatever obstacles impede the reception of the message. We have a better chance of doing that if we know what those obstacles are.

Gain the Attention

In order to listen effectively, the audience needs to be *ready* to listen, and that readiness may not always coincide with the beginning of the speaker's message. Communication breakdowns often occur at the very start of a presentation if the listener is thinking about something else when the speaker is providing orientation to the message.

Solution: The speaker must say something that will gain the attention of the audience before launching into the main idea of the message. We call this the *attention statement.* It might consist of a humorous anecdote, a quotation, a rhetorical question, a reference to the occasion, or just a word of welcome, but it is as important to an audience as a starter is to an automobile.

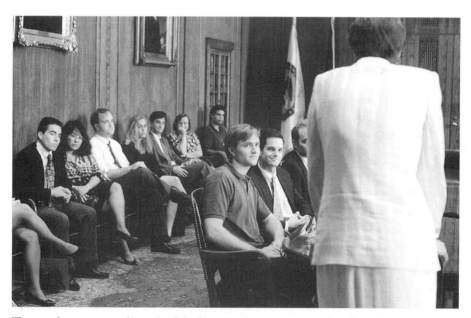

The speaker can ease the task of the listeners by overcoming the obstacles that impede reception.

Have a Clear Purpose Statement

If the audience fails to understand your main idea, the thrust of your speech will be lost. People will become confused, frustrated, and perhaps even antagonistic. They should not have to guess at your purpose or position, and they should not have to sort through a maze of obscure language to find it.

Solution: As soon as you are sure you have gained the attention of the audience, make a clearly phrased statement that provides orientation to the topic and to your point of view. The statement should be sufficiently qualified so that it focuses on what you want to say and excludes any tangential aspects of the topic that you do not plan to cover.

Emphasize Key Words and Important Points

It's easy for people to listen to what they already know; it's much more difficult for them to expand their fund of knowledge. They may find it difficult to perceive the value of a specific piece of information and may fail to retain the key words or important points.

Solution: Identify in your own mind what is important for the audience to remember; then think of ways to emphasize those items. For example, if you are going to use a key word that you think listeners might be hearing for the first time, you have to say it more than once. *Repetition* is the most effective means you have for facilitating audience retention. You could also *write the word* on a chalkboard or flip chart; you could use *vocal emphasis*—modulating your pitch or volume. A very easy device to use is a *pointer phrase* such as, "It's important to remember that . . . ," such a phrase calls attention to the fact that what follows is a significant part of your message.

Provide Connecting Phrases

It's not just the retention of specific information that is difficult, but also the ability to see connections. The audience needs to understand how the specifics relate to the main idea and how they support the thesis. Here again, the speaker must not rely upon listeners' being able to tie everything together by themselves.

Solution: Help the audience to see the significance of the information by using *connecting phrases* to link the data to the generalizations. The listening process is greatly enhanced when the speaker uses such expressions as "What we can see from this fact is that. . . ."

Build Attention Features into the Speech

You may believe that what you want to tell your listeners is the most important thing they need to know; however, there are going to be other matters on their minds. One listener is concerned about the unfavorable evaluation he has just received from his supervisor; another has remembered that

he is double-parked; and a third person has just found out that she is preg-
nant. All of these things are on the minds of the people who you believe
should primarily be interested in your speech on, say, the possible extinc-
tion of the spotted owl.

Solution: Build into your presentation features of interest that are designed to
capture and hold the attention of the audience. These *interest* or *attention features*
need to be woven into the speech so that they contribute to the content rather
than interrupt the flow. *Humor* is one of the best features to use—not jokes, necessarily, but humorous phrases and references. When you are researching your
topic, look for *unusual examples* that will grab the listeners' attention and try, if
you can, to *tailor the example* to an interest of the audience. Visual aids such as
slides, transparencies, or computer graphics can also be interest features; more
will be said about them in a later chapter.

Ease the Strain of Listening

What we know about listening is that it is not easy, and people who are not
highly motivated to pay attention may tune out if they are given an excuse to
do so. Certainly it is true that they should not give up on you even if your volume is a bit low or your voice is a monotone, but the fact is that they often do.
If listening to you becomes too difficult, or if they perceive something about
you that they don't like, they may conclude that it's not worth the effort, regardless of how important the message may be.

Solution: Don't give the audience a reason to stop listening. Speak loud
enough and clearly enough so that you can be heard, and modulate your voice
so that you are not talking in a monotone. Dress appropriately for the occasion.
Learn what behaviors are distracting to an audience and make an effort to
avoid them. Don't try to put on airs by bragging and showing off your knowledge, and don't "talk down" to people by speaking as though they were infe-
rior to you.

Penetrate Stereotyped Notions

People in the audience should not reject the message because of stereotypes
they have formed about the race, nationality, age, or sex of the speaker, but
sometimes they do. You can't always count on listeners' being tolerant and free
of prejudices. You certainly have a right to object if you experience intolerance
or prejudice, but complaining does not help the audience get the message.
What can you do if you perceive that your listeners are rejecting you because of
something over which you have no control?

Solution: Don't react in anger. You have nothing to gain by expressing hostility to an audience; in fact, doing that may reinforce audience members' prejudices. Try if you can to penetrate the stereotype by projecting yourself as a
person who is different from their preconceived notions. If you speak intelligently and convey a sense of reason and responsibility, you may succeed in
overcoming their biases and in gaining their respect in the long run.

Are we making progress in this area? Let's hope so. There was a time when black people could not even vote, let alone run for office; in many states women were not permitted to sit on a jury; long-haired men were not moved into corporate executive positions; and homosexuals were forced to resign from public service jobs. These conditions began to change when articulate people who belonged to such groups were able to break through the barriers of prejudice and convince those in positions of power that race, gender, hairstyle, and sexual orientation had nothing to do with a person's character or ability.

Observe the Time Limit

Any person in show business will tell you that timing is one of the most essential ingredients of a successful performance; the same is true of public speaking. If your speech runs long, the audience members may stop listening before you reach your conclusion. Even though they may politely remain in their seats, nothing is getting through to them after they have shut off their auditory receptors. Studies tell us that the attention of an audience peaks in the first twenty minutes of a presentation and begins to taper off after that. Does that mean that speeches should never be longer than twenty minutes? No. But you may have to work harder for attention if you are demanding a lot of the audience's time. Failure to observe the time limit became an embarrassment to Bill Clinton several years ago when he was governor of Arkansas. He was delivering the nominating speech for presidential candidate Michael Dukakis during the 1988 Democratic convention. Clinton was supposed to speak for fifteen minutes; instead, he talked for three-quarters of an hour. Delegates who were eager to hear the acceptance speech of the Democratic candidate began to shuffle about and whisper chiding remarks. Finally, Clinton came to the end and began his closing by saying, "In conclusion . . . ," whereupon the audience immediately began to cheer. Even he now admits that his timing was bad. What we can learn is that regardless of how vital your information may be, there is no point in talking if no one is listening.

Solution: Never go beyond the time that has been scheduled for you. Keep the speech as tight as you can; if you have a lot to say, you may have to talk at a fairly brisk rate. Don't go into so much detail that members of the audience miss the main point; they will listen better if your material is concentrated. The more time you consume, the greater risk you take of losing their attention.

RESPECT FOR THE AUDIENCE

Keep in mind that your function as a speaker is to meet the needs of the audience members. You are on the platform for their benefit, not for your own. You may be getting certain rewards from the experience—it may be gratifying and fulfilling—but basically your purpose is to provide information that your audience can use. If your listeners value your assertions, you can take satisfaction for having achieved your objective; however, if they don't, you must remember that they have the right to disagree. There is no way you can force your message upon them. You have an opportunity to be heard, but there is no guarantee that your message will succeed in persuading them. People will listen as long as they believe it is in their interest to do so. If you try to demand attention, you will probably meet with resistance. Recognize the fact that communication is a shared experience and can be accomplished only when the rights of both the speaker and the listener are acknowledged and respected.

good

THE AUDIENCE'S BILL OF RIGHTS

We, the people of the audience, in order to form a more perfect speaking environment, establish clarity, ensure attention and interest, provide common understanding, promote communication, and secure the blessings of reason and logic for ourselves and our fellow listeners, do ordain and establish this Bill of Rights for the Public Forums of the United States.

ARTICLE I
No speaker shall come to the podium unprepared. The speaker shall have given thought to the issue and shall be equipped with notes and visual aids as required.

ARTICLE II
The information contained in the speech shall be significant and useful. No excessive trivialities shall prevail on the podium.

ARTICLE III
The speaker shall tell the truth and nothing but the truth, and shall not intentionally deceive the audience by omitting necessary information.

ARTICLE IV
The speaker shall be punctual and not unnecessarily delay the audience. The speech shall begin and end on time.

ARTICLE V
The speaker shall articulate clearly and speak in a voice loud enough for all to hear. Attention shall be given even to those in the back of the room.

ARTICLE VI
The speaker shall be courteous to the audience at all times during the main address and during the question period.

THE SPEAKER'S RIGHTS
In accordance with this Bill, the speaker's rights shall not be abridged by the audience. Members of the audience shall not heckle or create distractions that interfere with the speaker's thoughts. The audience shall listen attentively even though they might disagree with the speaker's viewpoint. They shall participate during the question period with directness and brevity. They shall not make speeches of their own from the floor.

EXERCISE

Survey the class members and gather demographic information that will provide a statistical profile of the audience you will be addressing. Find out the average age, ratio of men to women, the nationalities represented, number of married people, and the average amount of time students spend working for pay. In your survey ask how many students voted in the last election and to what political party they are registered. You might also want to inquire about religious affiliations by having them check one of the predominant categories: Catholic, Protestant, Jewish, Muslim, Hindu, Buddhist, other, or none. After this information has been compiled, conduct a class discussion and speculate about the generalizations a speaker could make about the possible reactions the class might have to various topics and points of view.

QUESTIONS FOR REVIEW

1. What do we mean by the *demographics* of an audience?
2. What do we mean by the *logistics* of the speaking occasion?
3. How might age differences between the speaker and the audience affect the way a speaker's message is received?
4. How does the term *personal relevance* relate to changes in attitude and belief structure? What does a speaker need to do if the personal relevance factor is strong?
5. What is meant by the *peripheral route* to cognitive change? If the personal relevance factor is not strong, how might a speaker bring about change in a person's belief structure?
6. What is meant by a *single-issue* voter? What effect do single-issue voters have on political candidates?
7. What are some of the bad habits that interfere with good listening?
8. What does a speaker need to do before launching into the main idea of the message?
9. What do we mean when we say the purpose statement should be *qualified?*
10. What are several ways to emphasize key words and important points?
11. What are some ways of holding the listener's attention?
12. What do we mean by *stereotypes?* How can they be overcome?
13. What might be the consequences of speaking beyond your time limit?

THE AUDIENCE IN A PLURALISTIC SOCIETY

**AFTER READING THIS CHAPTER, YOU SHOULD
BE ABLE TO DO THE FOLLOWING:**

Understand the effects that recent immigration has had upon the
United States and how the concept of the *melting pot* differs
from the analogy of the *mosaic* or *salad bowl*.

discus

Participate in class activities to learn more about your own attitudes
toward people whose cultures are different from your own; discover
what stereotypes other people might have of you.

Appreciate the advantages of living in a pluralistic society; understand
how cultural diversity has enriched the lives of people in
the United States.

Keep from inadvertently exacerbating racial and ethnic differences; use
the speaker's platform to build bridges that bring people together.

Aristotle's teachings emphasize that "the central task for the speaker is to find or make common ground with the audience."[1] That is not an easy task in this country, because the United States has always been a *pluralistic* society—that is, a society having many different ethnic, religious, and cultural groups coexisting within its borders. We used to call ourselves "the melting pot," believing that it was desirable to have immigrants from all parts of the world blend the qualities of the society from which they came into a general "stew" that would become a culture of its own. In the early years of our history that appeared to be working, and we took pride in the fact that we were a mixture of nationalities with common goals and values. The reality, however, was that some ethnic groups were successfully amalgamated, but others were not. Furthermore, much of our diversity was being lost, as long-standing customs, traditions, and languages "melted" into obscurity.

STIRRING THE "MELTING POT"

The term *melting pot* was not coined until the beginning of the twentieth century, and then it became an important part of our national image. In reality it was the later European immigrants who were assimilated into our society—those whose ancestors had been the founders of the nation. They blended well into "the American way of life" because they looked and acted pretty much like the people of European descent who were already here. But our national tolerance for diversity was not unlimited. People who did not want to adjust to the cultural norm were callously told to "go back to where they came from" and were penalized by being excluded from the political arena.

Politicians in those times didn't worry about offending minorities and many referred to them publicly in derogatory terms. Stereotyping was commonplace, and people who suffered such indignity could do little about it, because they lacked social and political empowerment. The fact was that large segments of the population, notably African Americans, Asians, and Native Americans, were virtually disenfranchised, and public officials didn't feel they had to make an effort to win their support. Segregation was not only a standard practice, but in many states it was the law of the land, and many people believed that it was the "natural order of things."

Oddly enough, women were relegated to the same status as minorities; the fact that they were in the majority didn't seem to make any difference. They were not mentioned in the Fifteenth Amendment that was ratified in 1870 giving former slaves the right to vote. It wasn't until 1920 that the Constitution was amended to allow women equal voting privileges with men, and even then, they were not permitted to sit on a jury. In many states a woman could not hold a liquor license, even if she were the owner of a tavern. And, of course, business organizations and service clubs were for men only.

---

[1]Tom Schachtman, *The Inarticulate Society*, The Free Press, New York, 1995, p. 42.

Change in our national attitude has come about slowly. Women began to achieve some semblance of equality as a result of the role they played in the Second World War. For African Americans and other minorities, a turning point was the 1954 Supreme Court decision of *Brown v. the Board of Education of Topeka, Kansas,* which ruled that segregating schools on the basis of race was unconstitutional. The Civil Rights Act of 1964 gave still more legal muscle to the cause of ethnic fairness, and we began to hear the phrase, *"leveling the playing field."* At that time courts and legislatures were acting boldly to bring about social reform, though public sentiment lagged behind.

The Effects of Immigration

The United States has truly been a refuge for oppressed people from all over the world. We have given political asylum to thousands of people seeking to escape war zones and oppressive governments. We have welcomed other immigrants who came for economic reasons and brought with them their languages, customs, traditions, and lifestyles. This new foreign-born population has enriched our society by giving it greater cultural breadth than we have ever known, but it has also created a challenging task for our institutions.

According to the 1990 Census, 25 percent of the population growth in the United States comes from immigration; almost 30 percent of the people in this country describe themselves as being nonwhite; 9 percent were not born in this country but call it home.[2] Right now over 40 percent of elementary and secondary schoolchildren in New York belong to an ethnic minority, and in California, Asian, African American, and Hispanic students already outnumber Caucasians. In some schools on the Pacific Coast there are as many as twenty-seven different languages spoken by the children. These statistics say nothing, of course, about the cultural make-up of a specific audience, but they do suggest that there is a good chance the listeners in any given locale will not all have the same ethnic background.

Given the fact that we are a culturally diverse nation, what kind of assumptions can a speaker make about the probable reactions of a general audience, particularly when the topic of the speech deals with a social issue? First, we must be aware that not everyone perceives historical events in the same way. The attitude that members of the audience have toward events in U.S. history such as the winning of the west, the defense of the Alamo, and the use of Chinese labor for building the railroads may vary, depending on their individual ethnic origins. As a speaker you need to recognize that the perspective you have is not necessarily going to be shared by all the members of your audience. With that in mind, always act on the assumption that there is someone in the audience who represents an ethnic group that might be offended by a callous and insensitive remark. Rather than relying on "rules to be followed by public speakers," a better plan would be to work on changing any personal attitude or

[2]U.S. Department of Commerce, Economics and Statistics Administration, Bureau of the Census, 1990.

inclination you might have that denigrates anyone for their age, sex, race, religion, or national origin. If you have those thoughts running through your mind they are going to be revealed through your vocabulary or tone of voice— perhaps without your knowing it. Mark Fuhrman learned this lesson after trying to portray himself as being free from bigotry when he testified at the O. J. Simpson trial. The disclosure that he habitually spoke in racist terms resulted in his testimony being unequivocally rejected by the jury.

The Mosaic and Salad Bowl Metaphors

Over the years expression has been given to many points of view regarding the direction we should take in assuring equal opportunity for people of all races and nationalities in this country. Nevertheless, the vision is not yet clear, and the issue is still controversial. There are those who say we should hold onto the concept of the melting pot. They believe that people who make a commitment to live in this country should speak the English language and adopt the common value structure. Others regard that notion as too narrow-minded and xenophobic. They argue that the old way tries to force people into molds that may not fit and limits the scope of cultural richness. They would prefer to have our population compared to a mosaic or a salad bowl, a place where individual ethnic differences contribute to the blend but are recognizable as distinct.

Diverse Perception of Communication Skills

You can probably tell from what I have said so far that this text is written by someone whose cultural orientation has been configured by the influences of the western world. Literature on the subject of communication coming from Asia, Africa, the Middle East, or the Pacific Islands would have a much different perspective. For example, Dr. Milton Bennett of the Intercultural Communication Institute of Portland, Oregon, relates that, in Micronesia, a speaker would be taught to begin a speech by saying, "Excuse me for the great sin of having absolutely nothing to say to you."[3] That is the kind of opening the people of the Micronesian culture would expect, but it is not a recommendation that I would ever make in any of my classes.

Public speaking in a pluralistic society can be daunting, not only because of differences in language and cultural references, but also because of variations in styles of communication. Dr. Bennett tells of a young man from Nigeria who was participating in a group discussion. Other members of the group were U.S. Americans who spoke in the typical style of the western world, which is to relate information in a linear fashion and conclude by stating the point. The man from Nigeria began to tell a lengthy story. After

---

[3]Dr. Milton Bennett, of the Intercultural Communication Institute of Portland, Oregon, from a speech, "Beyond Tolerance: Intercultural Communication in a Multicultural Society," delivered to the "TESOL Conference, *Building Futures Together,* March 31, 1995.

about fifteen minutes, the other members interrupted him and said, "What is your point?"

He replied, "I'm giving you all the details you need to understand my point."

"Oh," they said, "then you will tell us your point?"

"No," he answered. "When I am through, you will know what my point is." He went on to explain, "In my country we say the point directly when we are speaking to children. Adults should be able to figure it out for themselves."

Having conveyed this example to you, I'm not sure that I can give you a good solution to the dilemma that is posed. All of us—from all cultures—must understand that these differences exist. I'm sure there are many of you reading this text who feel the frustration of realizing that what is being advocated in this course conflicts with the manners and customs that have been taught to you by your family. The challenge for those of you in that situation is to hold onto the patterns of behavior that are serving you well, but adapt your style to accommodate the methods of communicating that are prevalent in the society where you live. Remember that those of us in the western world followed the pronouncements of Aristotle, which led us into the methodology of problem solving; if we had been influenced instead by Lao-tse we might have taken a Taoist approach to public speaking.

Principal Attitudes

Let me advance several principal attitudes that are common among students of rhetoric who have had a western education. It's possible that these western attitudes will strike some of you as being self-centered, disrespectful, patronizing, inconsistent, and rude; however, they are not intended to be so. They are the reflections of people who desire to become effective in the art of persuasion.

1. "I have individual differences and I do not want to be regarded as being the same as everyone else in the society. I don't want to feel that I have to accept the ideas of other people for the sake of conforming."
2. "My information is important, and even older people can learn something from what I have to say. I have no reason to sound humble or apologetic."
3. "I want you to understand my point, so I'm going to tell you directly what I mean. I will relate to you all the details, but at the end I will tell you what conclusion I have drawn."
4. "I may make mistakes, but I do not regard that as being shameful. I am willing to accept criticism and change my position if the evidence shows that I am wrong."
5. "If we have a problem to solve, let's begin to analyze it right away and not waste a lot of time talking about personal matters. Time is valuable, and we can socialize on some other occasion."

The best I can advise at this point is to think about these attitudes and decide which of them fit into your own way of thinking. Don't make judgments about them, but recognize that they are pervasive among those who have embraced western values.

Assertiveness

There are values we prize in this country that are not necessarily embraced by people of all nations. For example, I encourage students to be assertive. In many of my class assignments I ask students to gather evidence on a controversial subject and then stand up and declare their point of view. That's very hard for some of them who have been taught always to agree with their elders and people of authority. However, the nature of a speech class is to teach you to make your own thoughts and ideas known to others. Those who choose to pursue a college education need to recognize that their lives are going to be transformed in the process. They may learn things that conflict with what they have previously been taught, and once something is learned, it can't be unlearned. Education necessarily makes cultural values subject to scrutiny.

To study public speaking in a pluralistic society we must consider variations in styles of communicating.

ETHNICITY IN THE CLASSROOM

The word *ethnicity* refers to the condition of belonging to a particular ethnic group. *Ethnology* is the study of socioeconomic systems and cultural heritage. These terms are relevant to students of public speaking, because failure to understand ethnic differences can impede communication. Since we must be able to recognize the obstacles to multicultural harmony, let's begin by looking in the *American Heritage Dictionary,* Third Edition, 1994, for a few pertinent definitions:

Stereotype. "A convenient, formulaic, and usually oversimplified conception, opinion, or belief; a person, group, event, or issue considered to typify or conform to an unvarying pattern or manner, lacking any individuality." Certainly there are generalizations that can and need to be made about groups of people, but we must understand that, although there might be some truth to them, a stereotype is not an accurate description of any particular person or event.

Prejudice. "An adverse judgment or opinion formed beforehand or without knowledge or examination of the facts." People who are prejudiced make up their minds about individuals before they really get to know them. They may or may not act on the prejudices. This word alludes to what people think rather than what they do.

Discrimination. "The ability or power to see or make fine distinctions; discernment." This word can easily be misunderstood. It is often used in a positive way to describe a person's intelligence or good taste. Take, for example, the statement, "She has a discriminating eye for fine artwork." This means she is able to perceive differences and recognize details that determine quality. On the other hand, a person who makes derogatory judgments on the basis of race or ethnic origin might be described as "racially discriminating," and that is synonymous with *unjust* and *narrow-minded.*

Racism. "The notion that one's own ethnic stock is superior." This is all the dictionary says about this word, but the connotations and implications are far more complex. Paradoxically, some people believe that efforts to compensate for racism are, in themselves, racist.

Learning About Yourself and Others

If you are in a multicultural class, you are fortunate, because you have an opportunity to talk with people of different backgrounds and get a broader perspective on the world. You might even discover that some of the preconceived notions you had about people of other races or nationalities are inaccurate, and if you are serious about your education, you will make adjustments in your thinking accordingly. There is also much to be gained by developing an awareness of the way you are perceived by others.

All of us have a cultural background that influences the way we speak and act. But we tend to regard ourselves as individuals first, and we may not be aware of the way our racial, ethnic, or national characteristics are perceived by others. We are probably more cognizant of the stereotypes we have of people from different cultures than of the ones they might have of us. As an exercise in dealing with this, get together with three or four members of your class who represent ethnic groups that are different from yours, and conduct your own multicultural study. Before you pursue this activity, it is important that you establish healthy solidarity among the members of the group. Begin by having everyone make an affirming observation about each of the others. This may be difficult if you are not a person who is used to relating in this fashion, but it is a good communication exercise. If you can't think of anything positive to say, find out from each person what kind of affirming comment he or she would like to have you make. This kind of validation of one another is important, because we cannot be completely candid with others unless they know that we have goodwill toward them and that our motives are sincere. When you have done this, identify what each person in the group regards as his or her culture. After that, proceed by asking questions that pertain only to those cultures that are represented in your group. Examples of some questions follow:

- *What are the common stereotypes that are associated with the people in your culture?* Now, remember, these are generalizations that we know are not going to apply to every individual in the category. Nevertheless, there had to be some basis for them even though the origin may have been misguided. For example, if you are talking to someone who came from Ireland, you and the other people in the group might identify the following stereotypes: Good sense of humor, poetic, musical, somewhat superstitious, heavy drinkers, quick to lose their tempers. Are those fair generalizations to make, and would anyone of Irish descent be offended?
- *Which of those stereotypes are positive and which are negative?* The answer to that is going to vary depending upon whom you ask. An Irish alcoholic, or perhaps one who abstains entirely from hard liquor, might not like the suggestion that people in his or her nation tend to be heavy drinkers. On the other hand, one who enjoys the camaraderie of the pub might view that characteristic with fondness.
- *Which of the stereotypes do you, as an individual in that culture, regard as applying to you?* We can do a little "reverse engineering" here. Ask the student of Irish descent to describe some personal characteristics and see if they translate into the stereotypes of his or her culture. It may be that this particular student is not the least bit superstitious, but might be willing to agree that it's a fair generalization to make of the Irish.
- *Which of the stereotypes have become obsolete?* Perhaps historically the Irish could have been described as superstitious, but maybe that generalization is no longer valid. Are there other descriptive terms that more accurately pertain to the new generation of Irish people?

- *Are you as an individual influenced in any way by a stereotype that has been applied to your culture?* For example, if you are an Irish American person and are inclined to lose your temper a lot, do you justify it on the grounds that you are Irish? Even if that does not apply to you, do you believe that it might happen to others of Irish descent?
- *Which of the stereotypes do you believe are unfair and wrongfully applied?* Answers to this question can be useful to the public speaker. What you learn from one person of Irish extraction will not tell you everything you need to know, but it could help you dispel some misconceptions that might otherwise get you into trouble.

Common Characteristics

The world *stereotype* has negative connotations, and we generally regard stereotypes as being building blocks of prejudiced thinking. We say, "Don't believe that; it's just a stereotype." On the other hand, there are such things as common characteristics, or cultural traits, that are often viewed in a positive way by those who share them. They can and do have a bonding effect on people to whom they are applied. Individuals who identify closely with their own particular ethnic group or culture feel a sense of community when they believe that they share with others a range of special qualities. They will cheer when a speaker who is one of them pays tribute to their common values, and they may scorn an outsider who doesn't comprehend what they stand for. An English politician, for example, is likely to have a difficult time rallying the support of an Irish audience.

THE CULTURAL EFFECTS OF DIVERSITY

Because of our cultural diversity we have a rich opportunity in this country to broaden our perspectives and improve the quality of our lives. There would probably be no disagreement with this claim when it comes to art, science, literature, music, and food. It's hard to imagine our society without the contributions that have been made by the talented artists, writers, scientists, musicians, and culinary masters from countries all over the world that have graced every neighborhood in the United States.

Diversity in the Workplace

In public and private corporations all over the country, sensitivity-training classes are being held to teach employees at all organizational levels how to relate to people in a pluralistic society. Large companies such as Colgate-Palmolive and many other of the Fortune 500 companies have full-time *cultural diversity managers* whose job it is to facilitate communication among and between members of a workforce who may have vastly different cultural backgrounds. There are practical reasons for doing this, of course, because a business will function more efficiently if the workers feel a community spirit. There will be fewer misunderstandings and work-related errors; there will not be as many interpersonal conflicts; there will be a higher degree of loyalty to the company and a greater sense of security among workers. But there is also a legalistic factor: A cultural diversity manager can help a business corporation stay within the scope of the laws that protect employees from racial or sexual discrimination. In effect, the people participating in these sensitivity courses are studying audience analysis in much the same way that a student of public speaking does. They are learning about the reaction they can expect from what they do and say.

Furthermore, there are economic advantages to cultural diversity. The *Wall Street Journal* reports that "tapping into diverse customers and markets" is an important consideration for U.S. multinational firms.[4] Writing for *Harpers Magazine,* David Rieff suggests that multiculturalism is more than just a theoretical concept of intellectuals. He points out that terms such as *cultural diversity* and *doing away with boundaries* resemble the stock phrases of modern business executives who talk about "product diversification" and "the global marketplace." In regard to human resources, Rieff says the fact that

> . . . non-white workers will be the key to the twenty-first-century American labor market is a given in most sensible long-range corporate plans. Like the multi-culturalists, the business elite is similarly aware of the critical role of women, and the need to change the workplace in such a way as to make it more hospitable to them. . . . As usual, it is the business community rather than the multi-culturalists who have taken the most radical steps toward acknowledging these new conditions.[5]

Social Implications of Diversity

Diversity is a prominent part of residential neighborhoods, too. Rather than detracting from what we have nostalgically referred to as the "American way of life," immigrants paradoxically are often more committed to "traditional American values" than are people born in this country, observes Ron K. Unz, chief executive officer of Wall Street Analytics in Palo Alto, California. According to Unz, "Whereas the traditional family consisting of a married couple with children is increasingly rare among white Americans—just a quarter of white households according to the 1990 Census—it accounts for nearly half of Asian and Hispanic immigrant households."[6]

Respecting differences does not mean that all customs from every culture are acceptable. For example, we are critical of parents who put their children to work in the fields and factories rather than sending them to school. We do not permit people to train animals to engage in mortal combat. We do not

---

[4]"Advocates Try to Tie Diversity to Profits," *Wall Street Journal,* February 7, 1996, p. B1.
[5]David Rieff, "Multiculturalism's Silent Partner," *Harpers Magazine,* August 1993, p. 62.
[6]Ron K. Unz, "Immigrants and American Values," *Ethnic Groups,* Social Issues Resources Series, vol. 5, 1995.

Martin Luther King was able to find
the common ground of all races.

allow the practice of having multiple spouses, nor do we let husbands beat
their wives with impunity. We scorn the caste system that creates untouch-
ables and locks members of the society into social or economic levels. We reject the practice of forcing women to undergo female circumcision. I cite these
examples to express my belief that we are selective in this country about the
kind of customs and practices we are and are not willing to accept. Speakers
need to know that there are limits to the range of notions that an audience
will applaud.

DIFFERENCES IN PERCEPTION

Learning to understand and accept the customs and values of people with ethnic backgrounds different from our own is a broadening experience for us, but
it is also a challenge. For one thing, we need to realize that not all failures to
communicate are due to misinterpretations or faulty listening. The really difficult breakdowns are those that are caused by fundamental differences of values
or perspectives. University of California sociology professor Bob Blauner cites
a poll that was taken just after the Rodney King beating in 1992:[7]

> While many whites saw the precipitating events as expressions of racist con-
> duct, they were much less likely than blacks to see them as part of some larger

[7]Bob Blauner, "Language of Race: Talking Past One Another," *Current*, January 1993, p. 4.

pattern of racism. Thus, two separate polls found that only half as many whites as blacks believe that the legal system treats whites better than blacks. . . . Whites and blacks see racial issues through different lenses and [use] different scales to weigh and assess injustice.

The same conclusion was drawn by polltakers who interviewed the public after the verdict was announced in the O. J. Simpson case. Many people in the general population agreed with the jurors that those who gathered the evidence were motivated by racism. But African Americans polled saw this as being the rule rather than an exception. In his study, Professor Blauner went on to say that there are two languages spoken by whites and blacks:

> Because of these differences in language and worldview, blacks and whites often talk past each other. . . . Whites locate racism in color consciousness and its absence of color blindness. They regard it as a kind of racism when students of color insistently underscore their sense of difference, their affirmation of ethnic and racial memberships. . . . Many black, and increasingly also Latino and Asian, students cannot understand this reaction. It seems to them misinformed, even ignorant. They in turn sense a kind of racism in the white's assumption that minorities must assimilate to mainstream values and styles.

This difference in perception might be the widest of all gulfs that separate blacks and whites. From the very beginning of the civil rights movement, well-meaning whites have been trying to find ways to assimilate blacks into the mainstream and have become frustrated when their efforts so often fail. Somehow they never really understood, or were unwilling to accept, that segments of the African American population did not want to be assimilated. The problem, as many whites perceive it, is that there is no other alternative; it's either assimilation or continued conflict. They don't know what else to do, so they persist in advancing the same thesis, even though it is regarded by some people of color to be racist.

Many blacks, on the other hand, continue to experience hostility and rejection when they try to enter the mainstream, and they can't understand why whites insist on preaching the same old theme.

> Much of the popular discourse about race in America today goes awry because ethnic realities get lost under the racial umbrella. The positive meanings and potential of ethnicity are overlooked, even overrun, by the more inflammatory meanings of race. Thus white students, disturbed when blacks associate with each other, justify their objections through their commitment to racial integration.[8]

This difference in perception was illustrated by the 1996 Million Man March on Washington led by Black Muslim activist Louis Farrakhan. It was certainly a successful event in many respects. Hundreds of thousands of black men raised their hands and vowed that they would treat their wives with respect and take responsibility for supporting their children. It was a proud moment for many blacks, because it was an achievement of their own and not something that was handed to them. Nevertheless, there were a great many white people, including

---

[8]Ibid.

liberals who were active in the civil rights movement and ethnic minorities favoring integration, who disapproved of the march because it excluded whites and women. It furthered the cause of empowerment for black men, but did not promote integration of the races.

The Speaker's Dilemma

How does knowing that differences exist help speakers to understand what they have to do when they step onto the podium with a topic that has racial overtones? For one thing, speakers may at least recognize the obstacles and perhaps adjust their expectations accordingly. Persuasion is possible when there is some common ground, and the task of the speaker is to find out what that is. But trying to reverse a fundamental belief by turning up the pressure is just not going to work, no matter how firmly you believe that you are right and others are wrong.

There is an expression that applies to people who do not understand the strength of the resistance against what they are doing. It is often applied to men who use sexist language and don't realize that their behavior is offensive to women. We say, "He just doesn't get it!" It's important to heed the meaning of that expression, because the more the behavior persists, the more the problem is aggravated. I remember how hard it was for many white students in the seventies to learn not to say to a black person during class discussion, "What is it that *you people* want, anyway?" The failure to recognize the offensiveness of that phrase did much to exacerbate the hostility between the races. If speakers have a sincere intent to make race or gender relationships better, they need to avoid saying things that will, by nature, make them worse.

Try to recognize how firmly entrenched a belief may be in the minds of the people you are addressing. For example, there is some leeway in an issue such as affirmative action because of its highly complex nature. Even those who support the policy may be willing to consider modifications in its implementation. On the other hand, the belief that racism is pervasive in the society is a conviction that is not likely to be adjusted on the basis of rational argumentation. There are no techniques, psychological ploys, or clever phrases that will reverse this kind of fundamental perception. This is not an issue that is going to be resolved by persuasive rhetoric. Don't expect that what you say in a speech is going to have a more powerful influence on people's thinking than what they experience directly in the real world. Change has to come from the way people treat each other on a day-to-day basis.

Common Ground

Certainly we have evidence of cultural barriers' being overcome. The best example is the one we see every four years at the Olympics. Athletes from all nations come together to compete, but also to draw strength from one another and to live by the common set of rules that governs the contests. For the period of time they are together, they set aside any cultural differences that may separate them and celebrate the remarkable capabilities of the human body. The respect they have for each other has nothing to do with race or creed; it comes out of their shared experiences. All of them know how much dedication, commitment, physical pain, and love for the sport was involved in the training necessary to measure up to the standards of the Olympics.

There is an important message here for speakers to observe: Set aside the differences that you know cannot be changed, and find the common ground.

The Challenge of Pluralism

To speak from a position of strength but at the same time lay the foundation for peace and reconciliation takes a truly exceptional orator. Such a person was Martin Luther King, Jr. It is proper, of course, that we honor the man for who he was, but, for the sake of rhetorical analysis, we also need to examine what he did and how he did it. The crowd that gathered in Washington, D.C., on August 28, 1963, to many observers resembled salt and pepper—it was more than 25 percent white. King was surprised by the mix, but not dismayed. Certainly, all 200,000 of the people in the audience would not be of the same mind, but that didn't matter. His message was tailored for all segments of the civil rights movement, rather than for a select few. His purpose was to find a common ground upon which all could stand. His strategy was not to narrow the focus of the issue, but to broaden it; to embrace everyone in the cause, not just those who had suffered injustices. He did not call for a change of purpose and direction, but for living out the true meaning of this nation's creed. Thus, he succeeded in pulling down the walls that separated one faction from another and in building bridges instead.

The legacy of Martin Luther King has been felt by ethnic minorities of every kind, not just by African Americans. And our nation is stronger because of it. Whenever we feel discouraged about our failure to resolve differences between the many cultures that are represented within our borders, we would do well to think about the challenge of the task. No other country of our size in the world has opened its doors as wide as we have. Whether we have a melting pot, a mosaic, or a salad bowl, the concept of ethnic inclusion is something that can be celebrated by all of us. Cultural diversity is our common ground.

EXERCISE

Prepare a short (three- to five-minute) talk that you can give to the class, telling what you would like people to know about the social contributions that have been made by the nationality or ethnic group (or groups) that you represent. You can use either current or historic examples. Your purpose is to promote respect for the people you are describing. Don't use a problem-solving format: You are not identifying social injustices, and you don't need to make any recommendations. Focus on the positive characteristics of your roots and not on the negative qualities of others. Be friendly and not angry; build bridges and not walls.

QUESTIONS FOR REVIEW

1. What is meant by a *pluralistic society*, and what are the implications?
2. What do we mean when we say America is a *melting pot?* Why has that image been criticized?
3. Why did earlier politicians not make an effort to seek the support of minorities?
4. What did the Fifteenth Amendment accomplish, and what segment of the population was not included?
5. What ruling did the Supreme Court make in the *Brown* decision in 1954?
6. What was the Civil Rights Act of 1964?
7. How does the analogy of a mosaic or a salad bowl differ from that of the melting pot?
8. What significant change has there been in the student population in elementary and secondary schools in New York and California?
9. What are the principal attitudes toward public speaking among people influenced by western culture? How might they differ from attitudes in other cultures?
10. What is meant by the word *stereotype?*
11. What is meant by the word *prejudice?*
12. What is meant by *racism*, and what are some of the implications of the word?
13. What effect has cultural diversity had upon the world of business and manufacturing?
14. What function does a cultural diversity manager serve in a business organization?
15. How was the beating of Rodney King perceived differently by blacks than by whites?
16. What was the rhetorical strategy used by Martin Luther King in his address on August 28, 1963?

LISTENING AND REACTING

**AFTER READING THIS CHAPTER, YOU SHOULD
BE ABLE TO DO THE FOLLOWING:**

Recognize that effective listening is a communication skill that can be
learned through instruction; that speakers rely upon the verbal and
nonverbal feedback they receive; that to be a good listener
means you must listen actively, rather than passively.

Become familiar with the 8 common obstacles to listening and not
allow them to interfere with your reception of a message.

Recognize the fallacies of logic; know how critical listening is
related to critical thinking.

Understand how semantics is involved in the reception of messages;
know what is meant by *operational meaning* and *semantic reactions;*
know that words can be high or low on the scale of abstraction
and that euphemisms can obscure meaning.

If you have ever become impatient while listening to a slow-talking college professor, you are not alone. Many times students tune out, not because they don't understand the material, but because they are able to grasp the idea before the speaker finishes the sentence and get tired of waiting for the next thought. The evidence shows that we can listen faster than people can normally pronounce the words. There is a remedy for this problem; it is called a *variable-speed compressor*. It's a device that records the message and plays it back at any speed you choose. You can take a lecture that plods along at 125 words per minute and speed it up to 275 or even 300 words per minute. In a study at Syracuse University students saved a third of their time normally spent listening to lectures and scored significantly higher on posttests than did the students who learned the same material at a normal speed.[1] That may sound good, but college lecture halls are generally not equipped with such devices, and, although the experiment apparently worked for students in the study, it may not work for you. You probably are going to be stuck having to listen to lectures, and that may not be a bad thing. Even though you can read the material faster than anyone can speak it, there are still advantages to acquiring the meaning through the spoken word. A person lecturing can elaborate in more detail, call your attention to the concepts and specific data that are most important, and bring you up to date on developments in the field. But, you need to have effective listening skills.

LISTENING HABITS

There have been studies indicating that people who are good listeners score higher on academic achievement tests than do those who do not listen well.[2] That being the case, it seems as though we should make a course in listening a prerequisite for all students in their first year of college. The fact is that some schools do require a class in oral communication, and listening is generally a part of the course content. Many institutions offer speech as an elective, but others do not put it in the curriculum at all, believing that students already know how to communicate by the time they get to college. That notion is subject to doubt, according to a report from Michael Cronin. Cronin says that it is a mistake to assume that because students can hear and talk when they enter school, they require no systematic instruction in understanding and using communication skills.[3]

[1]Carolyn Coakley and Andrew Wolvin, *Listening*, 4th ed., Wm. C. Brown Publishers, 1992, Dubuque, Iowa, p. 224.
[2]Carolyn Coakley and Andrew Wolvin, "Listening in the Educational Environment," in Deborah Borisoff and Michael Purdy (eds.), *Listening in Everyday Life: A Personal and Professional Approach*, University Press of America, 1991, Landham, Md., pp. 163–164.
[3]Michael Cronin, *The Need for Required Oral Communication Education in the Undergraduate General Education Curriculum*, Department of Communication, Radford University, Radford, Va., 1993. Updated August 8, 1996, by Ted Spencer, SCA Publications Manager, tspenser@scassn.org.

Feedback to the Speaker

But why should we be concerned about listening when the focus of this text is on speaking? One reason is that you will spend much more of your time in the audience than you will on the podium. Another reason is that you are studying *communication,* and that is a process dependent on the message being received. But there is yet a third reason: Anyone who does a lot of speaking to groups will tell you how important it is to get feedback from listeners. I know this is true for me, because I am personally energized by listeners who overtly react in a positive fashion. I like to see students looking at me while I lecture and taking notes when I make a significant point. I especially like to hear them laugh in the right places and see them nod in approval when they like something that I have said. I also believe that my lecturing improves when I observe positive feedback. Now, I'm not going to suggest that students do these things in order to stroke the ego of the professor, but I do want to call attention to the effect that the audience can have in the communication process. When students are the speakers, I want them to know that they are being heard. So, for the first round of speeches I sometimes assign a few members of the audience to give affirming nods from time to time while their classmate is making a presentation.

Nonverbal Messages

When you are the listener in the presence of someone who is speaking, it is impossible not to send messages of your own. *Nonverbal feedback*—the way you

As listeners, we need to be aware of the way our feedback affects the speaker.

sit or stand, the movement of your body, the expression on your face, the direction in which you cast your eyes—is an external indication of your internal reaction. It can be either positive or negative, and it can be an intentional or unintentional expression of your level of interest. An example of unintentional feedback would be a yawn. That kind of overt behavior on your part can have a demoralizing effect on a speaker, even though the yawn may have been an involuntary reaction having nothing to do with anything the speaker had been saying.

As listeners, we need to be aware of the way our feedback affects the speaker. And, as speakers, we need to recognize that the external reactions of audience members may make us feel good or bad, but they are not necessarily an indication of how well they are paying attention or whether they approve or disapprove of what we are saying.

Verbal Responses

The way people reply verbally to our message is a more reliable instrument for measuring reception than nonverbal feedback is. When listeners ask good questions or contribute relevant comments, we make the assumption that they were paying attention. But sometimes a speaker can be fooled. In social situations we learn how to make generic responses that fit all occasions even when we have no idea of what the other person has said. We can allow our thoughts to drift away, completely lose track of a story that is being told, and sound perfectly sincere by saying, "Oh, really, that must have been quite an experience." But this kind of "nonlistening" can also cause embarrassment, as illustrated by the following dialogue:

> Professor to a student in class: "You look like someone I've seen before. Do you have a brother who might have taken my class last year?"
>
> Student to professor: "No, it was me who took your class. I flunked it last year, and I have to repeat it."
>
> Professor: "That's strange, the resemblance is amazing."

That may be just an amusing story, but I was told that it really did happen. It's quite possible for us to look completely attentive without having the meaning of the message penetrate our consciousness. Let's analyze why this may occur.

- *We hear only part of the message and construct the rest of it ourselves.* In the example above, the professor heard the word *no* but didn't listen to the full explanation.
- *We focus on our own response.* We know that after the person has finished what he or she is saying, we are going to have to make some comment in reply. Instead of listening, we are framing in our minds what we are going to say when it's our turn.
- *Our thoughts go off on tangents.* Something that was said triggers an idea that launches us mentally in a direction that is not related to what the sender of the message is saying. It may be a very important direction for us to pursue, but it does not take us to the place where the speaker is going.

- *We want to disengage.* We stop listening when we really don't want to be in the conversation in the first place. Instead of trying to follow the road the speaker is taking, we are looking for an off-ramp.

Listening Passively

The next step up from nonlistening is *passive listening.* Receivers may hear what is being said, but they are not focused on the subject matter. In the passive mode, their attitude toward the message is neutral, and they have no intention of making an effort to remember what the speaker says. Any response they might make is noncommittal.

Early studies in listening behavior attempted to quantify the amount of time the average person spends listening to speech. A more important study for you, however, would be to keep track of the time you yourself spend listening to other people. As an exercise some evening, try to recall as much as you can from the things that were said to you during the day. You may remember having a conversation with the passenger sitting next to you on the bus or exchanging jokes with fellow employees at the water cooler, but you may have forgotten what was actually said. Don't judge yourself harshly for doing that, because sometimes the personal contact is more important than the message itself. What should concern you more is your ability to focus attention on the content of verbal messages that are important and to retain information that you need.

Listening Actively

Communication takes place only when the message of a sender is received. The professor who delivers an absolutely stirring lecture conveys no information at all unless someone in the room is awake. So, as an example, the student of communication would respond to the classic philosopher's conundrum by saying that if a tree falls in the forest, and there is no one there to hear, it does not make a noise. Ergo, the professor's lecture makes no impact if the minds of the students are elsewhere.

To be a good listener of speech, you must consider listening to be active behavior. You must be engaged in the process of communicating and regard your role as being equal to that of the message sender. Active listening means that you are focused on the present rather than the past or future, and are making a conscious effort to understand the sender's message at both levels of meaning, the cognitive and the emotional.

The Cognitive Level

First and foremost, you want to understand the meaning of the message on the basis of the words that are being spoken. Even with all of its limitations, language is the best means people have of expressing what they know and what they want. The listener must be attentive to the words used if he or she is to comprehend the denotative meaning.

The Emotional Level

To get the full impact of the message, the listener must be able to perceive the depth of the speaker's feelings. We are able to hear passion in the words of a poet, but we may have a more difficult time empathizing with an average person who has suffered a loss or experienced great joy. We must allow for the fact that emotion is often communicated by the *sound of the voice* rather than by the meaning of the words.

The emotional dimension of the message is often recognized by what we see rather than by what we hear. To be really good listeners, we must also use our eyes. Posture, gesture, and facial expressions are all part of what is being said. At the nonverbal level of communication, we monitor emphasis that is placed on words, and that can affect the cognitive as well as the emotional aspect of the message.

COMPREHENSIVE LISTENING

There are many different kinds of skills that can be learned in a course on listening, but we will cover just a few of them in this text. In this section we will discuss *comprehensive listening*, which means listening to understand and retain the substance of the message. It does not imply that we accept whatever is said; it suggests only that we comprehend the meaning. Later we will discuss *critical listening*, which adds the dimension of evaluating what we hear. There are two other kinds of listening that are important, but not closely related, to skills pertaining to public address: One is *appreciative listening*, which is behavior that enhances one's pleasure at a musical concert or poetry reading. The other is *empathic listening*, which is something we do when we are relating to friends who are expressing their personal feelings. Comprehensive listening is pragmatic and objective and addresses our ability to absorb and retain the content of the message.

Speakers, of course, need to be clear and direct in the expression of their thoughts, but we can't hold them completely responsible for getting the message across to us. Wolvin and Coakley say that, until recent times, ". . . little if any attention has been focused on the listener. As scholars have come to understand the psychology of processing human communication, they have also recognized the central role that the listener must assume in the . . . process."[4]

Not all communication breakdowns can be corrected by fixing the mistakes of the sender. A speaker can stand on the podium and perform flawlessly, but if the listeners have their receivers turned off, the transmission will not be completed.

---

[4]Andrew Wolvin and Carolyn Coakley, *Listening*, 4th ed., Wm. C. Brown, Dubuque, Iowa, 1992, p. 126.

Obstacles to Listening

There is an old saying that it is better to light a single candle than curse the darkness. We know that obstacles to listening exist, but there is no point in resenting the fact that they do. We have already spoken of the ways that speakers can compensate for the poor listening habits of the audience. Let's take another look at the list and see if we can give the same kind of help to people on the receiving end.

1. *Not listening from the beginning.* Speakers do not always tell you to start paying attention. They should do that, of course, but sometimes they don't. They assume you are listening, and they name the person, place, or thing that is the subject of their talk. They may do this too quickly; so be ready, and don't get caught napping. If you miss the antecedent, you will not know who, where, or what the speaker is talking about.

2. *Not getting the main idea.* The speaker may fail to express clearly the main idea of the speech. That is a serious omission on the part of the speaker, but nobody is perfect. If you miss the main idea, you are going to be confused until you get it. Try to construct in your own mind what you think the speaker wants to say. Let it be a tentative thesis until you are able to confirm that your interpretation is really what he or she meant.

3. *Listening only to what you already believe and not hearing new information.* Try to avoid falling into a pattern of not paying attention to facts that might expand your thinking. Partial knowledge may not be enough for you to draw a conclusion. Examples of this kind of abbreviated listening are sometimes found in court trials. Jurors may hear the opening arguments of the attorneys and make up their minds on the basis of the claims that are made. Later, they may tune out when the evidence is being presented and not hear the proof that is needed to determine the validity of the claim. This happens because details are more difficult to comprehend than generalizations. To keep this kind of obstacle from getting in the way of your forming a reasoned conclusion, you must believe that the decision you are called upon to make is important, and that hearing and weighing the evidence must precede your judgment.

4. *Not connecting important information to the main idea.* It's hard to know how many words are needed in order for an audience to relate information to the main idea. Sometimes the connection is not made by speakers when they think the receivers should be able to fill in the blanks. For example, a speaker may relate the details of the tearing down of the Berlin wall in 1990, and later comment that as a result, the United States has lost its national purpose. Would you, as a listener, be able to identify the national purpose as being the containment of communism if the speaker did not make the connection for you? According to Joanne Jacobs, half of America's twelfth-grade students couldn't do that on a federal government U.S.

history test.[5] One of the most difficult aspects of effective communication is "listening between the lines" and discerning what the speaker means—even when the words are not explicitly spoken.

5. *Dividing your attention with other thoughts.* It's quite possible that while you are trying to listen to the instructor in your speech communication class explain the requirements of the next assignment, your mind keeps drifting off to other areas of your life that are competing for your attention. Perhaps your room rent is due and you don't have the money to pay it; your boss has said you have to work the morning shift next semester and that will interfere with the classes you want to take; and, worst of all, the weather forecast calls for rain on the day you were planning to go to the beach. Effective listening means that you have to set extraneous issues aside and focus your attention on the matter at hand. Certainly, peripheral concerns are important, but you must convince yourself that they just have to wait their turn.

6. *Allowing a speaker's mannerisms to interfere with your listening.* It's not always easy for a person inexperienced in public address to place emphasis on key points and speak in well-modulated tones. When you are listening to a speaker who talks in a monotone and perhaps has a rather drab personality, you need to turn up the intensity of your own receptors. Concentrate on the content of the message, not the speaker's mannerisms. Take responsibility yourself for recognizing what is important.

7. *Discounting a speaker's message because of age, race, sex, or ethnic origin.* Prejudiced thinking has no place in intelligent dialogue. Get rid of any antiquated notions you might have that diminish the value of people who are not just like you. Stereotyping others on the basis of their being old, young, black, white, male, female, Muslim, Jew, Asian, or European is not only immoral and unethical, it is also ignorant.

8. *Not listening all the way through to the end of the message.* You might recognize this obstacle to listening if you have ever started to respond to a person in conversation before he or she had finished speaking. I must confess that I am guilty of doing this. I think I know how someone's sentence is going to end, and I react before I hear all of it. Often I'm wrong, and the person has to say, "No, that's not what I mean." In conversation this kind of listening error can be corrected right away, but in public address the speaker may not know that someone in the audience has jumped to a conclusion that distorts the intended message. Not listening through to the end may be something you do when a speaker is taking too much time to make a point. To be a good listener, you must be actively engaged in attending all the way through to the conclusion, even if your pacing is faster than that of the speaker

---

[5]Joanne Jacobs, "No National Consensus About What American Kids Should Know," *San Jose Mercury* (California), November 16, 1995, p. 7B.

CRITICAL LISTENING

We can learn a lot when we listen, as long as we listen with a critical ear. It is not enough just to absorb information; we must also be prepared to analyze it and determine whether or not it makes sense. Are we willing to accept the whole message, or only part of it? What kind of response do we want to make? Should we affirm or refute what is said? Critical listening is especially important in a political setting. Our ability to process information given to us by a candidate for office is vital in order for a democracy to function. Year after year, public officials are returned to office by voters who may have heard the voices of the candidates but did not listen critically to their arguments and reasoning.

Fallacies of Logic

Cleverness is not a substitute for substance. There are a number of rhetorical devices that can be used by a speaker to gain and hold attention, but they do little or nothing to contribute to understanding. Catchy phrases and humorous anecdotes make a speech appealing to listen to and are certainly not to be condemned. But, as a discerning listener, you may want to ask yourself, "Is the speaker using clever rhetoric to cover up a lack of substance, or to avoid confronting the issue directly?" Look for the smoke screens that are designed to conceal rather than illuminate the speaker's meaning. Here are several of such well-known devices, which are called *fallacies in logic:*

Red Herring. A diversionary tactic designed to prejudice the issue under consideration by relating it to a common fear is called a *red herring.* It is employed for the sole purpose of alarming the audience by claiming an improbable consequence that is only remotely connected to the issue. *Example:* People who oppose gun control in any form sometimes use the argument that if registration of firearms is required, the government will know where all the weapons are. Therefore, agents would be able to go around the country and confiscate them all so that citizens would have no way of defending themselves. *Analysis:* The issue of disarming the population is a red herring because it is a measure that would be taken only by a government that was hostile to its people. Legitimate gun owners who use firearms responsibly and do not intend to oppose the government by force should have nothing to fear from registration. We should note, however, that there are other, more reasonable, arguments that could be used against registration based on expense, red tape, and prejudicial denial of a license.

Straw Man. A strategy to divert attention away from the opposition's strong arguments to ones that can easily be attacked is called a *straw man* strategy. *Example:* Debaters who argue against capital punishment try to make it seem as though the main reason people have for wanting to execute criminals is to get revenge. *Analysis:* Although some supporters of capital punishment are motivated by the desire for vengeance, the stronger arguments, and the ones that need to be addressed, are those that deal with deterring thieves

from carrying weapons during a robbery, protecting prison guards from in-
mates serving life sentences who have nothing to lose, and making it impossible for the hardened criminal to return to society and commit further crimes.

Ad Populum. An argument that appeals to what a speaker knows to be the ex-
isting prejudices of the audience is referred to as *ad populum. Example:* Hitler relied
heavily on *ad populum* arguments in his diatribes against the Jews and the Bolsheviks because he knew that fear and hatred of those groups already existed in the
minds of most of his listeners. In *Mein Kampf* he wrote, "All propaganda has to be
popular and has to adapt its spiritual level to the perception of the least intelligent
of those towards whom it intends to direct itself."[6] In our own country, prior to the
Civil Rights Act, politicians in the southern states commonly loaded their speeches
with racist remarks because they knew that was the way to appeal to their con-
stituents on a feeling level. In fact, few candidates were able to get elected unless
they clearly supported segregation. *Analysis:* When speakers use prejudice as a ploy
to gain favor, they are exploiting the audience's weaknesses and are denying listeners exposure to rational arguments. Another word for this ploy is *demagoguery.*

Ad Hominem. A strategy that attempts to win a debate by making unsupported accusations to discredit an adversary's integrity rather than by

[6]Adolph Hitler, *Mein Kampf,* Houghton Mifflin, Boston, Mass. Translated by Ralph Manheim 1971,
p. 180.

Adolph Hitler played upon the fear and hatred that he knew already existed in the
minds of his listeners.

confronting the person's arguments with real refutation is termed *ad hominem.* In the political arena, this tactic is referred to as *name-calling. Example:* A speaker attacks the opposing candidate by saying he is unqualified to make decisions because he is a drunkard. *Analysis:* Terminology of this kind is meaningless, because it is entirely subjective. The person in question might simply be a social drinker by the standards of other people. The speaker is saying more about his or her own animosity than about the qualifications of the opponent.

Begging the Question. When the speaker asks the audience to accept a premise as though it were a foregone conclusion without offering supporting evidence, he or she is *begging the question. Example:* A speaker says, "Everyone knows, of course, that if the generals had been allowed to do their job, we could have won the war in Vietnam." *Analysis:* "Everyone" does not know that to be the case. The speaker is trying to make it seem as though the statement is not controversial when it is, in fact, highly argumentative. The point would have to be advanced as a thesis or a claim and be supported with reasons. It is not an assumption that can be accepted at face value.

Circular Argument. An argument in which the line of reasoning returns to the thesis as being its own proof is known as a *circular argument. Example:* "Marijuana should not be legalized because it is harmful. The reason it is harmful is that if people get caught selling it, they will go to jail." *Analysis:* A thesis must be proven with reasons outside of itself; otherwise, the arguer is simply repeating what has already been said.

Non Sequitur. The literal meaning of *non sequitur* is "not in sequence." In other words, a statement does not follow in a logical sequence from the previous one. *Example:* A parent says to a child, "Of course you have to go to college; your grandfather could never afford a new suit." *Analysis:* There may be a connection in the mind of the parent, but it is confusing to the receiver, who does not see the relationship between the two statements.

Post Hoc Ergo Propter Hoc. The Latin phrase for "After this therefore because of this," *post hoc, ergo propter hoc* denotes another type of illogic. The fallacy of this reasoning is based on the claim that because one event follows another, the first was the cause of the second. *Example:* People who live along the San Andreas fault in California try very hard to figure out when earthquakes will occur. Some projections are based on the weather, others on alignment of the planets. The reasoning is that because certain conditions existed just prior to previous earthquakes, there is a cause-and-effect relationship. *Analysis:* We cannot know whether one event is the cause of another unless we conduct a scientifically controlled study. Making a casual observation is generally not a reliable basis for forming a realistic belief. As listeners, we have a right to require more substantial evidence.

Critical Thinking

Critical listening is closely related to critical thinking. The arguments we hear expressed by other people are often incorporated into our own way of reasoning. In a complex society such as ours, we are bombarded continually by a barrage of words that urge us to buy, sell, vote, and behave in a variety of ways. We are exposed to more information than we can possibly process—some of it valuable, much of it useless or counterproductive. If we accept that which is illogical and laden with fallacies, our own thought and discourse will become equally contaminated. We must learn to be selective in what we accept as truth and to base our conclusions on evidence rather than on unsupported assertions.

SEMANTICS OF LISTENING AND REACTING

The study of all the ways that meaning is conveyed and received is called *semantics.* Using words is the most explicit method for making ourselves understood, but words by themselves are often not adequate. Language is an invention that evolved from human thought, and, as such, it is far from perfect. At best it is a tool that can be used with varying degrees of skill for conveying meaning. We know that effective oral communication relies heavily on applications that are nonlinguistic. For example, volume and vocal inflection can alter meaning when we place emphasis on some words and not on others. From the visual perspective, we are aware that posture, gesture, and facial expression influence the way our message is received.

If you have ever had to ask a question of a person unfamiliar with your language you know that it is difficult, but not impossible, to convey what you want to say without verbalizing. When you are in such a situation you probably rely on acting out the meaning, as you would do if you were playing charades. If your question pertains to a physical object that is close at hand, you can point to it; if there is an action verb in the message, you can go through the motions. You may even resort to drawing a picture for the person. One form of nonverbal communication that may be familiar to you is international signs that appear on highways and in public accommodations (Figure 4-1). Here we find an example of an important message that must be conveyed quickly and accurately, relying totally on the receiver's ability to interpret pictures. We call such symbols *icons.*

In the case of a "no smoking" sign, the message is clear even though no words have been used. However, if you are trying to get across an abstract idea, your task is more difficult. Imagine, for example, that you wanted to ask the person who does not speak your language if the journey across the mountain would be *strenuous.* There is nothing you can point to that conveys the idea of *strenuous.* Neither the sound nor the letters in the word have any relationship to the concept of strenuousness. Pronunciation of the word conveys meaning

FIGURE 4-1. One common form of nonverbal communication is the international sign, such as this icon for "no smoking."

only to those who have been taught to associate the word with the idea. This is why we say that *words are not containers of meaning;* they are simply *abstractions* to which we assign meaning.

Operational Meaning

When I say that words are abstractions, I simply mean that there is nothing about the sounds I make or the marks on the page that is inherently connected to the thing I am describing. S. I. Hayakawa suggests that some words are more concrete than others and that they can be examined on a scale of abstraction.[7] For example, I can use the word *cow* and have a fairly good idea that the image in my mind is probably quite similar to yours. When I use the word *livestock*, there probably will be some differences. When I start to talk about "farm assets," I am rather high on the scale of abstraction, and there is a good chance that you do not have the same picture in your mind as I do in mine.

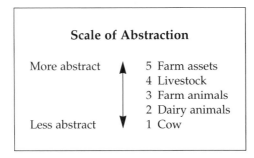

[7]S. I. Hayakawa, *Language in Thought and Action,* Harcourt, Brace & World, New York, 1949, pp. 168–170.

In the study of semantics we say that some word combinations have *operational meaning*—that means we are able to describe things in terms of size, weight, distance, volume, shape, number, or observable action. But when we get into the realm of aesthetic qualities, feelings, beliefs, values, categories, and concepts, we move higher up on the scale of abstraction.

Semantic Reactions

Communication is complex because we know that much of what we say does not have operational meaning. In many cases, the best we can do is to create *semantic reactions*—generating either a favorable or an unfavorable response. If I have good communication skills I should be able to get the kind of reaction from you that I want. If my intent is to have you to think favorably about a person, I might say, "He is firmly committed to his beliefs." To create an unfavorable response I would probably say, "He is stubborn in his opinions." Although the two statements may appear to be similar, the *semantic reaction* in one case would be significantly different from that in the other. This is a principle we must be able to understand in order to communicate effectively.

When the press reported that Hillary Clinton had participated in an exercise called *guided visualization,* many readers reacted to the term as though it were a belief in the supernatural. Other people, who were more familiar with personal growth workshop activities, recognized that this was a commonly used method of expanding someone's understanding of a person or an event. In this case, the First Lady had been asked to write a letter to Eleanor Roosevelt as a means of gaining insight into the thoughts of a woman she admired. If the phrase had been, *picture in your mind . . .* or *write an imaginary letter . . .* the semantic reaction might have been different.

Euphemisms

Discussing subjects that arouse strong emotional feelings often makes us uncomfortable, and we have a tendency to try to soften the impact created by stark or abrasive words. This generally happens when we are talking about something that we fear, such as death, or something that embarrasses us, such as sex. When we use an inoffensive term to conceal our emotional anxiety or embarrassment, we are speaking in *euphemisms.* For example, we don't like to say that a person died, so we say he "passed away." If we are too embarrassed to say that two unmarried people were having sex, we say they were "having an affair." Euphemisms such as these are generally regarded as proper because they are more polite and less offensive to the senses than are more coarsely worded terminology, but there are other euphemisms that are coined specifically to avoid confronting the real issue. A military action is sometimes called a "skirmish," and when bombs hit residential areas and civilians are killed, the news releases say that there has been "collateral damage." Language of this kind is defended by the press and by the military on the grounds that it communicates the message in a diplomatic way, but it is criticized by others, who say it insulates the listener and the reader from understanding the harsh reality of the events.

Shortcuts

People who know each other well, have similar interests, or work in the same professional or vocational fields are able to communicate effectively without having to be explicitly detailed in their conversation. If you are connected to show business, for example, you might refer to "the house" rather than to "the number of people who attended the theater," and you would shorten the titles of plays and musicals: For example, *The Phantom of the Opera* would become simply, "Phantom." In everyday language, a compact disc is a *CD,* and the World Wide Web is just *The Web.* Acronyms such as *FBI, FCC,* and *FDA* are all listed in the *American Heritage Dictionary* as though they were words. The shortcuts cited here are common enough for anyone to understand, but a speaker needs to be sensitive to the audience's background and not use jargon or initials that are not likely to be understood. For example, people in education may know that an "AP teacher" is one who has students in advanced placement classes, but the general public probably does not.

Legal Language

In legal matters it is often necessary to clarify vague terminology in order to translate abstract concepts into principles of law. This is particularly well illustrated in decisions the Supreme Court has made pertaining to the word *speech* as it appears in the First Amendment to the Constitution. Is the meaning of *speech* confined to verbal expression? No, says the Supreme Court. Speech can include certain forms of nonverbal communication; therefore, wearing a black armband as a protest gesture is protected under the First Amendment and is referred to as *symbolic speech.* That term was used again in 1989, when the Supreme Court handed down a decision that said the burning of the U.S. flag was also regarded as symbolic speech. If it had been deemed an "act of violence," it could have been prohibited. However, because it was construed as a political statement, a legal statute could not forbid it. Each court decision contributes to the legal definition of words, and, because law is based on precedence, the terminology from one ruling can provide the basis of understanding in subsequent cases.

A significant part of being an effective communicator is to understand the conventional meaning that society attaches to abstract words. Certainly there is a difference between art that is called "erotic" and that which is labeled "pornographic." *Erotic art* depicts sexual love, whereas *pornography* is intended to incite lascivious feelings. You might be inclined to say that the difference is only in the mind of the beholder, but that's not good enough when it comes to establishing public policy. Your community may want to place restrictions on one but not on the other. Therefore, the outcome of the language used in verbal descriptions that become codified into law makes a big difference to merchants and to patrons of the arts.

Intentional Choice of Words

Choosing words in order to create a desired impression is in itself an art, and no one knows this better than people in the world of merchandising. Advertising copywriters are paid big salaries for thinking of words that trigger positive responses. Exhaustive studies are conducted to discover what kind of effect certain words have on the public. Terms such as *all new* and *patented formula* are catch phrases specifically designed to make us want to buy the product, and a "preowned car" is more attractive to buyers than a "used car" is. Is this practice limited to advertising agencies? By no means—we all do it to one degree or another. If we are *intentional* in our communication, we choose words that generate the kind of feeling we want to evoke in the mind of the receiver of our message.

We say *the word is not the thing,* but we know that people react to a notion on the basis of the term that is used to describe it. For example, if we are able to change the name of a band of mercenaries to *Freedom Fighters,* we are more likely to get financial support from Congress. And if a nuclear missile is unpopular because it is viewed as an offensive weapon, we may be able to create a more favorable impression by giving it a name such as the *Peacekeeper.*

Certainly, the question of ethics is one that must be considered by serious students of public address. Speakers must know that when they are standing on the podium they have a responsibility to their audience. They are there because they believe they have something to say that will contribute to truth and justice. However, if they use words deceptively to create a false impression, they are engaging in sophistry. But, at the same time, there is a responsibility on the part of those of us who are the receivers. We can defend our integrity by learning to become intelligent, perceptive, and discerning listeners.

EXERCISE

Here is an exercise for testing comprehensive listening. Read the following paragraph out loud to someone who has not read it or heard it before. See if the listener can grasp the main idea and retain the information. This can also be regarded as an exercise in giving an oral explanation. Be as helpful as you can in making it possible for the listener to comprehend the message; speak slowly and emphasize the specifics that you think are important:

> There are $365\frac{1}{4}$ days in a year. That means every fourth year is designated as a "leap year" and we have to add an extra day. But each year of $365\frac{1}{4}$ days is actually 11 minutes and 14 seconds too long. That adds up to 3 excess days every 400 years. In other words, we have to skip 3 leap year days out of every 400 years. So, to even things out, we did not have a leap year in 1700, 1800, or 1900. However, we are now all caught up, and the year 2000 will be a leap year. We will not need to skip a leap year again until the year 2100.

QUESTIONS FOR REVIEW

1. If a student can read a textbook two or three times faster than a professor can speak, why is it still a good idea for the student to hear the lecture?
2. How can the audience improve the delivery of a professor's lecture?
3. What kind of nonverbal feedback might a listener give to a speaker? How reliable is that feedback?
4. What are some of the reasons "nonlistening" may occur?
5. What is meant by *listening passively?* What are three levels of listening actively?
6. What are eight obstacles to comprehensive listening, and how are they overcome?
7. How does *critical listening* differ from *comprehensive listening?*
8. What is a "red herring"?
9. What is a "straw man"?
10. What is meant by *ad populum?*
11. What is meant by *ad hominem?*
12. What is meant by *begging the question?*
13. What is a circular argument?
14. What does *non sequitur* mean?
15. What does *post hoc ergo propter hoc* mean?
16. What is meant by *operational meaning?*
17. What is meant by *semantic reaction?*
18. What is a euphemism?
19. What is symbolic speech?

THE MESSAGE

Good
Chapter

CHAPTER 5

THE TOPIC, PURPOSE, AND CONTENT OF THE SPEECH

**AFTER READING THIS CHAPTER, YOU SHOULD
BE ABLE TO DO THE FOLLOWING:**

Begin planning your speech by considering the appropriateness,
complexity, significance, and scope of the topic.

Know the distinguishing characteristics of speeches to inform, to
persuade, to motivate, and to entertain.

Know how to find information on the Internet and World Wide Web;
use a computer terminal or indexes in bound volumes to
access material in periodicals.

Recognize various forms of supporting information that add substance
to the main assertions you make in your speech; know how to use
"interest grabbers" to hold the attention of your audience.

About now you might be asking yourself, "Even if I decide I am willing to make a presentation, why would anyone want to come to hear me?" That's a good question to use as a starting point, because it orients your thinking toward the needs and interests of the audience. Public speaking is a *rhetorical* art, not a *performing* art. People are not going to come to hear how well you *deliver* a speech; they come because they are interested in the subject matter. You do, of course, want your delivery to be as good as you can make it, but, more important, you want the *substance* of your message to be worth the time that the audience is investing. People who make a lot of speeches know that it's not easy to attract an audience. If you are able to get twenty or thirty people together who are willing to listen to you for a half hour, you can regard yourself as being quite fortunate. They have made an effort for you, so it's your responsibility to make an effort for them.

THE TOPIC

Topic and purpose are interrelated, and it's hard to know which of those two should be your first consideration. The chances are that your instructor will be clear in assigning you either a speech intended to inform the listeners or a speech intended to persuade them. Or, if you are invited to speak to a community organization, the program chairperson will probably let you know whether or not the audience expects you to take a position on a controversial topic. It may be that the group just wants information and would rather not have you argue for one side or the other. In either of these cases, observe the guidelines that have been proscribed. If your intent is to give a speech that is intended to inform, be cautious about selecting controversial topics that would reveal your bias.

If public speaking is a new experience for you, selecting the topic may seem at first to be difficult. Begin by thinking of things with which you have had direct experience—hobbies you pursue, trips you have taken, jobs you have held, organizations you belong to, computer applications you use, and so on. Consider also topics that you have studied or read about in books and magazines. As you begin listing possibilities, you may be surprised at how many subjects there are that you can talk knowledgeably about. Here are a few suggested topics for a speech that is intended to inform.

- Job hunting on the Internet
- New evidence of life on Mars
- Experiments in extrasensory perception
- Government grants and academic scholarships
- The wealth of redwood trees
- Treatment for attention deficit disorder (ADD)
- How dinosaurs resemble birds
- Multicultural influence on U.S. business

It may be that you are given wide latitude in selecting your topic. Having lots of choices could make the task easier, but it could also make it harder. In order to be sure that you are meeting the criteria assigned to you, make for yourself a checklist.

Appropriateness

Be sure to consider the way the audience is likely to perceive your information. You may intend to give an informative speech on human fossils that were found a million years ago; however, your claims could be regarded as controversial if you happen to be speaking to a religious organization that believes literally in the biblical story of creation.

Complexity

Consider the complexity of the subject matter. You may know a great deal about a theoretical concept in physics or mathematics, but if the audience does not have the background that you do, your explanations might be too difficult for them to understand. Subjects that are extremely complex often lend themselves more to individual instruction than to public address. Giving a speech that is way over the heads of the listeners will lead them to believe that you are trying to make an impression by showing off your knowledge.

Significance

Select a topic that has some significance. Don't waste your time or the time of the audience on trivialities. You don't want to go beyond the listeners' capabilities for comprehension, but you don't want to insult their intelligence either. Remember that you are making a serious presentation, not performing a comedy act in a coffee house.

Scope

Don't overestimate the amount of material you can cover in the time you are allowed. If the subject area you are considering is too broad, you may find yourself under too much pressure to include everything you want to say. Bring your topic into focus. That means you must narrow the scope so that you have enough time to elaborate on the points you want to make.

THE PURPOSE

There are four general purposes for speeches in public address—(1) *to inform,* (2) *to persuade,* (3) *to motivate,* and (4) *to entertain.* The purpose you have in mind must not be equivocal, because you don't want your message to be misconstrued. Certainly, you can use humor in a speech to inform, but if you intend to leave your audience with information they can use, you must not let your jokes obscure the factual content. Decide what you want to accomplish, so that the audience doesn't have to wonder what you had in mind. There have been times when students in my class have given speeches that were absolutely hilarious, and all of us were thoroughly amused; nevertheless, a comedy routine is not the same thing as a speech that is designed to inform.

The general purpose of the speech does not need to be stated directly. It's not a good idea to say to your audience, "My purpose is to persuade you . . . ," because you may set up resistance to what you want to accomplish. Often, your general purpose will be suggested by the nature of the occasion. The person who invites you to speak will give you some indication by asking you to explain a procedure, support a recommendation, get a program moving, or lighten the mood of the audience. Try to accommodate your listeners by giving them what they want and what they expect. It is not good form to launch into a persuasive speech when you have been asked to simply provide information.

We'll be discussing speech to inform and speech to persuade in detail in later chapters, but let's take a brief look at all of the four general purposes.

The Speech to Inform

Almost all speeches contain some information, but the *speech to inform* has that characteristic as its primary function. Your speech falls into this category if you are making an effort to present your material objectively, without trying to persuade your audience to accept your solution to a problem. The subject matter might deal with controversial material, but when you are giving a speech to inform, you are not trying to influence the decision of the audience one way or another. You are simply giving them the information they need in order for them to make up their own minds. Sometimes you hear this type of presentation referred to as an *expository* speech.

The Speech to Persuade

If you were making a speech in a courtroom or legislative hearing room you would probably be giving a *speech to persuade.* Your purpose would be to try to get your audience to think favorably about your cause and to believe as you believe. You would still be giving information to your listeners, but you would also be adding an interpretation that would lead them to a particular conclusion. In this type of speech you would anticipate opposition, and you would be prepared to refute it. You would probably be using both emotional and logical appeals.

The Speech to Motivate

The kind of speech that is designed to inspire people is called the *speech to motivate.* When it is delivered from a pulpit it is called a *sermon* or a *homily.* It might also be a presentation made by a marketing manager who is introducing a new promotional campaign or is trying to generate enthusiasm on the part of the sales staff. It may contain some factual evidence, but the most successful speeches of this kind rely heavily on appeals to universal values, metaphorical language, and illustrations that reach people at the emotional level. The audience would probably be made up of people who already agree with the basic premise of the speaker but who are looking for inspiration. The purpose here is to move people to action: to live a better life, to work for a cause, to contribute their money, to join an organization, or to vote for a candidate.

The Speech to Entertain

If you were an actor or a comedian and liked to perform on the stage, you might be asked to give a *speech to entertain*. Such a presentation is often referred to as an *after-dinner speech* and is designed primarily for the sake of amusement. You would not expect the audience to learn anything of significance or to be persuaded to a point of view; you would simply want the listeners to enjoy the experience. This kind of speech generally consists of humorous references, anecdotes, and narrations worked around a central theme. It is appropriate when an audience is in a relaxed or perhaps frivolous mood.

THE CONTENT

Now you have selected your topic and established your purpose: Next, you need to gather information to make up the substance of your speech. Probably you already have a few ideas in your head, but those must be augmented by material found in published sources.

Start by recalling what you already know. Think of what you might have learned by working at an interesting job, traveling, talking to others who are informed on the topic, watching a TV documentary, or reading books and periodicals. Then make a visit to your library. Be sure you start your research early; you may find that the topic is more complex than you had thought. You might also discover that what you thought was true, actually is not. When that happens, you may have to change your thesis altogether. Begin your research with an open mind, and allow the information you gather to lead you to your conclusion. You will want the most reliable data, and also the most current.

The Internet and the World Wide Web

To find up-to-date information on your topic, use your computer to get onto the Internet and the World Wide Web. Most libraries will have several terminals that will give you access to the Internet through *servers* that are "on-ramps" to the information superhighway. Once you're on, you need a "browser" in order to connect with a Web site. The one that is most widely used at this time is Netscape, which allows you to download graphics as well as print. You will also need a "search engine" such as Yahoo or Alta Vista, to help you locate Web sites that contain information on the topic of your choice. You can go directly to a particular Web site if you know the address; it's called an *URL—Universal*

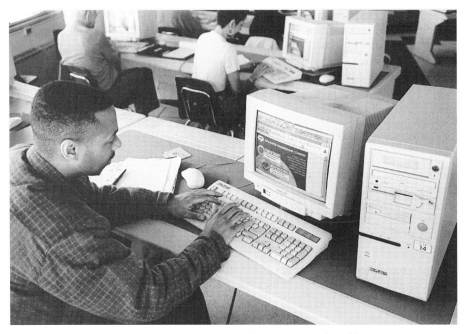

The Internet will give you current information, but you must be able to recognize what is useful and reliable.

Resource Locator. A daily newspaper, for example, will publish its Web site address so that readers can go to it and find background material or in-depth reports. If you don't know the specific site number, you can use the search engine to help you find what you want. Type in a few key words, and you will get a list of what is available. Try to be as specific as you can; otherwise, you may find that your choices are in the tens of thousands. If you have trouble locating what you want, ask a library assistant to help you. Most colleges have computer labs staffed with knowledgeable personnel who are trained to guide the novice "surfer" in finding useful Web sites.

The World Wide Web has made, and will continue to make, a remarkable difference in the way we send and receive information. The quantity of words and pictures out there in cyberspace is immense, and that is a problem as well as an opportunity.

Retrieval

The sheer volume of data available to us makes the task of retrieving information a bit overwhelming. First of all, we need to have the technical expertise that is necessary in order to operate the computer software; we need to be analytical enough to know what questions to ask and what key words to use in our search; we must be able to recognize useful information and separate it from the mounds of garbage; we need to evaluate the content and the source of the material; and we must know what to do with it after it has been downloaded. But there is yet another frustrating characteristic that you will discover when you begin doing research on the Internet: When you try to go back to the same site you had used a few days before, you often find that the information you want is no longer there. A Web site does not have the same permanence as a magazine article. There are not thousands of copies of it in libraries and bookstores, and the words can be changed or completely deleted with a few flicks on a keyboard. So, once you find something of value, be sure you save it. If it is print rather than graphics, you can download it to your hard drive; that way you can return to it easily. You can also print a hard copy of it, or simply take good notes.

Quality of the Source

The fact that the World Wide Web is so expansive means that we must be extremely alert when we use it. Think about the implications: Individuals or groups who have a product or a cause to sell, a little money, and a personal computer can set up a Web site. If they have some skills in graphic design, they can make up a really attractive Web page. It's like having their own magazine or newspaper. They can write whatever they want and make it available to thousands of people. What's more, they don't have to go through the evaluation or editing process that writers must when they submit work to professional journals. Then, you come along doing your research, and the Web site of someone with an ax to grind pops up, along with all the others. Therefore, when you gather information from the Web, you must read very critically; otherwise, you might find yourself quoting radical and one-sided assertions.

The Time and Expense

You may have access to the Internet through your home computer. You're fortunate if you do, because that's like having your own personal library. The danger, however, is that you may spend so much time on-line that you run up a big bill. That can easily happen. If you are using a computer at a library, you won't have the expense, but you will be consuming time looking at the monitor while others might be waiting. Some libraries have only two or three terminals, and there may be restrictions on access time. It may be more fun to get your information from a cathode ray tube (CRT), but don't forget how to read from the printed page.

Access to Periodicals and Books

Information that appears in periodicals may not be as current as that which is on the Internet, but it is sound and reliable. Generally, libraries carry only publications that have high integrity and credibility. Although the volume of material might be limited and the periodical you want may not be on the shelves, the chances are that what you do find can be trusted. Again, you will probably need to use a computer terminal to conduct your search.

The system used by the library might be called *Magazine Index* or *InfoTrac.* It will be able to access four or five hundred periodicals, plus newspapers such as the *New York Times* and *The Wall Street Journal.* To find the sources, simply enter a subject title and press the SEARCH key. A list of articles will appear on the screen, and you can pick the one you want. You can also get a short summary of the article, so that you can see if it really is something that would be useful. It may be that your library has a system that will allow you to download the entire article.

Indexes in Bound Volumes

Yes, these are still available in many libraries: The *Readers' Guide to Periodical Literature* may be handy if you are looking for material that is more than fifteen years old. Other good sources, also in bound volumes, are the *Social Science Index,* the *Humanities Index,* the *Business Index,* and the *Education Index.* These references are cross-indexed by title, author, and subject headings, similar to the *Readers' Guide.* They will direct you to the more scholarly articles and recent studies that appear in professional journals such as *Political Science Quarterly* and the *Journal of Philosophy.* The *New York Times Index* is an extremely useful library reference that can be used when you know the approximate time of an event and want specific information about the details. The volumes are arranged according to subject and in a chronological sequence. You will find a brief summary of the event itself and also a reference to the *New York Times* edition that carried the story in detail. For in-depth research you could go into the archives of the newspaper and retrieve the original article.

Social Issues Resources Series (SIRS)

SIRS is a source that includes current articles on social issues, and it's available at many libraries on CD-ROM. It will provide you with a description of a given problem, an analysis of causes, and possible solutions. It is supplemented with new material every year. Among the social issues listed are crime, family, population, human rights, and others that are frequently used as speech topics.

Reference Books

There are a great many other sources you can use for background information: the *World Almanac, Facts on File, Statistical Abstract of the United States,* and the *Congressional Quarterly Researcher,* to name just a few. As you progress in your college work, learn to use research tools other than just encyclopedias and dictionaries. And, by all means, don't hesitate to ask the librarian for assistance.

Taking Notes

Library research can be time-consuming and still not be productive if you fail to keep track of what you read. The beginning speech student may spend many hours in the library pouring over books and periodicals, yet fail to include any concrete information in the speech. Don't rely on your memory alone; take notes as you read. Record names of people, places, and things; professional titles and positions; dates and times; costs and quantities; court cases and scientific studies; and any details you might need to put into your outline to help

Reference books in bound volumes are still available in libraries.

you develop and substantiate the explanations or historical accounts that you plan to include in the speech. Be sure you make note of your sources. On some occasions, the audience may be skeptical about what you say, and being able to cite the source will help to validate the data.

If you find that your research takes a good deal of time and effort, you are probably going about it in the right way. Most preachers will tell you that it takes about an hour of study to prepare for every minute of a sermon.

FORMS OF SUPPORT

A speech that is well-balanced is one that has variety in its development. You would not want to give or hear a speech that is composed entirely of quotations or statistics, although those are both substantial forms of elaboration. Let's examine the kinds of supporting material that you can look for when you are gathering information and taking notes on what you want to include in the speech.

Definition of Terms

Formal debates often begin with a definition of terms so that there is no misunderstanding of the issue. Normally, you don't need to start a speech that way, but there may be words and phrases used in specific ways that are outside the listener's frame of reference and must be explained at some point. While you are in the process of gathering your information, make note of what you think may need to be defined.

Technical Words. A speech dealing with electronic equipment will be difficult for members of an audience to understand if they do not have a technical background. Listeners may give up trying to follow you if the terminology is not clear. You might need to explain to novices, for example, that *peripherals* refer to hardware such as scanners, modems, printers, and CD-ROM players that are attached to a computer.

Legal Terms. If you were giving a speech dealing with legal issues, there might be specific terms that you would have to define, such as *reasonable doubt* or *probable cause.* Ordinary reference books would not be much help to you; you would have to consult a source such as *Black's Law Dictionary.*

Words in Other Languages. We are used to people borrowing words from other languages when the English word is not adequate to convey the idea. We are all conversant with the Hawaiian word *aloha* or the Hebrew expression *shalom.* But if a foreign word is not well-known, it requires a definition. For example, if you say that it's important for students to have *ganas* in order to learn, you might have explain that *ganas* is the Spanish word meaning "desire" or "willingness."

Common Words with Specialized Meanings. We may think we know the meaning of a word, but if it is used in a specialized way we may not understand it at all. In education, for example, the word *articulation* does not mean the ability to speak clearly. In that context, it refers to the arrangements two schools make in order to coordinate their programs.

Words Defined by Quantitative Measure. If you were to make a speech in favor of giving federal aid to people living in poverty, you would have to define quantitatively what you meant by the term *poverty.* In this case, the definition is continually changing as the cost of living changes. In 1995, for example, the poverty level was set at $15,569 per year for a family of four.[1] Five years earlier it had been $13,359.[2] You can see how the number of people considered to be living in poverty could be modified by raising or lowering that economic index.

[1] U.S. Census Bureau, www.census.gov/, 1996.
[2] Ibid.

Specific Instances

As you read, look for specific instances that are interesting and related to the point you want to make. Include details of the illustration in order to add credibility to your statement. You may wish to cite a number of such examples or take just one and elaborate on it. If your topic is controversial, you will have to point out how the incident you have selected leads to the conclusion you want to draw. This kind of rhetorical support is sometimes called *anecdotal,* and it is an excellent device for gaining and holding the attention of the audience. People like to listen to stories, particularly those that have unusual or mysterious characteristics.

Sometimes theories are based on anecdotal support: For example, the mystery of the Bermuda Triangle was created by an Associated Press reporter named E. V. W. Jones. He noted an instance that occurred on December 5, 1945, when five Navy torpedo bombers took off from a base in Fort Lauderdale, Florida, and were never seen or heard of again. That incident, by itself, might not have attracted attention, but Jones discovered that there were a number of other mysterious disappearances that also occurred in the same triangle marked by Bermuda, Puerto Rico, and Fort Lauderdale. The story captured the imagination of people all over the world.

Anecdotes are fun and interesting for the storyteller as well as for the audience, but let's make sure we put their value and significance in perspective. By themselves, they cannot *prove* a generalization; they are simply indicators that a condition may exist. Too frequently people jump to conclusions based on anecdotal support, without asking for more substantial evidence. Medical theories, for example, may cite instances when people were cured of a disease by a particular herb or vitamin. The theory may begin to develop credibility if there are a great many reports of circumstances that produce the same result, but unless there are controlled studies to verify the theory, the scientific world is generally skeptical.

Controlled Studies

When we conduct a controlled study, we are using what is called the *scientific method.* We start with a hypothesis or a theory. Then we proceed to test it by setting up a series of experiments in which we control all of the variables. By modifying one variable at a time and observing the results, we begin to learn what the outcome will be when a particular adjustment is made. To find out what causes cancer in rats, for example, we control the conditions of their environment and then proceed to make one change at a time in their diet or exposure to chemical substances. If we get to a point where we can repeat the experiment and are able to predict what result will be produced by a particular change, we say that the study has *reliability.*

As an undergraduate college student you will probably not be called on to conduct original research; you can simply examine the studies that have already been made. But you want to know how such studies are conducted so that you are able to tell if your information is really substantial. Studies conducted in physics and chemistry, of course, are going to be more reliable than those conducted in the behavioral sciences; however, the same methodology is used. Studies frequently have to be qualified by language that acknowledges that there are exceptions to the generalizations being made. You can cite studies, for example, that show that smoking cigarettes causes lung cancer, but you would have to acknowledge that there are people who smoke who do not get cancer and that there are people who get cancer who do not smoke. But even though there are exceptions to the findings, scientific studies are more reliable than the casual observations we make.

Statistical Data

By *statistical data,* we mean any kind of information that can be expressed in numbers. It is sometimes called *quantitative information*—that is, evidence that can be counted or measured. It may be in the form of totals, percentages, averages, rates, or other numerical values. It can be obtained by actual count or from random samples. Statistics may be important in order to establish the validity of a claim. If you try to persuade without using quantitative evidence, your listeners may begin to believe that you are simply trying to sell them "blue sky" notions that have no substantive meaning. Consider the following claims that a speaker might make:

1. "There is a great deal of oil that can still be drilled off the coast of California."
2. "Most people are in favor of capital punishment."
3. "Students who go to parochial schools score higher on achievement tests than do those who go to public schools."

All of these claims require quantitative support; specific instances or anecdotal evidence alone would not be sufficient. In the first example, you might report on the barrels of oil that have already been pumped from one well. But, in order to make the claim that a lot is still available you will need an estimate from an expert in the field who has conducted reliable studies. Even if you had that figure, listeners might also want to know how much that is in comparison to other oil fields and how long it would last at the present rate of consumption.

The second statement would also have to be supported by statistical information. It would not be enough to ask eight or ten people whether they favored capital punishment. You would have to present figures gathered from a recent survey that was conducted using a random or representative sample of a given population. And then you would have to restrict your generalization so that it applied to people in the particular area that was surveyed.

In order for the third statement to be an acceptable claim, you would have to compare the scores of the parochial students with those of students in public schools. The comparison would have to be based on the same test given to a significant sample of students under identical conditions.

Use statistics to support a generalization when it is necessary, but use them in such a way as to provide clarification and credibility to what you are saying. Here are some suggestions:

- Don't inundate your listeners with more statistics than they can retain. If you have a long list, put the figures on a chart for them to see, write them on a chalkboard, or distribute copies of a handout sheet. Doing this will help them remember and will also impress on them that the numbers are important.
- Round off large numbers when it's possible to do so without distorting the information. For example, an expenditure of $1,468,216.00 can be expressed in a speech more easily as "almost one and a half million dollars."
- Don't use figures deceptively. Avoid the habit of substituting percentages for adjectives. Although you may have reason to believe that a large portion of the staff favors a four-day workweek, don't say, ". . . and 90 percent of the people on the staff like the idea," unless you have actually taken a survey.
- Don't compare absolute numbers with percentages. It is not very useful to say "a neighboring district cut its expenses by $200,000 whereas our reduction was only 6 percent."

Accuracy

Statistics can be misleading if you are not careful. For example, figures that show a rising crime rate may not necessarily indicate an increase in crime; they may merely reflect an increase in arrests. As a similar example, records show that more automobile accidents are caused by men than by women. However, this doesn't mean that women are better drivers; it just means that men do more driving. Recognizing such fallacies in the use of statistics is not just the responsibility of the audience, it is also the responsibility of the ethical speaker.

The advantage of employing statistics is that they give the listener the "big picture" and add significance to your assertions. The danger is that statistics can be carelessly used. Numbers can be manipulated by words, as illustrated in the following example:

> Three men decided to share a hotel room that cost $30. They each paid the clerk $10 and went up to the room. Later, the clerk remembered that the room had been reduced in price to $25, so he told the bellhop to take $5 back to the three men. On the way up to the room the bellhop decided to keep $2 for a tip. He gave the men $3, so they each got a dollar back. The room then cost each man $9 instead of $10. Three times nine is twenty-seven; the bellhop kept $2. What happened to the other dollar?

In this example, the arithmetic is accurate, but the conclusion is false, because the words used to relate the story are deceptive. (The men paid more than nine dollars for the room, because they each gave a third of a dollar tip to the bellhop.) The point is that *figures do not speak for themselves.* The speaker has an obligation to interpret statistical evidence in a responsible way so that the numbers clarify an issue rather than obscure it.

Emphasis

The emphasis you place on the statistical data and the way you state the evidence will have a lot to do with the impact the numbers have on the listeners. For example, it may be true that a corporation's profit increased 100 percent. But it could also be true that its net profits went from 2 to 4 percent. Both of those statements might be perfectly accurate; the speaker has the prerogative of selecting which one to use.

There are certain extrapolations you can make from statistical data. For example, if a survey indicates that 54 percent of the eligible voters cast a ballot, you can assume that 46 percent did not. But there are precautions you must take in making assumptions. A speaker might claim that in the past decade the number of marriages per 1,000 population remained the same, but that the number of divorces doubled. The ratio of marriages to divorces in this country is now about 2 to 1. That evidence does not mean, however, that 1 of 2 marriages will end in divorce, because many people get married and divorced more than once. What's more, it is not a reasonable extrapolation to say that any particular couple has a 50 percent chance of getting a divorce. Statistics, no matter how accurate they may be, are not able to predict individual behavior.

Interest

Another thing we can say about statistics is that they tend to be dull. You can make them more interesting if you can provide an illustration that listeners are able to visualize. For example, if you want to impress people with the size of the world's oil supply, you could tell them that all of the petroleum we have taken out of the ground in the past 150 years would fill a lake the size of Chicago to a depth of 300 feet. Then you can add that it is estimated there is still enough oil in the world to raise the level of the lake to 2,300 feet.

Testimonial Evidence

Much of the evidence you will want to include in your speech will not be quantitative and will need to be expressed in words rather than numbers. Again, you will want to go beyond your own experience and relate observations that have been made by other people. This type of support is called *testimonial evidence* and can be divided into two categories:

Eyewitness Accounts

Suppose an issue under consideration at your college is whether or not security officers should carry guns on campus. Because it is a topic of local interest, you will need to have the perspective of people who have had direct experience with the situation in your particular area. Probably the best person to talk to would be a campus security guard. He or she might tell you that there is no reason for an officer to carry a gun, because there have been very few instances of physical attacks. In the cases when an officer has had to intervene, the perpetrator was unarmed, and either ran off or submitted without resistance. A different impression, however, could be given by a guard who has been on night patrol. "It may seem like a safe campus in the daytime," the guard might report, "but at night it becomes a meeting place for drug dealers. They carry guns, and they know that we do not." Which of these two eyewitness accounts would you use? If you were giving a persuasive speech and advocating a position, you would have to pick one or the other.

Court trials rely heavily on eyewitness testimony. Witnesses will often be called upon to describe in detail precisely what they saw or heard. They must testify only to that which they actually experienced—what other people told them is called *hearsay evidence* and is not admissible. Although eyewitness accounts are given great weight by judges and juries, such testimony is not infallible. Many experiments have been conducted showing that wide discrepancies can appear in the accounts of different witnesses to the same event. When there are several eyewitnesses who all testify to having seen the same thing, the evidence is very strong. But if one person saw something that no one else did, the evidence may be open to some question.

Expert Testimony

Often, courts will call to the stand people who are referred to as *expert witnesses.* These are people who have expertise in a particular field and are able to verify the results of a study, experiment, or observation. They are able to understand technical data and relate scientific findings that are pertinent to the case. A ballistics expert, for example, can testify that two bullets were fired from the same gun. The jurors do not need to witness the actual test; they only need to hear the testimony of the expert.

For a speech you are preparing on the cost of education, for example, you might want to gather information from the bookstore manager. Rather than relying on your own observations about the cost of books, you can add credibility to your speech by quoting someone who is directly involved in pricing policies. That person becomes your "expert" and might be able to give an explanation that is better-informed than your own could be. It may be that the cost of a large volume containing highly specialized material with many color illustrations would be priced even higher than it is, if the expense were not balanced by increasing the markup on smaller books that are sold in larger quantities. That's a policy that could be modified, perhaps, but any change would need to be based on the testimony of an expert.

Explanation

In both the speech to inform and the speech to persuade you may need to provide explanations. As the speaker, you must be sure you understand the material thoroughly yourself. Explanations can be regarded in a number of different ways.

Analysis

When we analyze an event, we try to discover what happened, what worked, and what didn't work. Football coaches do this all the time when they watch the playback of a game. They observe what each player did on every down, and from this analysis they can develop strategies for future games. Conducting an in-depth analysis on a complex issue is probably not something you would do as an individual; instead, you might report on an analysis made by an institution or an expert in the field. The National Academy of Sciences, for example, completed a fifteen-month study on the *greenhouse effect*—a global condition that traps harmful gases within our atmosphere. The conclusion of the Academy's analysis was that the danger of the greenhouse effect was real, that it could adversely affect the weather patterns of the entire world, and that carbon dioxide produced by the burning of fossil fuels was the most serious offender. The value of an analysis of this kind is that it tells you what questions need to be asked in order to find a solution: How can we generate electricity in the quantity we need without producing carbon monoxide? Do we have to stop relying on the burning of fossil fuels? What other energy sources are available to us? Questions of this kind are extremely important in the process that leads to workable solutions.

Historical Background

At the time you are doing your research, try to think of what historical background your audience will need in order to understand the point you are trying to make. In an earlier chapter, for example, reference was made to the Supreme Court decision of *Brown v. the Topeka Board of Education* in 1954. Some audiences would understand that reference; others would not. You might have to elaborate by explaining that ever since the end of the Civil War, the South claimed that it was the right of the states to determine if they wanted to maintain separate facilities for blacks and whites. Until 1954, federal law allowed the southern states to do that. But, in the *Brown* decision, the Court said that the Constitutional rights of black children were violated when state law required that they attend separate schools from white children, even if the facilities provided were equal.

Providing this kind of background information might be necessary if your audience is composed of people who are new to this country or perhaps are young and have not studied the social conditions of earlier generations.

Description

Another form of explanation is *description.* If you have the ability to paint word pictures, you can create images in the minds of your listeners. You may want to tell what it is to live in an urban slum; or you might wish to describe the beauty of Yellowstone National Park. This form of rhetorical development can be extremely effective if you are skillful in selecting relevant details and using vivid language. Description can be a powerful persuasive device if employed for that purpose.

Narration

Examples can be conveyed to an audience simply by presenting the bare facts, but you can generate more interest and create a stronger impact by relating the information in narrative form. Vice President Al Gore did this in his acceptance speech at the Democratic Convention in 1996. He related how his sister Nancy Gore Hunter died at the age of forty-five from lung cancer. He said she had begun smoking at the age of thirteen and had been unable to quit even though she knew she had a life-threatening disease. He concluded his narration by saying, "Tomorrow morning, another thirteen-year-old will start smoking."

In order for a narration to be effective, it needs to have a "punch line" at the end, so that your audience will get the point. Be aware that a narration of this kind may be emotionally moving for some people, as this one was for Democrats; however, others may find it overly dramatic.

Analogy

An effective aid to explanation is *analogy*. Most people can learn better when new information is compared to something they already understand. For example, if you wanted to explain the flow of electricity through a wire, you might compare the concept to the flow of water through a pipe. In a speech on this subject, you could say that the water's motion is called the *current*, the pressure that pushes the water is the *voltage*, the valve that controls the flow is the *resistance*, and the work done by the water is the *power*. With this picture in mind, the listener might better be able to understand your explanation.

In addition to simplifying complex material, analogies can also be used to add color and vividness to your language. In doing this, the points you make and the ideas you advance are more likely to be remembered. In a speech on career planning, for example, you may want to say that sometimes it is necessary to move on to a new occupation, even though there may be some risk in doing so. Your analogy could be that of a circus aerialist who must let go of one trapeze and spend an agonizing few seconds in midair without any support before grabbing onto the next bar. Having established the analogy, you can reinforce the point by making reference to the trapeze artist again later in the speech.

Analogies can be used in comparing any two concepts that have similar characteristics. Suppose you wanted to recommend that the United States extend free or low-cost health insurance to all citizens. You could say that good health is just as important to the citizens in a democracy as a good education is, and that because we provide free public schools, we should also see that every citizen has access to affordable medical care.

Interest Grabbers

In either the speech to inform or the speech to persuade, it is necessary for the speaker to hold the listeners' attention. In doing your research and gathering your thoughts, look for *interest grabbers*—examples or references that are not only informative but will make the audience want to listen. Here are a few ideas along those lines:

Humor

One of the most effective means of establishing rapport with the audience is humor. When you get people to laugh, they are actively participating in the communication process. You don't need to be funny all the way through the speech, and your jokes don't need to be sidesplitters. But work your humorous remarks into the theme of the speech so that they're relevant to what you are saying. *Example:* "One of my colleagues recently asked me if I believed in free speech. I told him that I certainly did. 'That's good,' he said, 'because I'd like to have you give one to my class next week.'"

Suspense

The reason adventure stories are popular is that they keep us in suspense. We read or listen through to the end in order to find out what is going to happen. In the *Tales of the Arabian Nights,* Scheherazade was such a good storyteller that the king let her live as long as she continued to keep him in suspense. Take a lesson from this ancient tale and learn to hold the attention of your audience by not revealing the ending of your story until you build it to a climax. The same principle applies to telling jokes. Don't give away the punch line until you have sparked the curiosity of the listener.

Unusual Examples

Not all examples have to be unusual ones, but if you are able to add a few that have really interesting features, you can change an ordinary speech into one that people will remember. Some topics lend themselves to unusual examples more than do others. For example, new products in the high-tech industry provide us with a wealth of material. One of my students described in his speech a new electronic device that would help keep people from losing their credit cards. It was designed in such a way that it started playing a tune after it had been exposed to light for several minutes. It continued to play until it was programmed to stop. An added feature was that you could pick from among a hundred tunes one that you wanted it to play. Presumably, you could program it to cry out for help if it were stolen.

Familiar References

Have you ever been daydreaming during a lecture and then snapped back to attention when the speaker mentioned the name of a friend, or a place you had visited, or an incident you were involved in? This is a phenomenon that good speakers recognize and use as an effective attention grabber. It's not always possible for you to know what will be familiar to your audience, but you can make some good guesses. To start with, you can use references to other speeches that have been made in class, personality traits of your instructor or other students, or names of local places and events. Mentioning the names of popular entertainers, musical groups, or sports figures is another way to get the attention of the audience, or you might tie your information to an item that has just recently appeared in the news.

Personalized Connections

People generally pay attention to things that are going to affect them directly. This is why newspapers try to find a "local angle" when reporting the news. If U.S. military troops are being sent on a mission, people want to know if the reserve unit near their city will be called. And if a large corporation announces that it will be downsizing, workers want to know if their local plant will be affected. When you are planning your speech, try to think of how you can respond to the question that you know will be in everyone's mind, "How is this event going to affect me and my family?"

Selecting Your Material

At this point in the preparation stage you should have the material for your speech spread out in front of you. You have now selected what may be the hardest part of the process. The next thing you need to do is to become as familiar as you can with your information. You may find that you have more than you can use. In that case, you will have to select the best and leave the rest for another occasion. Resist the temptation to squeeze it all in if you have too much; you don't want to run the risk of going over your time limit or talking so long that the audience loses interest.

On the other hand, you may discover that you don't have as much information as you thought you did, and you don't have time to gather more. In that case, go with what you have, and keep the speech short. Don't try to pad your material just to fill up the time. The quality of the speech is not determined by its length.

Your next step is going to be to arrange the information in a logical and coherent sequence. This will help you to make sure that the ideas you want to include are clear in your mind.

EXERCISE

Find five Web sites or five sources from the computer access terminal for periodical literature in your college library. Prepare a bibliography of five sources of information pertaining to one of the speech topics suggested in this chapter. In addition, find an example from one or more magazines to illustrate the five forms of support: (1) definition, (2) controlled studies, (3) statistical data, (4) testimonial evidence, and (5) explanation.

QUESTIONS FOR REVIEW

1. Why do we say that public speaking is a *rhetorical* art rather than a *performing* art?
2. What are the four general-speech purposes?
3. What is meant by a *homily?* Where would you expect to hear such an address?
4. What is meant of an *expository speech?*
5. What kind of speech might draw on universal values and metaphorical language?
6. Why would you probably not want to say to your audience, "My purpose is to persuade you . . ."?
7. Why do you need a server, a browser, and a search engine to find information on the Internet?
8. What are the reasons you might want to be cautious about doing your research on the Internet?
9. What are the computer programs that many libraries use for locating articles in periodicals?
10. What are the indexes that will direct you to articles in professional journals?
11. What is meant by *anecdotal* information?
12. What is meant by *quantitative* information?
13. Why do we say that figures do not speak for themselves?
14. How can you make statistical data more meaningful to the audience?
15. In a court trial, what is meant by *expert testimony?*
16. What is the value of using analogy as a means of support?
17. What are "interest grabbers," and what value do they have in a speech?

ORGANIZING AND OUTLINING

AFTER READING THIS CHAPTER, YOU SHOULD BE ABLE TO DO THE FOLLOWING:

Recognize the importance of making an outline when you prepare a speech; understand the basic structure of a speech outline.

Prepare an introduction that includes an attention statement, a purpose statement, and a presummary.

Write main headings for the body of the speech; find a place under each of the main headings for supporting information; know how to include transitions in your speech.

Plan a conclusion to your speech consisting of a brief summary, a statement that reinforces the thesis, or a relevant quotation.

Write your outline in finished form; prepare note cards.

Information has become the principal economic commodity of our social structure. The year that began to happen was 1956, when white-collar workers in technical, managerial, and clerical positions for the first time outnumbered blue-collar workers. Today, most of us in the workforce occupy our time gathering, creating, and distributing information rather than producing goods. Consider the huge quantity of data that is available to us on the World Wide Web, plus all the print material from the time of Johann Gutenberg. Add to that the fact that Americans spend as much money on computers as they do on television sets. There is so much data available to us that the problem becomes one of selecting and sorting material to make it useful.

THE NEED TO BE ORGANIZED

Don't ever think that people who are well-organized lead boring lives. Actually, the contrary is more likely to be true. They are better able to expand their breadth of knowledge, fill their lives with enriching experiences, and communicate in greater depth than those who move through life at random. The same is true in public address: When you are a well-organized speaker, you are able to gather and assemble interesting examples, hold the attention of the audience, and convey a great deal of information in a short period of time. You also raise your confidence level when you have the sequence of your ideas clearly in mind, because you have less fear of forgetting what you planned to say. The advantage to listeners is that they can easily follow a logically constructed speech and are more inclined to assimilate and retain the information.

The Value of an Outline

Writing an outline is the most effective means of organizing your material, because you can see the *structure* of what you want to say. Plan on making a rough draft first; you can't expect to get all your ideas down on paper in a neat, well-organized fashion the first time. When you do make your final copy, you may decide it is something you want to keep and use on more than just one occasion.

The Basic Structure

The outline you develop will be composed of several divisions. Think of them as boxes that you are going to use for the sake of sorting out your material (Figure 6-1). Each box has its own purpose: Use the one labeled "Introduction" for words that will gain the attention of the audience and launch the main purpose of the speech. In each of the boxes labeled "Body," provide a main heading, supporting information, and a transition statement that leads to the next thought. In the box labeled "Conclusion," put material that will summarize or reinforce what you want your listeners to remember. Let's look at each of those elements separately.

INTRODUCTION

> A Attention statement
> B Purpose statement

BODY

> I Main heading
> A Supporting information
> B Supporting information
> (Transition)

> II Main heading
> A Supporting information
> B Supporting information
> (Transition)

CONCLUSION

> A Summary statement
> B Reinforcement of thesis

FIGURE 6-1. The basic structure of an outline.

THE INTRODUCTION

Think back to what we said earlier about the obstacles to communication. People do not always listen well. One reason they don't is that they often tune in late. They may not hear what the speaker says in the beginning, and they may therefore fail to grasp the central purpose of the message.

The Attention Statement

You don't want to run the risk of having your listeners think about something else when you are stating your thesis. Therefore, plan something to say that will get their attention. There are several ways you can do this:

The Humorous Anecdote. The *humorous anecdote* is a fairly standard method of getting listeners' attention, because laughter helps to relax both the audience and the speaker. When you get a response from your listeners early in the presentation, you will feel more confident, knowing that you are off to a good start. Make sure, however, that your funny story has a point to it that is related to the purpose of the speech. It's quite possible that your anecdote will not get a laugh. If that happens, you are still all right as long as you can relate the punch line to something you want to say in the speech. For example, if you are speaking on the subject of education, you might start with a remark like the

Bill Cosby knows how to use humor to gain attention.

one Bill Cosby made. He said that when he finally graduated from high school he found that all the jobs had been taken by the dropouts. The point is (and you can say this even if no one laughs) that a high school education is not enough preparation for today's job market.

It's not a good idea to make the opening remark too long, because you risk losing the audience's attention. And if the joke is not funny, you have wasted a lot of time. Be cautious about off-color jokes; they may backfire if the audience does not appreciate that kind of humor. And don't tell ethnic or sexist jokes; they could do a great deal of damage to your integrity.

An Illustrative Anecdote. One type of introduction that can be used if you don't want to begin by setting a mood of levity is an *illustrative anecdote.* In all cases, when you relate a story of any kind, plan the way you are going to tell it; think especially of how it should start and how it will end. The impact of all anecdotes, humorous or serious, depends on the phrasing of the punch line or climactic statement. Here's an example, again on the topic of education:

> A young man came into my office recently who had been in my class several years earlier. He had been just an average student when I had him, but he must have improved a lot. He had managed to get his B.A. degree and was planning to enter graduate school. Of course, he wanted me to know that. We talked philosophically for a while, and at one point he said, "You know, if truth were

self-evident, there would be no need for persuasion." I recognized the line because it is my paraphrase of what Aristotle said, and I have used it often. But the student had forgotten that he had learned it in my class. I was pleased, however, because he had made the idea his own.

A Surprising Fact or Claim. Beginning a speech with a *surprising fact* or *claim* is a device that works well, because it creates what might be called the "gee whiz" effect. For example, you might begin a speech on education by saying, "According to the California Department of Education in 1994, almost 58 percent of the students enrolled in public schools in this state are listed as minorities." That fact could also be used as supporting evidence for the claim that the public school curriculum must be adjusted to the needs of a changing student population, and you certainly would want to reaffirm the point later in the speech. But because of its surprising nature, the fact can serve effectively as an attention statement.

A Rhetorical Question. An opening line that you can use when you want to gain the audience's attention before you advance an argument or an assertion is called a *rhetorical question.* For example, you might begin by saying, "Why does the United States—a nation that spends more money on education than any other nation in the world—have such a high rate of illiteracy?" When you pose a rhetorical question you are not asking for a response from the audience, you are leading into what you want to say. Such a question serves as a transition as well as a method of gaining attention.

A Response Question. When you want answers from the audience, you might begin by asking a *response question,* such as, "How many of you have lived in this community for more than ten years?" When you say this, raise your own hand to indicate what it is that you want the people to do. This method is quite effective because the audience members become actively involved, and those who respond help you gain the attention of the others. What's more, you can tell by the show of hands if they are really listening.

Reference to the Occasion. An easy way to get started is by making *reference to the occasion.* You can begin by thanking the person who introduced you and letting the audience members know that you are happy to have the opportunity to address them. If the day is a special occasion—an anniversary or the beginning of an event—let people know you are aware of that. If you can make a connection, tie the occasion into the topic of your speech, as in the following example:

> I'm pleased to be here on the occasion of this school's fortieth anniversary. It might be interesting to note that some of the students who attended this school when it first opened are now heading up corporations that are making products that weren't even invented when the foundation of this building was poured.

Any of these methods can be used as an attention-getting device. The important thing is for you to give the audience the opportunity to get ready to listen.

The Purpose Statement

Once you have gained the audience's attention, you can move on to the second phase of the introduction—the *purpose statement*. It is at this point that you provide the audience with orientation to your topic. You let your listeners know where you are going and how you are going to get there. To do that, you should try to phrase your statement so that it is brief, clear, and well-qualified.

Brief. You don't want to go into detail right at the outset, because people will think you are beginning your speech in the middle. The body of the speech is the time for you to elaborate on your purpose statement.

Clear. Don't use sentence structure that is too long and complicated. The audience must be able to understand your intent. If the listeners don't understand it, they will lose interest right at the start.

Well-Qualified. A well-qualified purpose statement means that you tell your listeners how you have limited the subject matter and what you are going to emphasize. Sometimes this is referred to as setting the *parameters* of the topic. Because the purpose statement is so important, let's start at the very beginning when you are deciding on what the substance of your speech will be.

Giving Focus to the Subject

Your interest and involvement in a particular activity may be the reason for your being invited to speak. Suppose you have been asked to make a presentation because of the work you have been doing in the public library. It may be that you have training in library science and know a lot about the subject. You have to be careful that you don't go into so much detail that you lose the attention of your audience. On the other hand, you have to be specific enough so that the information you present is fresh, useful, and thought-provoking. Your own experience may be your primary source of information, but you might need to gather more material from published sources. Always use more than just one source, and arrange the material in a way that makes the presentation distinctly your own. As you begin to read and take notes, you may discover that there is a particular aspect of the issue that is especially important; that's when you start to narrow your topic down to a central idea. At this point, you can phrase your purpose statement.

Phrasing the Purpose Statement

The purpose statement is the keystone of the speech; it lets your audience know what it is that you are going to talk about. If the topic is controversial, it is called a *thesis statement,* and it serves to prepare the listeners for the point of view you want to express. The statement brings the subject area into focus and lets the audience know what limitations you have placed on the topic. Give a lot of consideration to the way you phrase the purpose statement; it is important to the listeners, but it is also important to you. It will help you get a good firm handle on what it is that you intend to say. I suggest that you write the purpose statement on your outline pretty much the way you plan to say it and *keep it in the back of your mind the whole time you are delivering the speech. Everything you say should be related to that purpose statement.* If you follow this guideline, you will be less likely to go off on tangents—that is, areas that are not related to the central idea of the speech. Here are several ways you can phrase the purpose statement. Notice that each has a different emphasis and suggests a slightly different focus.

- The people of our county are fortunate to have one of the finest library systems in the nation.
- Library facilities in our county have been severely cut in recent years, and residents of this community must find a way to restore the services that were once provided.
- In the past ten years we have seen tremendous growth and development in our county, and it's essential that we expand our library facilities in order to keep up with the times.
- Some areas in our county have excellent library facilities, but others need a great deal more help than they are getting.
- Let me explain some of the new services that are now being provided by our local library.

The Presummary

The purpose statement conveys to the audience the particular aspect of the topic you plan to cover, but you also may need to tell your listeners how the speech is organized and what sequence you will follow as you progress from one point to another. To do that, you add what is called a *presummary.* This is a list of the main ideas that will be contained in the body of the speech. On your outline, you would write just a few words to suggest briefly what you are going to say:

Today I would like to report on . . .
   Our funding
   Our facilities
   The use of our services

In order for the audience members to listen well, they must be able to recognize the speaker's organizational pattern. The presummary will help them do this. Be sure that the items listed in your presummary follow the same sequence as your main headings. The main headings form the basic skeletal structure of the speech and need to be arranged in a pattern that accomplishes the intent of the purpose statement.

THE BODY OF THE SPEECH

The body of the speech is the substantive portion of the presentation. It needs to contain main headings and supporting information. Each *main heading* is a generalization that leads the listener into the portion of the speech you want to discuss. The purpose of the main heading is to introduce one section of the speech at a time and lay the groundwork for the more detailed material that follows. The *supporting information* consists of the evidence or examples used by the speaker to elaborate on the thought expressed in the main heading. There is a third element, and that consists of the *transitions* in the speech. These are the phrases that connect one item to another. They are extremely important; however, they do not necessarily need to be written into the outline.

Main Headings

Writing the main headings is the first step in working out the organizational structure of the speech. There are several things you should note:

- Make sure the main headings are phrased so that they are easily recognized when you deliver the speech. I suggest that you designate them with Roman numerals in the outline.
- Limit the number of main headings to five or six. If you have too many, your speech will become fragmented.
- Remember that the main headings must be directly related to what is said in the thesis or purpose statement of the speech.
- Make the main headings broad enough to cover what you want to say, but not so vague as to be meaningless. Saying "Let me give you some statistics" doesn't tell the audience what you are thinking.
- Don't make your main headings statements of fact, make them generalizations. The factual information comes after you tell the audience your main idea.
- The main headings must follow some sort of logical organizational structure. Using the library topic as an example, here are a few possible patterns:

The Topical Pattern

Often your material will break down into clearly divided subject areas that form a natural organizational pattern. The subject areas might be the main reasons that support your thesis. The example below could be used when you are giving an informational speech to the people who use the libraries and to the taxpayers who provide the funding.

- The people of our county are fortunate to have one of the finest library systems in the nation.

I	We are well-funded.
II	We have modern and convenient facilities.
III	Our services are well-used.

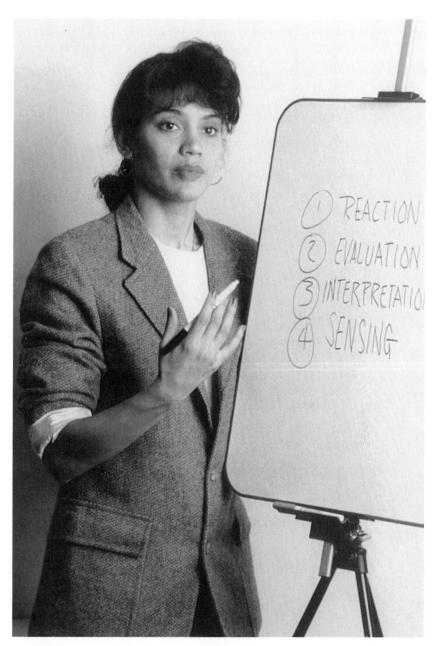

Main headings will help the audience follow the organizational pattern of the speech.

The Problem-Solution Pattern

It might be that the libraries in your county need help. In this case, the first heading should make the claim that there is a significant problem; the second heading should tell why the problem is there; the third heading should suggest alternatives and possible solutions. This organizational method is called the *problem-solution* pattern.

- Library facilities in our county have been severely cut in recent years and residents of this community must find a way to restore the services that were once provided.

    I   Our libraries are not being used.
    II   Budget cuts have forced us to reduce our services.
    III   We need to take measures to restore our facilities.

The Chronological Pattern

In the organizational pattern termed *chronological,* you follow a historical progression. Start with the earliest incidents, and proceed to those that are the most current.

- In the past ten years we have seen tremendous growth and development in our county, and it's essential that we expand our library facilities in order to keep up with the times.

    I   Ten years ago our county launched a campaign to improve our library system.
    II   Five years ago we won a state award for having a high-quality program.
    III   Since then we have fallen behind, and today our facilities need a greal deal of improvement.

If the focus of your speech is on the solution, you might use the chronological pattern so that it progresses from the first step to the second step to the third step.

    I   First, we must set goals for improvement.
    II   Next, we must raise the money we need.
    III   Finally, we must recruit a well-qualified staff.

The Spatial Pattern

The problem you are describing might differ from one locale to another, in which case you could use the *spatial pattern* for organizing your material. Notice that the example below could also be one that moves from most severe to least severe.

- Some areas in our county have excellent facilities, but others need a great deal more help than they are getting.

    I   Our county libraries are best-equipped in the northern area.
    II   Facilities in the western part of the county are average.
    III   We need to give more help to the southern section.

When you have settled on the wording of your main headings and the order in which they are to be arranged, you can look at the information you have gathered and see where it fits.

Supporting Information

Main headings cannot stand alone; they must be supported by items of information. The kind of material you need to elaborate on in your main headings is that which was described in the previous chapter: *Definition of terms, specific instances, statistical data, testimonial evidence,* and *explanation.* Look over the rough notes you have made from the books, periodicals, and other documents that you have used. Your job now is to figure out where each piece fits into your outline. Be sure to write down *all the details that you don't want to commit to memory.* This is an important point, because you are not going to deliver a memorized speech and you are not going to read it word for word. You are going to explain what you want to say in your own words as you do in conversation, but you are going to include more specific details than you usually carry around in your head.

The important thing is that you have your information arranged in a clearly organized sequence so that it makes sense to your audience. Your speech would be a disaster if you were to recite the specifics at random, as they appear in your initial notes. Here is how the items might look in your notes before you begin to sort them out:

- Libraries in Palo Alto are open sixty-eight hours per week.
- Eighty-six percent of our public library capital referenda have been approved by voters.
- Residents can check out CD-ROMs.
- Over 230,000 books are in the Palo Alto library—four for every person.
- Survey of nine library systems.
- Palo Alto spends $8 per resident on new materials.
- Theme for National Library Week is "Libraries Change Lives."
- Palo Alto libraries spend three times more than the national average.
- Libraries in other cities are open only about 38 hours per week.
- Twenty-two copies of best-selling novel, 14 "holds" on it; one-month wait.
- Catalogs are accessible by modem from home.
- Almost 1,000 magazines, 4,000 CDs, over 5,000 videos.
- "From my earliest years, libraries have been a source of inspiration for me." Carole Simpson
- Palo Alto residents visit the library three times more often than the national average.
- In some counties residents wait five months for a best-selling novel.

As you can see, it would make no sense to relate the information in this sequence. Each item must be connected to an appropriate main heading. We'll see how that is done in the sample outline at the end of this chapter.

Transitions

The organizational structure of your speech is going to be clear to you, because you are the one who planned it, and you can see what it looks like on the outline in front of you. You know that there are divisions in the speech and that each division has a main idea; you also know the point at which you complete one main idea and begin to develop another one. However, this may not be as clear to the audience as it is to you.

In order for the listeners to be able to follow the flow of your organizational structure, you have to provide for them signposts that we call *transitions*. A transition is a phrase that leads the audience to your next idea. For example, you might use a statement such as one of the following:

- "But there are other problems to consider. . . ."
- "Now, in order for us to understand, we need to look at. . . ."

As you begin to get more experience in public speaking, you will develop a sense for where transitions need to go. Transitions do not have to be written down in your outline; they are easy enough to extemporize. The main point is to be aware of their importance.

THE CONCLUSION

When you reach the end of the presentation, you will have to let the audience know you have finished. If you conclude with a piece of specific information such as ". . . in some libraries, residents wait five months for a best-selling novel," the audience is going to look at you with the expectation that you say something more. You can't end a speech that way; you need to pull your ideas together either by summarizing what you have said or by reinforcing your purpose statement. The conclusion is important because it may be the thing that the audience is most likely to remember. As evidence for that claim, let me ask you what you recall from the famous speech of Patrick Henry. I'm sure you are able to remember "Give me liberty or give me death," even if you have forgotten all the rest.

When it comes to the speech you are preparing, remember that you have to *plan* what you are going to say in the conclusion. Don't expect that the right words will come to you in a moment of inspiration. Think about how you are going to end the speech, and write it on the outline pretty much the way you plan to say it.

The Summary

If your speech is fairly long and contains detailed and complex material, you might want to end with a summary of the general ideas. This is a good practice when it is important that the audience be able to remember what you have said. Be careful, however, that your conclusion does not recapitulate too much of the speech itself.

Reinforcement of the Thesis

When you have a short speech, it might be a better idea to simply paraphrase your thesis as a means of reinforcing your main idea. Be sure that your conclusion is *consistent* with the thesis. I have heard speakers who have negated the effectiveness of their presentation by using words in the conclusion that seemed to contradict what they said in the body of the speech. It's very important that you have a clear understanding yourself of what it is that you want to reinforce.

Quotation

An effective way to conclude a speech is to use a quotation. This works well for two reasons: first, because the quote you selected will probably be one that is pithy, clever, or has emotional impact; second, because you are bolstering your own credibility with the words of someone else who supports the point you want to make. To quote Brendan Francis, "A quotation in a speech, article, or book is like a rifle in the hands of an infantryman. It speaks with authority."[1]

THE FINISHED OUTLINE

We have examined all of the elements of an outline; now let's put it together. This sample outline contains everything that has been described: The attention statement, the purpose statement, the presummary, the main headings, the supporting information, and the conclusion.

Computer-Generated Outlines

The sample outline that you see in the box entitled "National Library Week Speech Outline" was prepared on a word processor, but there are other ways you can do it. Many computer programs have outlining applications that are available on pull-down menus. Actually, if you prefer a simpler method, you can do the same thing with a pencil and a yellow notepad.

There are several computer programs that are specifically designed for preparing speeches. One of these is called Power Point and has several attractive features for making your presentation look and sound professional. On the main menu is a heading called *AutoContent Wizard.* There you will find several suggested ways to organize your material, depending on the kind of speech you want to design. There are patterns such as *Recommending a Strategy, Selling a Product,* and *Communicating Bad News,* among others. Choose one that comes close to what you have in mind. It does not have to be an exact match, because you can modify the main headings and subheadings

---

[1]Edward F. Murphy (ed.), *Crown Treasury of Relevant Quotations,* Crown, New York, 1978, p. 500.

NATIONAL LIBRARY WEEK SPEECH OUTLINE

INTRODUCTION

Attention statement: The theme for this year's National Library Week is, "Libraries Change Lives." Libraries launch children into the world of education, sustain the intellectual momentum of young people, provide depth of understanding for adults, and serve as havens for senior citizens.

Purpose statement: The people of our county are fortunate to have one of the finest library systems in the nation.

- We are well-funded.
- We have modern and convenient facilities.
- Our services are well-used.

BODY

I   Funding is an important part of the success of a library system.
- A Eighty-six percent of our public library capital referenda have been approved by voters.
- B Palo Alto is able to spend $8 for every resident each year on new materials.
- C Overall, the city spends three times as much as the national average.
- D Over 230,000 books; four for every person in the city.

II   The most modern and convenient facilities are available in our county libraries.
- A Catalogs are accessible by modem from home.
- B Residents can check out CD-ROMs.
- C Almost 1,000 magazines, 4,000 CDs, over 5,000 videos.
- D Twenty-two copies of the best-selling novel.
  - Fourteen holds on it.
  - One-month wait.
  - Residents of other counties wait five or six months.

III The investment is worthwhile because the services are well-used.
- A Survey made of nine library systems.
- B Libraries in Palo Alto are open sixty-eight hours per week.
- C Residents visit the library three times as often as the national average.

CONCLUSION

Carole Simpson, anchor for ABC's *World News Sunday,* can testify to the theme of National Library Week. She worked for several years at the Chicago Public Library after she graduated from college, because in those days there were no jobs in journalism for black women. She says, "From my earliest experience, libraries have been a source of inspiration for me." So they can be for all of us—they can change our lives.

to suit your needs. One thing I like about this program is that it helps you put each item of your material in the right place with the proper indentation and "bullets."

Before you open Power Point, you should make a list of all the specific items of information that you want to include in the speech. You can do that on a word processing program that is compatible with Power Point. Then, when you open Power Point and start building your outline, you can pull the information, one item at a time, out of your file and put it where it belongs. Another way to do it is simply to have your information written out on a sheet of paper; then type it under the appropriate main heading.

The best feature of Power Point is that it does several jobs at once. While you are writing the outline, the program will be preparing slides that you can use as visual aids, and can also generate note cards.

The Outline on Note Cards

If there are a lot of facts and figures in your speech—names of people and places, dates, numbers, percentages, amounts, and so on—you probably will want to use note cards. What you put on your note cards will be arranged the same as your outline. However, you might not need to use as many words as you do on your outline, because you will be able to extemporize around the basic information. But you probably want to include each main heading so that you don't take a chance on forgetting any of the important generalizations you want to make. You could, of course, deliver the speech directly from the outline, but sometimes a full sheet of paper is cumbersome and keeps you from having good audience contact. Using 3 by 5 or 6 by 8 note cards works better.

The Framework of the Speech

It's important that the outline say what you want it to say and that you be familiar with the material. Read all the way through the outline. Then, go over it again and practice extemporizing around the main ideas. Remember that the outline is just a framework, not a complete manuscript. When you deliver the speech, you are going to elaborate on the specific information and use verbal transitions to make it all fit together. As you practice the speech out loud, listen to how the ideas are expressed, and make your own critical evaluation of the organizational structure. If changes are needed, make them in the preparation stage; don't expect to do it spontaneously at the time of delivery. *Plan the speech you want to give, and give the speech you plan.*

EXERCISE

Select any speech from the periodical *Vital Speeches* and analyze its organizational structure by answering the following questions:

- What did the speaker say to gain the audience's attention?
- What did the speaker say to establish the main purpose of the speech?
- What are three main ideas developed in the body of the speech?

- What is the most significant piece of evidence presented by the speaker?
- What did the speaker say in order to bring the speech to a conclusion?

QUESTIONS FOR REVIEW

1. What was the significant change in U.S. industry that occurred in 1956?
2. What are three reasons that good organization is essential in public speaking?
3. What are the three basic structural elements of a speech outline?
4. What are the two important functions of the introduction?
5. What are the attention-getting devices that can be used at the start of the speech?
6. How does a rhetorical question differ from a response question?
7. What is meant by a *presummary?* What is the purpose of it?
8. What are you doing when you qualify the purpose statement?
9. What are you doing when you focus the topic?
10. Why should you keep the purpose statement in the back of your mind while you deliver the speech?
11. What is the function of the main heading in the outline?
12. Name four patterns for organizing the main headings in an outline.
13. What is the conclusion of the speech designed to do?
14. Why is a quotation often a good way to end a speech?

THE SPEECH TO INFORM

**AFTER READING THIS CHAPTER, YOU SHOULD
BE ABLE TO DO THE FOLLOWING:**

Know how to focus the topic and subject matter of a speech
to inform so that it is distinctly your own; understand that
a speech to inform is defined by the way it is
presented, rather than by the topic.

Know how to give a speech to inform on a topic that has controversial
aspects; to hold the audience's interest while giving information;
to give unbiased information on political issues
to voters before an election.

Be able to outline and deliver a one-point speech.

Be aware of the speaking opportunities in business; know how to
prepare for a job as a training specialist; be able to participate
effectively in a group discussion; know what you have to
do to make an informative presentation to a
decision-making group.

As members of the audience we have certain expectations when we go to hear someone speak. If we visit a courtroom and listen to lawyers pleading their case, we expect to hear persuasive speaking; when we go to church and see the preacher in the pulpit, we expect that he or she will be delivering a motivating sermon to inspire us to become better people; when we are at a dinner show, we expect to be entertained by a comedian. We don't want to hear a sermon at a comedy club or a string of jokes in the closing arguments of a court trial. Expectations also apply when we attend a lecture on an academic topic. We are not there to be persuaded, inspired, or amused—we are there to be informed. It's true that the speech may contain brief expressions of each of those three elements, but none of them should dominate over the primary purpose of conveying information. If the audience comes to hear a speech to inform, that's the kind of speech you should give. It may be more fun to do a comedy routine, and more exciting to debate a controversial issue, but you are not in front of an audience to meet your own needs; you are there to meet the needs and the expectations of the listeners.

THE QUALITIES OF EXPOSITION

As we noted in Chapter 5, a speech to inform is sometimes referred to as an *expository* speech, because it deals with the *exposition* of information rather than the *interpretation* of it. The essential qualities are fairness and objectivity—speakers must not favor one side over another, and they must not be subjective in their evaluation. A speech to inform can be given on a controversial topic, but it must be done with thoughtful consideration to questions that are disputable. If you select such a topic, be sure to examine your own motives. Are you willing to take a neutral position and trust the listeners to make their own decisions on the basis of the information that you provide? You will have to bring into the speech evidence that supports each side of the issue and present all of it with equal emphasis. You must not indicate with your words or with the tone of your voice that one contention carries more weight than another.

The Focus Makes it Your Own

You don't have to feel that you must be an expert in a given field or have scholarly knowledge in order to deliver a speech to inform. If you know enough about the subject matter to converse intelligently and if you understand the vocabulary and terminology, you should be able to make a respectable and competent presentation. What's more, it's not necessary for you to have all the information committed to memory; your statistics and specific examples can be written on note cards. It's quite possible that some people in the audience may know more about your subject than you do. Don't let that shake your confidence. This is your speech, not theirs. The focus you give to the material is what makes it distinctly your own.

People who are truly experts might be able to present more facts, but that doesn't mean that their speeches would be better than yours. If you can explain something in a way that others are able to understand, you can perform a service that may be more valuable than that of a genius who can't communicate.

Being Familiar with Your Subject

Speaking to a group can be intimidating, especially when you know there are high-status people in the audience. You may never be as smart as they are, but what you can do is tell them something they don't know. One of the first public speaking experiences I can remember occurred when I was thirteen years old and a member of a Boy Scout troop in Berkeley, California. The occasion was our annual dinner, and I was scheduled to do a slide show presentation. I learned, to my dismay, that in the audience was the man who designed and built the first cyclotron and nuclear reactor—Dr. Ernest Lawrence. Fortunately, my topic had nothing to do with atomic science; I was talking about our summer camp in the Sierra. Even though Dr. Lawrence was perhaps one of the smartest people in the country, I like to think that I was the one who taught him how to pack a donkey and tie a diamond hitch. My point is that you can be an expert even to the best-informed people if you pick a subject that is familiar to you but new to your audience.

If you can explain something in a way that others are able to understand, you can perform a valuable service.

Speaking Opportunities

In real-life situations (as opposed to classroom settings), there probably will be more opportunities for you to give a speech to inform than there will be for you to give a speech to persuade, entertain, or inspire an audience. Let's look at a few examples:

- Explaining the features of a new product to a company's sales representatives
- Reporting to members of an organization what happened on a field trip
- Giving information to a board of directors who have to make a decision
- Outlining a new policy or procedure to fellow workers
- Presenting the findings of a special committee or task force
- Teaching new employees how to operate equipment they will need to use
- Making an announcement of a coming event

These are the kinds of presentations that you are very likely to be called on to give, and a speech class will prepare you for the experience. Notice that, in most of the situations listed above, the information could probably be communicated by a written directive or memo. Why is it necessary to make an oral presentation?

For one thing, you can see the faces of the people who are being exposed to your message. You may not know for sure that they are listening, but you know that the information was expressed in their presence. A written memo, on the other hand, might be ignored.

Another reason is that the oral presentation allows listeners to ask questions—something that is not easily done when the message is written.

Finally, the oral message can be more emphatic. The speaker can place emphasis on key points, and the writer has less chance to do that.

Topics for a Speech to Inform

The topic you pick for a speech to inform might pertain to something that you have experienced directly, or it could be one that requires some research. Look at a few example titles:

- Cross-Country Travel on a Mountain Bike
- The Potential of Electric Automobiles
- Making Movies with a Camcorder
- Animal Life in our Local Nature Areas
- The Culture of the Navajos

These are all good subject areas—as long as you can be objective about them. That means you have to set aside your personal biases and opinions and just stick to the facts. If you identify a controversy within the topic and begin interpreting your information to support a point of view, you are treading into the area of persuasion. This leads us to an important observation: *A speech to inform is defined more by the way it is presented than by the topic itself.*

Any subject can be made into a speech to persuade or a speech to inform, depending on the way the information is presented. A speech with the title, "Cross-Country Travel on a Mountain Bike" certainly seems to be noncontroversial, and it is—unless the speaker suggests that bikers should be given the right-of-way over hikers. "The Potential of Electric Automobiles" appears to be safe enough—unless the speaker begins to criticize federal standards and quotas imposed on car manufacturers. What about "The Culture of the Navajos"? That sounds all right, too, so long as the speaker does not dwell on unflattering characteristics of the tribe. It probably is impossible for the speaker not to have a bias, but the speech can still be regarded as informative in nature if the subject matter is treated fairly and objectively.

TAKING A NEUTRAL POSITION

Consider issues such as capital punishment, welfare, birth control, national health care, assault weapons, or drug testing. It would be hard not to have an opinion on these questions, and they would all make good topics for persuasive speeches. But if you are able to remain neutral, you could make any of them into a speech to inform. The variable that makes the most difference is the way you phrase your purpose statement. You would not begin an informative speech by making the claim that the death penalty has a history of preventing violent crime. However, you might say in your purpose statement that you want to clarify the federal and state court rulings made in the past two decades that pertain to capital punishment.

In addition to the phrasing of the purpose statement, there are other factors that will determine whether the speech is to be classified as informative or as persuasive.

- *The balance of evidence.* You are being persuasive if you have more evidence or stronger evidence on one side than you do on the other.
- *The objectivity of sources.* You are tilting the scales in favor of one side if you get most of your information from sources that have an intentional bias.
- *The language you use.* Your speech will not be regarded as truly expository if you treat one side of the issue with sarcasm or contempt.

Priming the Audience's Interest

To say that you must take a neutral position when delivering a speech to inform is not to say that enthusiasm is unimportant. You must prime the audience's interest in what you are saying, and to do that you need to project excitement and commitment. For the speech to be successful, the audience must believe that you regard the subject matter to be worth an investment of time and effort. If you really believe your material is important, you will want your listeners to pay attention and try to retain the information you are giving them. Don't imitate the boring lecturer who drones on and on as though there were no one else in the room. And, conversely, don't be in such a hurry to get through your speech that you leave the audience behind. To be really effective, you must be aware of how the audience is receiving the message. Pace your speech so that you hold the listeners' attention, and give them a chance to digest what you say. Be pleased if audience members ask questions afterward, because it means they are interested in your subject. The challenge to you as the speaker is to give an answer that resonates with a listener's question and perhaps adds information that may illucidate the issue. If you know your topic well and sincerely want your listeners to be able to grasp and retain your information, you should have no trouble with this part of the presentation. There will be more said later in the text on the question period after a speech.

Helping to Inform the Voter

Every time there is an election, our mailboxes fill up with literature advising us how to vote. There is so much information in newspapers and magazines that we can't absorb it all. Sometimes we don't read as thoroughly as we should in order to be well-informed; then, a few days before the election, we quickly try to catch up on the background of the candidates and issues. What we discover is that almost everything we read or hear has a point of view. The flyers in the mail, the radio and television announcements, the columns and editorials in the newspaper—all try to give an interpretation to events that will lead us to the conclusions that the advocates want us to draw. It is for this reason that the Speech Communication Association launched its program to promote *media literacy*.[1] One of the goals is to teach students to process information they receive and test it for its objectivity. The problem is that information that is not tainted with opinion is extremely rare.

Speakers who can uncover information on candidates and ballot measures, and then make clear and unbiased presentations at election time, perform a valuable service for electorates. One group that is noted for its efforts to do this is the League of Women Voters (LWV). The LWV sponsored the first presidential debates on television, and, over the years, it has acquired a well-earned reputation for fairness. The LWV has local chapters in many of the communities in the country. These chapters can be contacted by organizations who wish to have speakers come to talk to small groups. Their mission is to see that voters make informed choices when they go to the polls.

A Short Speech to Inform

The sample outline in the box entitled "The One-Point Speech" is for a short speech to inform that could be delivered in less than three minutes. It could be a stand-alone speech, because it contains an introduction, a body, and a conclusion. However, it could also be one part of a longer speech. For example, you could

---

[1]Speech Communication Association, Annandale, Va., "Standards for Speaking, Listening, and Media Literacy Released," June 4, 1996, <http://www.scassn.org/k12stdspr.htm, October 30, 1996.

THE ONE-POINT SPEECH

The body of a full-length speech is composed of several main points connected in a logical fashion; a good way for the beginning student to practice is by presenting just one main point at a time. We call this a *one-point speech*. In the example below, notice that the speech starts off with a broad statement pertaining to wildlife, and then narrows down to one point concerning a bird called a *murre*. The one point is indicated by a single Roman numeral.

THE RESCUE OF THE MURRE

Purpose statement: If we are going to preserve wildlife and allow animals to live in their natural habitats, we must think of creative ways to protect them from the ravages of human beings.

I   I'd like to tell you about the rescue of a seabird called the *murre*.
  A   A murre is a member of the auk family.
    1   It is related to the puffin.
    2   Looks like a penguin.
  B   Murres make their living underwater.
    1   Dive and swim to catch small fish.
    2   Go to depth of 240 feet.
  C   A colony that was living off the coast of California was driven out by an oil spill.
    1   Oil barge spilled 20,000 gallons.
    2   Killed 6,000 murres; the rest driven out.
    3   Oil company paid $4 million in fines for cleanup.
  D   Rescuers launched an ingenious plan for bringing the murres back.
    1   They mounted 300 life-size models of murres made of wood and plastic.
    2   Placed a dozen mirror boxes.
    3   Battery-powered stereo played murre mating calls.

Conclusion: The plan worked. The murres returned to their rock island home, attracted by the sight and sound of what appeared to them to be other murres.

---

elaborate by adding more examples of birds and wildlife that have been rescued. The one-point speech is a useful model, because it helps us to examine each main idea separately to see if it contributes to the support of the purpose statement and fits into the overall plan of the speech.

Delivering a short speech to inform is a good way to begin practicing your public speaking skills, because such a speech is less demanding than the speech to persuade. However, this does not mean that the speech to inform is easy. You must have concrete information that is organized well enough for your audience to follow what you say. Good organization helps listeners fit the information into their thinking and retain what you have told them. It also contributes to gaining their favor, because it lets them know you put some effort into the preparation.

A speech to inform could be a full fifty-minute lecture that you might hear in a college classroom, or it could be a three-minute announcement made at a business meeting. The length is not what determines the purpose. Sometimes students will gather too much information and try to squeeze it all into one speech. A better idea is to be selective, so that the points you make have greater impact.

SPEAKING IN THE BUSINESS WORLD

Sometimes students ask me, "How am I going to use the skills I learn in this class? Is it likely that I will ever be asked to give a speech?" My answer is that there are indeed opportunities for those who are willing. You don't have to be in one of the "high-profile" professions—there are many people who prepare and deliver speeches every day as part of their work. Classroom teachers do this, of course, but there are also an increasing number of business and professional people who are regularly called on to make presentations.

Training Specialist

In this age of technology, companies that sell computer software and highly specialized electronic equipment must do more than simply provide their customers with a user's manual. If the equipment is extremely complex and highly specialized, companies often need to hire professional people to give lectures and demonstrations to the users as part of the sales package. When a library purchases and installs a new retrieval system, for example, all of the personnel who use the equipment and teach others to do so would need a training program to learn about its operation and capabilities. The supplier of the product would send someone who has a facility for making presentations to do this kind of instruction. Such a person can be called a *training specialist* and may work full-time at developing course material and making presentations. This may be one of the best examples of a practical application of the speech to inform. The specialist would prepare for a lecture in the same way that you do for a class assignment. He or she would consider the following questions:

- What do the customers already know, and what new information do they need?
- How much information can I give in the time that is available?
- What is the best way I can organize the material?
- How can I help them understand and retain the information?
- What handouts will I need to give them?
- What sort of graphics and visual aids should I prepare?
- What questions will they ask, and what are the best answers I can give?

If it is a high-tech item you are going to be explaining, you will need to have some technical background in addition to teaching skills. That doesn't necessarily mean that you have to start out being an expert on a particular product, but you must have enough education in the field so that you can learn what you need to know. Large companies or consortiums will hold workshops and seminars to teach training specialists how to conduct classes and make presentations.

Speaking to a Committee

Learning how to function effectively as a member of a discussion or decision-making group is an area of speech communication that is different from public speaking; however, there are certain elements of similarity. Normally, you do not need to make the same kind of preparation for a committee meeting as you do when you are going to be a principal speaker, but there might be occasions when you have very specific ideas you want to contribute. Rather than relying on your ability to speak in an impromptu fashion, make a few notes beforehand. By doing that, you will be sure to include all the details that you want the other members to know. There are some differences, of course, between group discussion and public speaking. One is that in the former situation, you will do your speaking sitting down rather than standing up. That has both advantages and disadvantages. The advantage is that you may feel less nervous; the disadvantage is that other members of the committee will probably interrupt you from time to time with their own comments, and that may throw you off stride. There's an observation that we can make here about nonverbal communication: If you stand when you speak, you are saying nonverbally, "I have the floor and I expect to be heard all the way through before you respond." Sitting down

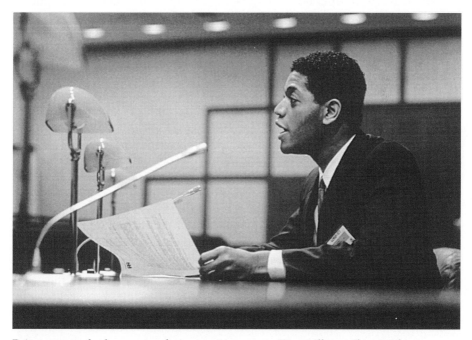

Being prepared when you make a report to a committee will save the members valuable time.

says, "We are communicating on an equal basis, and I invite you to speak if you want to comment on what I am saying."

There is another important difference between public speaking and group discussion: Public speaking is an individual endeavor in which you arrive at a conclusion that is based on your own thought and research; you then defend the position you have taken with the best evidence and reasoning you can produce. Group discussion is thought in process. That means you come to the meeting with a tentative idea, but you know that your conclusion is subject to change on the basis of the input you receive from other members of the committee. You may prepare your presentation in the same way you prepare for a public speech, but you may have to modify your position after you hear what others suggest.

The Informative Presentation

The complexity of our society places a heavy burden on committees and individuals who have authority in a broad area of responsibility and who need to make policy decisions based on specific information. When neither the chairperson nor the members of the committee feel that they have the expertise to make such a decision, a specialist may be called in to provide the information that is needed. You may be the person chosen to make a presentation that serves this purpose, not necessarily because of your skill in public speaking, but because of your knowledge of the subject matter.

Although your presentation may be essentially informative, you might be asked to make a recommendation. Be prepared to do so, but remember that ultimately it is the committee's decision and not your own. Your job is to tell your listeners what they need to know in order for them to make an informed choice; therefore, give them a complete picture, and don't gloss over the obstacles.

Let's say, for example, that you are employed by a company that has been contracting out its printing jobs, and now it is considering producing its own brochures and flyers using an in-house operation. Assume that you have had some experience in this field and have been asked to describe the feasibility of purchasing printing equipment and hiring personnel to operate a shop to do this work. You would have to take into consideration the capital investment, office space that would be needed, and the impact that hiring new employees would have on the company's budget. You would need to know what volume of work there would be and the quality that the company expects. Let's further assume that you have been given a limited amount of time to make your presentation and that you will be talking to a group of busy and high-paid executives.

> *Plan your strategy.* Talk with people beforehand who understand the goals of the company and the standards of quality that are expected. Learn as much as you can about the equipment you would need to buy, the cost of its operation and maintenance, and its dependability. Also be prepared to explain what operating skills the personnel would need and what the hourly wage would be for people who do this kind of work.

Find out the group's level of understanding. Determine how much members of the committee already know and how much they need to know. It is necessary for them to have a clear comprehension of cost and quality, but they do not need to know the details of operation.

Put together a set of visual aids. The impact of your presentation will be enhanced if you use visual aids. Let the audience see samples of the quality of work that could be produced. If there is going to be an additional cost in order to obtain better quality, the members of the committee will have to weigh that differential. They must be able to see what the finished product will look like in order to make a judgment.

THE HUNDRETH MONKEY

Sometimes you may feel as though there is nothing you can say that will have any effect on what people do or what they believe. If you have a concern for social issues, you may get discouraged when you read about government policies that seem to ignore human needs, business ventures that perpetuate greed and corruption, or industrial practices that pollute the environment. But before you become resigned to accepting what appears to be the inevitable, consider the notion that has been advanced by Ken Keyes, Jr., in a book called *The Hundredth Monkey*. He describes a study made of a Japanese monkey that had been observed in the wild on the island of Koshima for a period of thirty years. The study began in 1952, when scientists began dropping sweet potatoes into the sand on the island to add to the monkeys' diet. The monkeys liked the potatoes, but didn't like the taste of the dirt on them. One monkey solved the problem by learning to wash the potato in a stream. This practice was picked up by a few other monkeys, but after several years the scientists observed that there were still a great many monkeys who had not learned the trick. Keyes relates:

> *Then something took place. In the autumn of 1958, a certain number of Koshima monkeys were washing sweet potatoes—the exact number is not known. Let us suppose that when the sun rose one morning, there were 99 monkeys on Koshima Island who had learned to wash their sweet potatoes. Let's further assume that later that morning the hundredth monkey learned to wash sweet potatoes. Then it happened. By that evening almost everyone in the tribe was washing sweet potatoes before eating them. That added energy of this hundredth monkey somehow created an ideological breakthrough.**

You never know when you might be the person who provides insight to the "hundredth monkey" by saying the right thing at the right time. If there is validity to the theory that Ken Keyes proposes, and if it does indeed apply to human behavior, your efforts to make constructive social changes by sharing your thoughts and ideas can make an important difference.

---

*Ken Keyes, Jr., The Hundredth Monkey, Vision Books, Coos Bay, Ore., 1982, pp. 11–15.

Have your specific data available in printed form. You can display the figures on a computer screen, a flip chart, or an overhead projector, or you can give each person a handout sheet. The members of the committee may need to have time to think about what you will tell them, and quantitative information is difficult to retain if it is presented only by the spoken word. Before the meeting adjourns, be sure you know what further service is expected of you.

EXERCISE

Select a topic similar to one that is mentioned in this chapter and develop a one-point speech to inform. Check to see that it discusses only one point by examining the evidence you have gathered and seeing that it all fits logically under one main heading. Even though the body of the speech is short, there should still be an introduction, a purpose statement, and a conclusion. Deliver the speech in three minutes or less.

QUESTIONS FOR REVIEW

1. How does a speech to inform differ in purpose from other types of speeches?
2. Why is presenting information orally more effective than writing a directive or a memo?
3. Why is a speech to inform sometimes called an *expository speech?*
4. How can a speech to inform be defined other than by the topic?
5. Can a speech to inform be given on a controversial topic?
6. What is one of the goals of teaching *media literacy?*
7. What function is performed by the League of Women Voters?
8. What are the characteristics of a one-point speech?
9. What opportunities are there for giving speeches in the business world?
10. What questions should a training specialist consider in preparing for a presentation?
11. Under what circumstances might you prepare notes for yourself before participating in a committee meeting?
12. How does speaking at a committee meeting differ from making a regular, "stand-up" presentation?

THINKING AND REASONING

AFTER READING THIS CHAPTER, YOU SHOULD
BE ABLE TO DO THE FOLLOWING:

Give serious thought to social issues, and examine what you
believe to be true; test for accuracy what you read and hear;
be aware of what you need to know in order to
draw rational conclusions.

Be able to tell if a piece of evidence is a *sign* of something or a *cause;*
be able to reach a conclusion through the *inductive* process.

Be able to reach a conclusion through the *deductive* process by using
a syllogism; understand how syllogisms can be used in
rules of law; be able to construct a *prima facie* case.

Develop a framework for problem solving by defining and analyzing a
problem, establishing criteria, considering alternatives, and
selecting the best solution.

Presentations that are of real value to an audience are not the clever platitudes of a glib stage personality, but the intelligent deliberations of a person who is well-informed and has a sincere commitment to the topic and to the interests of the listeners. Becoming an effective speaker requires that you develop your ability to recognize the significance of the information you hear and read, interpret its meaning, file it away in your mind, and retrieve it when you need it. The most effective speakers are those who have a good grasp of their own beliefs. They are well-informed and are able to organize their thoughts when the occasion demands. As you acquire the skills of public address, you will also be training your mind to *think critically*. You will learn to approach problems in a logical fashion, evaluate your data, correct for error, and avoid jumping to irrational conclusions. These are important capabilities for you to refine, because ideas must make sense to you before you are able to express them persuasively to anyone else.

CRITICAL THINKING

The term *critical thinking* refers to our ability to go beyond mere rote learning. Formal education is often faulted for teaching facts without regard for developing the student's capacity to analyze, interpret, challenge, and see the implications and consequences of the data. If we are going to be able to write and speak intelligently, we must be able to think critically. Richard Paul sees this as being an essential part of our education:

> What we say or write . . . is only a small portion of the thinking process—the proverbial tip of the iceberg. Surrounding any line of thought is a large substructure of *background thought*, logical connections not lying on the surface of reasoning, but prior to it, underlying it, or implied by it. In the background of all thinking are foundational concepts, assumptions, values, purposes, experiences, implications, and consequences—all embedded in lines of thought radiating outward in every direction.[1]

What this theory implies is that the roots of public speaking go deep into the cerebral processes, and in order to make substantive changes in your rhetorical skills you must learn more than methods and techniques.

Selective Learning

First of all, we must understand that the substance of our learning goes through a selection process. Because we cannot possibly assimilate all the information that we are exposed to, we must open our minds to that which seems to be useful to us and close our minds to the rest. Even data we have mentally processed are not always retrievable, so that we are limited to what

---

[1]Richard Paul, *Critical Thinking*, Center for Critical Thinking and Moral Critique, Sonoma State University, Rohnert Park, Calif., 1990, p. 70.

we can recall or rediscover through experience or research. We can expect that our information is always going to be incomplete; what we would like to know may be unavailable to us, or it may not yet be discovered by science. No matter how hard we try, we will never know it all. Nevertheless, we must make evaluations and judgments based on the best information that we have.

Examining Beliefs

By the time you become an adult, your brain contains an abundance of information; some of it is accurate, and some is inaccurate. That which you believe to be true is what you call "reality," but it may be simply a belief pattern and not resemble the real world at all. For example, the "reality" of a man who believes that women biologically are not capable of understanding principles of finance is quite different from the "reality" of a woman who knows she has a talent for such work. Even though facts and evidence do not support his conclusion, the man will be inclined to act on what he believes to be true. Because reality forms the basis of our behavior, such a man would probably not hire a woman to be his budget director, regardless of what qualifications she may have. Thinking critically means we can learn to avoid making these kinds of irrational mistakes that adversely affect our lives and the lives of those around us.

Direct Experience

Some of our information comes to us by direct experience. We perceive it through one or more of our five senses—hearing, seeing, touching, tasting, and smelling. Knowledge that we acquire through personal experience has more impact on us than does what we learn indirectly. It is also more apt to affect our thinking and will be retained for a longer period of time. For example, being in an automobile accident would surely have a profound effect on the way you think about traffic safety. Being witness to an accident also makes a strong impression. Other forms of learning, such as seeing a film, hearing a lecture, or reading an account, may to some degree influence your thinking, but not nearly so much as the direct experience will.

Influence of Other People

Although direct experience may be the most powerful form of learning, it is not always possible, necessary, or even desirable, to acquire knowledge firsthand. A great deal of what we believe to be true comes about as a result of information we receive from other people. As small children, we learn from parents, siblings, other relatives—even eccentric relatives—and peers; later in life we also learn from books, from teachers, and from the mass media. Because our information comes to us from such a variety of sources, we can assume that a certain portion of it will be inaccurate, biased, or misleading. The quality we call *wisdom* depends to a large extent on our ability to perceive the difference between information that is valid and that which is faulty.

Testing What You Hear and Read

Some reports you hear and read in the mass media are more reliable than others, and if you are to base your beliefs on what appears in newspapers, on television, and on line, you must have some way of knowing whether or not you can trust the source. The validity of material that is printed, broadcast, or published electronically can be tested by asking the following questions:

1. Is the source reputable? Has other information from the same source been found to be accurate?
2. Does the source have any obvious bias? Is it financed by an organization in support of one side or another of an issue?
3. Has the source provided complete information, or have important data been left out? Have quotations been taken out of context? Would the rest of the context change the meaning?
4. Has the source given the most current information? Have later events changed the circumstances?
5. Does the information meet the test of reason, or are there internal inconsistencies? Does the information contradict something else you know to be true?
6. Do other sources corroborate the information? If so, are those other sources reliable? Are there reasons that one source would possess facts others do not have?
7. Is the language of the source objective? Does the information contain emotionally loaded terminology designed solely for the purpose of arousing fear or hatred? Is the source attempting to discredit a person or a cause with diatribe rather than reason?

Be suspicious of sources that do not meet these criteria. If you are not sure that the information is accurate, seek verification. If you find that you have been misinformed and have arrived at conclusions based on erroneous data, don't hesitate to make corrections in your thinking.

Learning What You Need to Know

By itself, memorizing words, theories, and facts is not a path that leads to critical thought. However, you cannot test data and draw conclusions unless you have a foundation of knowledge to use as a starting point. You can argue that there is no need to learn a lot of big words and commit facts to memory, as long as you know where to find the information when you need it. That's true to a certain extent; however, unless you have some fundamental background, you will be unable to determine which specific words, theories, or evidence you need to investigate or uncover.

Vocabulary

Words and their definitions are important, not just for the sake of expressing ideas, but for thinking about them. For example, the word *xenophobic* means

"fearful of strangers," but the implications of the word go beyond its literal trans-
lation. The term does not make reference to people who run away from someone they don't know; it refers to those who feel threatened by people of different cultures who move into their neighborhood. Knowing the terminology not
only helps us to understand the concept, but also opens up possibilities for talking about things such as cultural diversity and immigration. Memorizing
words and definitions out of a dictionary certainly does not contribute to our
capacity for critical thought, but reflecting on their meaning and implications
will expand the horizons of our thinking. Words have limited value unless they
are used in context. We must learn to recognize the significance of their meaning in relationship to other words.

Literary References

Communicating effectively requires more than just having a broad vocabulary and knowing the meaning of a lot of words. It is also incumbent upon a
speaker to be familiar with the historical and literary references that are common to the culture. In the *Dictionary of Cultural Literacy,* E. D. Hirsch says,
"Successful communication depends on understanding the text's literal meanings as well as its implied meanings. These all-important implied meanings
can only be constructed out of a shared knowledge between writer and
reader."[2] In one of Hirsch's tests a group of community college students read
a passage from a book referring to a meeting between Ulysses S. Grant and
Robert E. Lee in the parlor of the Appomattox Courthouse on April 9, 1865. Although the students knew the meaning of all the words in the passage, many
of them failed to grasp the gist of the story because they did not connect the
facts to the U.S. Civil War. Those who do not have discernment for the significant events of the Civil War cannot be fully conversant in contemporary matters such as civil rights and the centralization of power in the federal government. Therefore, consider knowledge of this kind in the same way you regard
the importance of vocabulary.

Interpreting Information and Drawing Conclusions

Educators continually strive to find the most effective mix of pedagogical methods that will stimulate the critical thinking process. Do students need to learn
facts? Certainly they do; otherwise, they will believe that everything is simply
a matter of opinion. Do they need to learn how to interpret information and
draw conclusions? Absolutely. If our schools rely totally on rote learning, they
are engaged in a conditioning process rather than education.

Thinking critically is difficult and is frequently rejected in favor of easier
and less taxing methods of reaching conclusions. All too often people rely on
platitudes or simplistic slogans—a thought process that might be called
"bumper sticker mentality." This is a term that refers to applying some cleverly
phrased statement to a situation without analyzing the meaning of the words

---

[2]E. D. Hirsch, Jr., et al., *Dictionary of Cultural Literacy,* Houghton Mifflin, Boston, Mass., 1993.

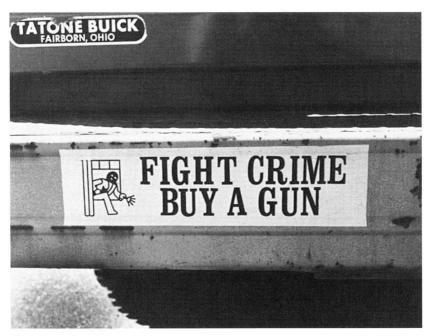

"Bumper sticker mentality" leads to simplistic conclusions.

or their validity in a given application. The man in the earlier example who had a fixed belief about women and the principles of finance may have drawn his conclusion from the saying, "A woman's place is in the home." Such a statement is not based on evidence or reason but on mindless repetition. The problem is that we tend to listen to people without making a critical evaluation of what we hear.

THE INDUCTIVE PROCESS

One way we can arrive at a reasoned conclusion is by using a method called the *inductive process.* This method is similar to the *scientific method,* in that conclusions are deferred until the evidence has been gathered. The process starts with the formation of a *hypothesis.* That means you make a guess about what the conclusion might be, but you do not rely on it until you have examined the data. For example, the man who believed that women were not capable of comprehending principles of finance might have reached a different conclusion if he had first considered the facts:

1. Standardized tests indicate that women score just as high as men on instruments that measure quantitative reasoning.
2. Colleges and universities report no difference in grade point averages between men and women in classes dealing with financial matters.

3. Women who have pursued careers in finance have proved to be equal to men in every respect.

All these facts conflict with the hypothesis; consequently, the man mentioned earlier would have had to alter his conclusion and acknowledge that a woman could be just as good a budget director as a man could be. When you follow this procedure, you are using the inductive method of reasoning—allowing the evidence to lead you to a conclusion rather than accepting a notion because of previous beliefs.

The scientific method works in the same way. When a study is conducted, researchers set up a series of experiments, being careful to control the variable factors. Let's say the research involves the effects of the omission of a particular nutrient in the diet of laboratory rats. The researchers will then make alterations in the conditions by varying the diet of the rats. After observing the results, they will form a hypothesis and conduct the study again. If the same results occur each time the experiment is performed, and if the researchers are able to predict each time what the outcome will be, they are able to say that the study has *reliability*. If the results are consistent with the results of other studies of the same nature, a conclusion can be drawn that there is a cause-and-effect relationship between the variable and the result.

Signs and Causes

All too frequently we draw conclusions on the basis of insufficient evidence. If several of our friends were to lose their jobs, for example, we might be tempted to say that the country is in a recession. Certainly, the loss of a few jobs is not sufficient reason to form a generalization. If we were to look at nationwide statistics, however, we might get a more valid indication. When unemployment figures climb to 6 or 7 percent, we might be able to say, with greater confidence, that a recession is occurring, but still we would be basing our conclusion on just one index. There is other evidence we need in order to support a declaration concerning the economic health of the nation. We would look at the gross domestic product, the balance of trade, and perhaps the number of new housing construction starts. If all of the evidence were consistent with our hypothesis, we might be able to see a pattern. Even then, we would need to recognize that in a subject area as complex as the economic condition of the nation, the claims we make are going to be based on subjective values as well as quantitative evidence.

Data we use to form a belief that a problem exists are called *signs*. We must be careful not to confuse signs with *causes*. Sometimes the language we use distorts the logical progression of our thoughts. For example, we might say, "The nation is in a recession, because the unemployment rate has risen to 7 percent." We don't mean that the high unemployment rate has *caused* the recession; we mean that the 7 percent rate is a *sign* that a recession exists. It is for this reason that we need to study the use of language simultaneously with examining the processes we use in interpreting data and forming conclusions. We must be able to speak clearly and logically to ourselves as well as to others.

THE DEDUCTIVE PROCESS

When we are reasoning through the inductive process, we don't begin with a premise or a generalization; we begin with specific evidence and then follow it to see where it leads. This is why we say that inductive reasoning proceeds from specific information to a general conclusion. When we reason *deductively*, we start with a general principle that we believe to be true and apply it to a particular situation. You may read, for example, a story in which Sherlock Holmes notices a bit of red mud on the boot of a suspect and concludes that the person has been walking through the moors. That's when Dr. Watson says, "Brilliant deduction, Holmes." The master detective is using what we call *syllogistic* reasoning, which is constructed in the following manner:

> Red mud can only be picked up on a boot by walking through the moors.
>
> That man has red mud on his boot.
>
> That man has been walking through the moors.

Holmes would probably reply, "Elementary, my dear Watson." Indeed, it does appear to be elementary; however, it is the *method* of reasoning that we want to examine.

A *syllogism* is a rhetorical device that can be used to analyze the validity of a conclusion. We won't go too deeply into the rules for syllogisms, because they can get very complex; all we need at this time is to have a basic understanding of the theory behind them. A *categorical* syllogism has three parts:

1. A major premise that must be accepted as an unqualified truth
2. A minor premise that is a specific case governed by the major premise
3. A conclusion

The classic example is as follows:

1. All men are mortal.   (Major premise)
2. John is a man.   (Minor premise)
3. John is mortal.   (Conclusion)

If the major premise is true, and if the minor premise is governed by it, the conclusion must *necessarily* be accepted as true. Be sure to note, however, that both the major premise and the minor premise are subject to refutation. If you wanted to reject a conclusion drawn from syllogistic reasoning, you would have to demonstrate either that the major premise was not true or that the minor premise was not governed by it. To challenge Sherlock Holmes's reasoning, for example, you might argue that red mud could be picked up somewhere other than on the moors or that the boots had been worn by some other person.

It's not just in detective work that we find applications for syllogistic reasoning. The syllogism is a rhetorical tool that can be used whenever you want to argue that a specific example is or should be included in the category of a major premise. It can become a way of making the social system work for you, as shown below:

1. All children are entitled to an education.
2. Jane is a child.
3. Jane is entitled to an education.

As long as there are no exceptions to the major premise that all children are entitled to an education, and as long as Jane is included in the category of all children (minor premise), the conclusion must logically be accepted.

The *rule of law* provides for us another example of where syllogistic reasoning can be applied. In this country we say that all people are "equal under the law." That means that everyone is entitled to *due process* of the law; it also means that the *penalties* for violation of the law must be applied equally. The law, then, can be used as the major premise in a syllogism:

1. All persons using a gun in committing a crime must go to jail.
2. The defendant used a gun in holding up a liquor store.
3. The defendant must go to jail.

This example leads us to an important principle of our social structure. If we are to have a fair system of justice, the rules of law must be based on reason rather than on the inclination of judges. In this country we say that a person is innocent until proven guilty and that the burden of proof is on the prosecutor rather than on the defendant. Even before a case is allowed to come to trial, the district attorney must be able to satisfy a judge that there is evidence against the person charged. Then, the prosecutor must be able to present a prima facie case in order to get a conviction.

A *prima facie case* is one that is inherently complete at its face value. It is constructed in such a way that the conclusion must necessarily be accepted unless one or more of the major contentions is rejected. Normally, the prosecuting attorney would begin the trial by presenting to the jury an outline of the case that the state has against the defendant. If the charge were armed robbery, for example, the following claims would have to be proved:

- That a robbery was committed
- That the defendant was the one who committed the robbery
- That the defendant carried a weapon at the time of the robbery

The next step would be for the prosecutor to support all three of those claims with evidence. If the jury members believed all of them to be true, they would have to return a verdict of guilty. And if the law were to be upheld, the defendant would have to go to jail. In order to discredit the case, the defense attorney would have to successfully refute the evidence that supports one or more of the main contentions.

As you can see, there is a similarity between the prima facie case and the syllogism. In both circumstances the conclusion must necessarily be accepted unless the opposition is successful in demonstrating that one or more of the main contentions are not true.

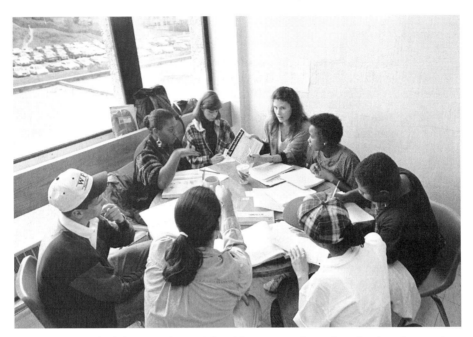

You are likely to find that complex social problems are easier to describe than they are to solve.

FRAMEWORK FOR PROBLEM SOLVING

Every time we pick up the newspaper we read about problems that need solutions. The word *problem* should not be regarded as a synonym for *trouble*. We are imperfect people living in an imperfect society, and problems are part of our everyday life. We can look at problems in several different ways: We can ignore them and pretend they don't exist, we can worry about them and do nothing, or we can confront them and find solutions. The last choice seems to be the most sensible, as long as we use effective methods in dealing with them. Sometimes our gut-level response works all right, but complex issues call for a more rational approach.

The philosopher and educator John Dewey has given us a method called the *reflective thinking process*.[1] It has been adapted in a number of ways to a variety of situations, but here is the basic framework:

- *Define the problem.* State the problem in a way that clearly identifies it. If you can't put it into words, you probably don't really understand what it is.
- *Limit the problem.* Bring the problem into focus so that it is distinguished from other issues. The better you are able to pinpoint the problem, the better chance you will have to find a solution.
- *Analyze the data.* Gather and examine information that is related to the problem. Your data may suggest how the problem developed, how serious it is, and what effect it is having.

---

[1] John Dewey, *How We Think,* Heath, Boston, Mass., 1933, pp. 106–115.

FRAMEWORK FOR PROBLEM SOLVING

- *Establish criteria for solutions.* Before you decide on a solution, you need to have some idea of what you want the solution to achieve.
- *Consider possible solutions.* Here you have a chance to think creatively. Don't get locked into believing that there is only one answer to a problem; open your mind to more possibilities.
- *Select the best solution by checking each possibility against your criteria.* Consider all the alternatives in light of what you said you wanted your solution to accomplish; then pick the one that fits best.

This framework can be a useful tool in dealing with complex problems. But, remember that you have to be realistic. There is no such thing as a perfect solution.

THINKING THROUGH A PROBLEM

To illustrate the problem-solving framework, let's look at the issue of street drugs. Everybody has an opinion on how to deal with this problem, but often the conclusion people reach is based on oversimplified thinking that doesn't take into consideration the complexities of the issue. Don't make the mistake of making a speech on a topic such as this before you have pursued in your mind a logical progression of thought.

Define the Problem

Begin by identifying in a general sense what you perceive the problem to be. Do you want to address the debilitating effects that drugs have on the individual, or are you more concerned about the damaging consequences to the society? A broad definition of the topic might be something such as this: "The sale and use of street drugs in the United States continues to be a serious social problem."

Limit the Problem

Once you have the general idea, you can begin thinking about how to limit the problem, or topic. The scope of the problem as stated is too extensive for you to handle in one study, so that you will have to be more specific in order to make an effective report. The limitations you put on the topic might be to evaluate it in terms of the particular drugs and the specific segments of the society that are affected. For example, you might sharpen the focus of the topic by posing the question in the following way: "How extensive is the sale and use of crack cocaine in the public schools, and what methods work best to deal with the problem?"

Analyze the Data

Begin by doing some reading on the subject, and talk to people who are informed on the topic. You may also want to structure your research by posing a list of questions:

- What effect does crack cocaine have on the people who use it?
- How much does it cost, and how do students get the money to buy it?
- How many students use the drug, and how old are they when they start?
- What motivates students to begin using crack cocaine?
- How much crime is related to drug trafficking?
- What role do students play in the gangs that supply the drug?
- Where does the drug come from? How does it get into the country and into the schools?
- What effect does the drug problem have on the quality of education?

FRAMEWORK FOR PROBLEM SOLVING

- What are school officials doing to curtail the use of drugs?
- What happens to a student who is caught using or selling drugs?
- What are the courts and law enforcement officials doing about the problem?

You may not be able to find answers to all these questions, but at least the list will help you to think about what you need to know and what the audience might ask.

Establish Criteria for the Solution

Establishing the criteria for the solution is an important step and one that is too often left out. It is a hard step to take because it requires insight, judgment, and objective thinking. What frequently happens is that solutions come to mind while you are analyzing the data. Those solutions may appear to be very attractive, and you might be tempted to start right away to build a case in their support. Before you do this, however, consider what goals you want your solution to accomplish. Here are six possible criteria:

1. Significantly reduce the sale and distribution of crack cocaine in public schools.
2. Modify the attitude of students so that they are not motivated to use drugs.
3. Improve the learning environment for students.
4. Provide rehabilitation for those addicted to drugs.
5. Punish the offenders and prevent them from repeating their crime.
6. Provide a means for students to earn money without having to sell drugs.

Some of these criteria may be more important than others, and you will have to decide which ones you want to focus on in this particular study.

Consider Possible Solutions

Now you are ready to start thinking about possible ways to solve the problem. This step in the process calls for *creative thinking* as well as *critical thinking.* You very likely will find that complex social problems are much easier to *describe* than they are to solve. Open your mind to possibilities, and get them down on paper. Your list might look something like this:

1. Develop support programs and rehabilitation centers for students who want to quit the drug habit.
2. Give special privileges to students who stay off drugs.
3. Provide job opportunities for students who would otherwise be tempted to sell drugs.
4. Close the campus so that no one is allowed in or out until school is over.
5. Require that students who are caught using drugs attend school in separate facilities.
6. Prosecute students in adult courts when they are caught selling drugs.

Select the Best Solution

The way to select the best solution is to measure each one of them against your criteria and see which one comes the closest to accomplishing your goal. In addition to producing the most effective solution, this method also gives you one that is *defensible—* that is, you will be able to explain why you selected that solution over the other possibilities. This is an important feature of the method, because it is quite likely that you will be called on to do precisely that.

DISCOVERING WHAT YOU BELIEVE

The process of discovering what you believe is sometimes referred to as *dialectical thinking.* Richard Paul says,

> Whenever we consider concepts or issues deeply, we naturally explore their connections to other ideas and issues within different domains or points of view. Court trials and debates are dialectical in form and intention. They pit idea against idea, reasoning against counterreasoning in order to get at the truth of a matter. As soon as we begin to explore ideas, we find that some clash or are inconsistent with others. If we are to integrate our thinking, we need to assess which of the conflicting ideas we will accept. . . .[3]

There is some risk involved in this practice, because the evidence and the logical thought process may lead you to a conclusion that you don't really want to accept. Oliver Wendell Holmes said, "What is true is what I can't help believing." Being in that position may make you uncomfortable at first, but it will also make you a better and a more reasonable public speaker.

Do not expect to receive unanimous approval when you make specific declarations on a controversial issue; you may gain the favor of some, but you are bound to lose the support of others. You can urge your listeners to protect the environment or fight to preserve their freedom, for example, but such assertions have no functional application. It isn't hard to get people to see the value of some abstract virtue; disagreement occurs when you begin to talk about details. For example, you can easily say in your speech that unnecessary expenses must be cut, and every person in the audience will thoroughly agree. But if you are forced to be specific about where those cuts should come, you are likely to confront opposition.

Learning to think critically helps us to appreciate those who have the responsibility for inventing and implementing solutions to social problems. Lawmakers, administrators, and people in positions of authority have more difficult jobs than we sometimes believe: After they win the office or appointment and receive the cheers of the crowd, they must translate their political rhetoric into operational procedures that deal with real problems in a real world.

EXERCISE

Review the steps in the section "Framework for Problem Solving" and the issue of the sale and use of street drugs in public schools. Note that there are six choices under the subheading of "Establish Criteria for the Solution." There are also six choices under the subheading "possible solutions." For each criterion, there is a corresponding solution, and your task is to match the ones that go together. Remember that when you develop a speech on an issue of this kind, the solution you advocate must correspond to the problem you have described.

[3]Richard Paul, *op. cit.*, p. 254.

QUESTIONS FOR REVIEW

1. What do we mean by *critical thinking?*
2. What do we mean by *selective learning?*
3. Which has more impact on us, direct experience or reports we read? Why?
4. What are questions we should ask in order to test the validity of sources?
5. Why is vocabulary important in both the thinking and speaking processes?
6. What does Hirsch mean by *cultural literacy?* How can it affect our understanding of messages?
7. In order to become educated people, what do we have to do in addition to learning facts?
8. What is another term for *inductive reasoning?* Describe how the process works.
9. What is the difference between a *sign* and a *cause?*
10. What are we doing when we reason deductively?
11. What are the three parts of a categorical syllogism?
12. What do you have to do before you can logically reject the conclusion of a syllogism?
13. How can a syllogism be applied to the rule of law?
14. In what way is a syllogism similar to a prima facie case?
15. What are the steps in the problem-solving framework?

THE SPEECH TO PERSUADE

**AFTER READING THIS CHAPTER, YOU SHOULD
BE ABLE TO DO THE FOLLOWING:**

Know how persuasion differs from coercion, manipulation, bribery,
and deception; understand what Aristotle meant by the
modes of proof—logos, pathos, and ethos.

Be able to construct an argument that defends or opposes the status
quo; identify evidence that creates the condition of *cognitive
dissonance* in the minds of people you are attempting to
persuade; phrase information in a way that contributes
to the support of your argument.

Know how to construct an argumentative case by advancing a claim,
using evidence, providing a warrant to reinforce the evidence,
forming and qualifying a thesis.

Apply emotional appeals to a persuasive speech by calling attention
to shared values that you have with the audience and establishing
your own personal integrity; know how to talk about your
feelings and experiences using emotional language that
contributes to your sincerity.

You might say that every speech you prepare is designed to persuade in one respect or another. Even in a speech to inform, you try to persuade your audience that you are a credible person, that your information is accurate, and that your message has significant value. In terms of rhetorical categories, however, the speech to persuade is classified as a message that favors one side of a controversial issue. When you prepare for this kind of speech, you must assume that there will be people in the audience who will be opposed to your thesis; your intent is to persuade them to reevaluate their thinking and accept what you want them to believe.

THE PERSUASIVE MESSAGE

Before going any deeper into this subject, reflect a bit on how you feel about the term *persuasion*. You may be one of those people who believe that persuading others is the same as trying to get them to do something they really don't want to do. "After all," you might ask, "what right do I have to tell people what they should believe or how they ought to behave?" You may personally resent having someone try to persuade you to do something—particularly if you have had bad experiences with high-pressure salespeople. Even if the persuaders have your best interests at heart, you may object to their insistence on your doing things their way. And it probably doesn't reduce your irritation much when they tell you they are doing it "for your own good."

The Inherent Qualities of Persuasion

In order to discuss the art of persuasion intelligently, we must understand that, in its pure classical or academic sense, it is neither coercive nor deceptive. If it were, its methods would certainly not find a proper place in a college textbook. The reason the term sometimes evokes a negative reaction is that it frequently is associated with practices that *are* designed to threaten or deceive. What we need to do is to qualify the definition of *persuasion* and show how it differs in nature from terms that appear to be similar.

> *Coercion* is one way to get people to do what you want them to do. Here you are using force or the threat of force to get them to comply. It is different from persuasion in terms of the end result. People who are coerced may do what they are told to do as long as the pressure is applied, but they will usually return to their former behavior when the threat is removed. They conform to your wishes, not because you have offered persuasive evidence, but because they fear the consequences if they do not. Coercion is not persuasion; it is the exercise of power.
>
> *Manipulation* is a devious tactic for getting what you want. It plays on emotional insecurities such as guilt, shame, fear, or a sense of obligation. People who are manipulated may comply—albeit reluctantly—but they may not respect themselves very much for having done so. For example, an

encyclopedia salesperson might say to a customer, "Now, you don't want to deprive your children of all the educational advantages they deserve, do you . . .?" This is not persuasion; it is a manipulative device designed to get a sale rather than to meet the needs of the customer.

Bribery is the offering of gifts with a view to gaining a favor. It is probably the easiest way to influence people, but the person who bribes is employing an underhanded, rather than a persuasive, method. The person who accepts a bribe is making a choice based on personal gain rather than on the merits of the proposal itself.

Deception is another practice that can be used to change a person's belief or behavior, but deliberate falsehoods certainly have no place in the legitimate art of persuasion. *Deception* means distorting the facts or exaggerating the claims when you know that a true statement would not be effective. This does not meet the definition of *persuasion,* because it denies recipients the ability to make a choice based on accurate information. When people realize they have been deceived, they will reject not only what you have told them, but also any further efforts you may make to try to influence them.

When we practice the art of persuasion, we are expressing what we honestly believe to be true. We are not trying to take advantage of our listeners—we want them to be the *beneficiaries* of our message, not the *victims.* We share with the audience the evidence, the reasons, and the logic that we, ourselves, have used in arriving at a conclusion. And we recognize that our listeners have *free choice* to accept or reject what we are saying. If we do anything that deprives them of that choice, we are using devious, rather than persuasive, methods.

Modes of Proof

Aristotle analyzed persuasion in terms of the elements that affect the people to whom the message is directed. He contended that those elements or modes were the *logos,* the *pathos,* and the *ethos.* These terms correspond roughly to the *argumentation,* the *emotional appeals,* and the *ethical qualities* that the speaker brings to the speech.

Logos

The term *logos* refers to the efforts the speaker makes to prove a case argumentatively by offering facts and reason. If the controversial aspect of a speech can be addressed at the cognitive or rational level, a speaker might be successful in changing the minds of the listeners by offering evidence that refutes what they had previously believed. By Aristotle's definition, *persuasion* has a broader meaning than *argumentation.* This may seem to be a fine point of difference, but when you are sitting on a jury, for example, it is important for you to know whether the prosecutor is attempting to persuade you by appealing to your reason or by appealing to your emotions. Certainly, emotional appeals are legitimate as a means of persuasion, but rhetorically they are not the same as the proofs that Aristotle calls the *logos.*

Pathos

An appeal to the emotions is what we call the *pathos*. A speaker may be able to influence an audience by arousing feelings of fear, anger, or compassion, or a sense of justice. Here again, we can use the courtroom as an example. An attorney for a plaintiff in a personal injury suit has to prove through evidence (logos) that an act of violence was committed, but the extent of suffering that was endured by the victim can only be measured on an emotional scale. The jury might agree that the defendant was responsible for the act, but individual jurors might differ in terms of their compassion for the offended party. The difference here might be quite real when it comes to the amount of damages awarded to the plaintiff. The U.S. Supreme Court ruled that testimony pertaining to "victim impact" could be considered by juries in cases that involve the death penalty. This decision allows the punishment of a person convicted of a capital crime to be influenced by emotional appeals.

Although we certainly strive to be logical in what we say and do, a great many of the issues of our time are judged by emotion rather than by reason. We are called on to make decisions based on whatever evidence is available, but we frequently find that facts are not enough. One of the most powerful speeches of this century is the one delivered by Martin Luther King on August 28, 1963, from the steps of the Lincoln Memorial. In that address he said:

> I have a dream that my four little children will one day live in a nation where they will not be judged by the color of their skin, but by the content of their character.

Consider the influence these words had upon civil rights legislation in this country. There is nothing here that could be called factual evidence; yet, people were profoundly moved by the power of the statement.

Ethos

Neither of the first two modes of proof mentioned—the logos or the pathos—would influence an audience unless the speaker displayed a sense of ethos. To use Aristotle's words, "There is persuasion through character whenever the speech is spoken in such a way as to make the speaker worthy of credence; for we believe fair-minded people to a greater extent and more quickly than we do others. . . ."[1] The evidence that is presented in a speech or the phrases that are used to create an emotional impact have a much greater effect on listeners who have confidence in the integrity of the speaker. Certainly, words themselves have influence of their own. However, in order to explain why it is that Martin Luther King was able to achieve the success that he did, we have to look beyond the words and give credit to the persona of the speaker. It is unlikely that the same words spoken by someone else on the occasion of the 1963 civil rights rally would have had the same effect.

---

[1]Aristotle, *On Rhetoric*, trans. George A. Kennedy, Oxford University Press, New York, 1991, p. 38.

TAKING A POSITION

At an early stage in your preparation of a speech to persuade you must decide which side of the issue you are going to take. Are you going to attack the prevailing conditions, or defend them? To know that, you need to have a clear understanding of the status quo.

Status Quo

The term we use to mean "the way things are" is *status quo.* That could refer to the laws that are in effect, the generally accepted standards of morality, or any other present state or condition. Your argumentative position will either be to support the status quo or to call for some modification of it.

Let's say, for example, that you are giving a speech on teenage pregnancy. You have examined the evidence and have found that a great many teenage girls are impregnated by men who are in their twenties or older. Often, the young girl is left with the baby, and the father is allowed to get away without taking any responsibility. Men are hardly ever prosecuted for doing this, but states do have laws on the books against statutory rape and child abuse. However, these laws are seldom, if ever, enforced. If you were to recommend in your speech that the state begin to bring charges against older men for having sex with teenage girls, you would be advocating a change in the status quo. But

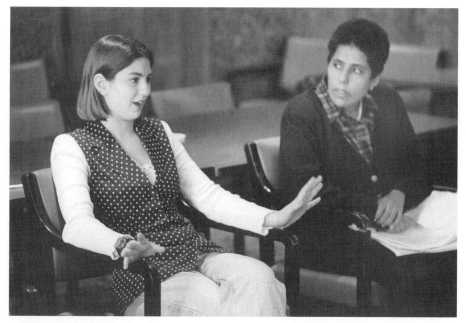

When we practice the art of persuasion, we want listeners to be the *beneficiaries* of our message, not the *victims.*

you have to be careful about which side you are on: If you are debating with someone who says that statutory rape laws should be abolished, you would be supporting the status quo in maintaining that the laws should remain in place and that they be enforced.

The status quo is also an important consideration when you are deciding whether to support or oppose a proposition that is on an election ballot. Sometimes, the wording of a proposition is misleading, and if you are not careful, you may wind up voting in favor of something that you actually oppose. Remember this: Any time you vote "yes" on a proposition, you are voting for a change in the status quo; when you vote "no," you are voting to retain the status quo. Therefore, it is necessary that you know what the status quo is. For example, the proposition may pertain to the construction of a new dam, and you may want to prevent it from being built. The status quo may be that previous legislation has granted rights to build the dam, and the proposition would be to repeal that action. Therefore, you would vote "yes" on the proposition because you are *opposed* to the dam.

Once you have established in your own mind what side of the issue you want to be on, you can begin to consider what information you need to include in your presentation that will have an effect on the way the people in your audience draw their conclusions.

Conflicting Beliefs

When people establish for themselves a belief structure pertaining to issues they regard as important, they like to hear facts supporting their concept of truth. They also want to feel assured that they are acting in accordance with what they are convinced is the truth. For example, if they are making contributions to a television evangelist, they want to believe that their money is going for a good cause. To reinforce their convictions they likely will associate with other people who have similar beliefs and tune in to media presentations that say what they want to hear. When they are confronted with information that conflicts with their beliefs, they will probably try to find a way to reject it or refute it. If the evangelist is accused of having an illicit love affair or is charged with misusing funds, supporters may have a difficult time reconciling the new information with what they want to believe to be true. Some of them might attempt to discredit the source of the critical information and claim that the charges are false; others might try to minimize the importance of the accusations, maintaining that the evangelist was doing such good work that a few minor infractions and indulgences should not be cause for criticism. On the other hand, there may be people who allow the new evidence to change their minds.

The painful experience of being confronted with irrefutable evidence that conflicts with a deep-seated belief structure is what sociologists call *cognitive dissonance.* It is sometimes referred to as "buyer's remorse," because it is similar to the feeling you have when you are dissatisfied with a purchase you have made. The feeling is especially strong when the purchase was an expensive item and was something you thought you wanted for a long time. TV viewers who "buy into" an evangelistic movement may not give up easily, even when the evidence of a scandal is strong; in fact, many of them may continue to support the movement while all the time they know that the leaders are squandering their money. When people don't really want to change, they can always find a reason for not doing it.

The condition of cognitive dissonance does not necessarily bring about the alteration of a belief or commitment, but it frequently is the step that precedes such a change. This is why we say that cognitive dissonance is the first stage of persuasion.

What you need to recognize when you are delivering a speech to persuade is that some people in the audience may have an intense commitment to the point of view that you are about to attack. You are not going to be successful if you make unsupported accusations. For example, to claim simply that a charitable institution has been irresponsible with its money is not going to have any effect on those who fervently believe in what it is doing. You will have to provide documented evidence that significantly challenges the credibility of the institution. The information must be damaging enough so that opponents are required to refute the charges in order to logically maintain the allegiance that they previously held. Even when you are able to produce this kind of evidence, the people you are trying to persuade may still not be sufficiently persuaded to change their minds. If, however, you create in them the condition of cognitive dissonance, you can consider your efforts to be successful. Persuasion generally does not occur immediately after a single speech, so be patient.

Persuasive Information

In its raw state, information is rhetorically neutral. That is, it can be employed to develop any kind of a speech, whether the purpose is to inform, to persuade, to entertain, or to motivate. The significance of the material you gather is not always self-evident—it can enlighten, convince, amuse, or inspire, depending on the way it is used.

Information that is intended to be persuasive must be presented in a persuasive framework. The listener must be able to perceive two things: (1) that the new evidence is valid and (2) that it conflicts with previous beliefs. It is up to the speaker to facilitate both of these conditions in order for the first step of persuasion to take place. The perceived validity of the information will depend on the confidence the listener has in the speaker, as well as in the source of the speaker's information. The extent to which the information conflicts with previous beliefs depends on the way the speaker integrates the information into his or her claim.

The information used to support a speech to persuade is called *evidence.* Evidence could, of course, be physical as well as rhetorical, but right now we are primarily concerned with the latter. Rhetorical evidence can be in the form of statistics, testimony, specific instances, case histories, or any of the other forms mentioned earlier. When your purpose is to lead audience members to a conclusion you want them to accept, your evidence must be presented in a way that will accomplish that end. Extraneous information should be deleted from the speech, and contrary material should be justified in some way. What do you do when you come across evidence in your research that seems to contradict your postulate? You could leave it out, of course, but then someone might ask you about it during the question period. A better plan would be to include it in the speech, but refute it. If you can't refute it, explain to your audience how you are still able to take the position you do in the light of what seems to be conflicting evidence.

Part of the strategy of developing a speech to persuade is to phrase your information in a way that supports your claim. It's important to remember that facts do not speak for themselves; the interpretation you give to the facts is what will influence the audience. For example, you might be giving a speech in support of government-funded health insurance. While researching the topic, you discover that 87 percent of the people in the United States are already covered by some sort of medical plan. If you simply present the evidence and let it stand without comment, you are suggesting that there is not much reason for your proposal. But you don't have to phrase it that way. You can say that 13 percent of Americans—33 million people—have no coverage at all. With such wording, the same information communicates a much different message.

CONSTRUCTING AN ARGUMENTATIVE CASE

The speaker who addresses an audience that is listening critically must know how to construct an effective argumentative case. To persuade an audience through reason rather than through emotion requires that we have an understanding of the theory behind argumentation. An argument is more than just a statement of fact or the expression of an opinion. It is a combination of parts, each with a specific function, and all of them have to work together. Let's begin our analysis by defining some of the commonly used terminology.

Advancing a Claim

A *claim* is a sentence or phrase that expresses a belief that you have arrived at through reason. By itself, it does not constitute a statement of fact, but it does imply that there is factual evidence that supports it. It could also be called an *assertion* or a *contention*. In your outline, it might be one of the main headings. For example, a claim would be as follows: "Cigarette smoke is harmful to the health of people who breathe it." Note that a claim is different from an opinion. You can express an opinion anytime you want—with or without evidence. When you say, "I don't like cigarette smoking," you are not constructing an argument, you are simply stating your opinion. It's your right to do that, whether you have evidence or not. But when you advance a claim, you are required to provide factual support.

Using Evidence to Support a Claim

Evidence is the factual support behind the claim, and it must be linked to the claim before we can say that an argument has been advanced. In other words, evidence does not speak for itself. The reason it does not is that it can often be interpreted in a number of different ways. It is your job as a speaker to provide that interpretation in order for the audience to know what you mean. Here is an example of a piece of evidence: "Cigarette smoke contains tars." If the statement were allowed to stand by itself, we would not know what significance the speaker might be attaching to it. The evidence needs to be *linked* to the claim in order to form an argument:

> Cigarette smoke is harmful to the health of people who breathe it, because it contains tars.

Providing a Warrant to Reinforce the Evidence

In order for an argument to be firmly established, the significance of the evidence may need to be reinforced. In other words, the audience members might be saying to themselves, "Why is that evidence so important?" Remember, we observed in an earlier chapter that listeners may not be able to see how a piece of information is linked to the idea that you want them to accept. Therefore, it might be necessary to explain how the evidence contributes to the support of the claim. In the theory of argumentation, a linking statement of this kind is called a *warrant*. To establish that the evidence in the smoking argument is really important, the speaker might add, "Tars in cigarette smoke are carcinogenic."

Forming a Thesis

When you develop a series of arguments, they will begin to form a pattern, and you can start thinking about phrasing your *thesis*. The thesis is the main proposition of a persuasive speech, and is the one you want your audience to accept. It needs to be expressed in such a way that it embraces all of the assertions you make and accounts for all of the evidence. On the subject of smoking, your thesis might be phrased this way:

> If smoking is to remain legal in the United States, we need to do everything we can to help people quit the habit, to prevent young people from starting to smoke, and to protect the health of nonsmokers, who are forced to live and work with those who smoke.

Qualifying the Thesis

There is one final element that you might need to add in order for your argumentation to be complete. You may find it necessary to take exceptions into consideration and deal with them by making a *qualifying statement*. In the example used above, the qualifying statement is "If smoking is to remain legal. . . ."

What you are doing here is saying to your audience that you are not suggesting that smoking be outlawed. The qualifier gives credibility to your thesis so that listeners know that you are taking a reasoned and responsible point of view.

When you combine the claim, the evidence, the warrant, the thesis, and the qualifier, you have a strong argumentative *case*. "Avoiding the Hazards of Smoking" shows the way the example case would look in outline form.

Avoiding the Hazards of Smoking

Attention statement: Everything we know about cigarette smoking tells us that it is harmful to health and has no socially redeeming qualities.

Thesis statement: If smoking is to remain legal in the United States, we need to do everything we can to warn people of the dangers, prevent the younger generation from starting to smoke, help smokers to quit, and protect the health of those who are forced to live and work with people who smoke.

I   Smoke from cigarettes is harmful to everyone who breathes it.
  A It is life-threatening to the smoker.
    1 Cigarettes contain tars and nicotine.
    2 There are 350,000 deaths per year from lung and heart disease.
  B It is harmful to other people who breathe the smoke.
    1 Effects of secondary smoke.
    2 Effects on people with lung problems.

II   Every day new smokers are taking up the habit.
  A More people are starting than are quitting.
    1 About 51 million smokers in the United States.
    2 Tobacco industry targets specific groups.
    3 Most new smokers are young people.
  B Smoking is addictive.
    1 Nicotine has proved to be habit-forming.
    2 About 85 percent of smokers want to quit but can't.
    3 A 75 percent relapse rate; harder habit to break than the drug habit.

III   Education is not enough; we need to enact controls.
  A Label products and advertisements with warning that smoking is addictive.
  B Ban cigarette machines.
  C Remove government subsidies of tobacco industry.
  D Restrict smoking in public places.

Conclusion: We certainly must have compassion for smokers: they are victims, not offenders. But their habit is placing themselves and others at risk, which makes smoking a social problem as well as an individual problem.

EMOTIONAL APPEALS

The best approach for developing a speech to persuade is to present strong supporting evidence whenever it's available, but there are occasions when it may be more effective to base your appeals on values you hold that you know are shared by members of the audience. Attorney Clarence Darrow said that when the defense of a person on trial is a matter of justice, you do not have to give the jury reasons to acquit the client; you make them want to vote for acquittal and they'll find their own reasons.

Shared Values

There are times when our convictions are founded upon emotions rather than on fact, and the message that we want our audience to accept may not be one that can be supported by evidence and clinical studies. For example, we all share a belief in justice and the protection of human rights, and we don't require that documented proof of their value be provided. People in the audience are going to be moved by a speaker whose appeal is founded on the same principles to which they, themselves, subscribe and who conveys a sincere and dedicated commitment to the moral tenets that are basic to their belief structure.

There may be times when rhetorical evidence does not tell the whole story and may actually be counterproductive to achieving the purpose of the speech. Facts alone do not have the inspirational quality that moves people to take courage when hard times and even disaster are facing them. During the depression years of the 1930s the social conditions in this country were extremely bleak. If Franklin Roosevelt had done nothing but relate statistics to describe the economic circumstance, people might have fallen into a state of despair. Instead, he was able to reach them at the emotional level by speaking to them on a regular basis in the comfortable setting that came to be known as a "fireside chat." Instead of stock market quotations, he gave them words of encouragement and told them, "The only thing you have to fear is fear itself." To a large extent, it was the personal integrity and sense of confidence that President Roosevelt projected that gave people hope and eventually led the country out of the depression.

In order to be successful in making emotional appeals work for you, it is necessary that you identify the values you share with the audience and project them with a sense of conviction. Probably the most important quality you need is sincerity. If you attempt to apply lofty values to trivial issues, the phoniness will become immediately apparent to your listeners. To make the claim that you are fighting for freedom against totalitarian aggressors who are raising the parking meter fees, for example, will not inspire confidence in your sincerity.

Shared values are much easier to establish at a high level of abstraction. For example, we might all be able to agree with the generalization that the lives of innocent people should be protected. It's when we begin to apply those values to specific cases and define what we mean by "innocent lives" that we find ourselves confronted by differing opinions. Those who oppose the legal status of abortion would include an unborn fetus in the definition of "innocent lives." People who support a woman's right to have an abortion would argue that life does not begin until after birth. This issue is a particularly difficult one, because the underlying principle that forms the basis of what people believe is not a matter that can be established with factual evidence.

Personal Integrity

The use of emotional appeals in a speech is, in itself, a controversial issue. There are some critics who contend that decisions ought to be based on reason alone and that attempts to arouse emotional feelings are rhetorically unscrupulous. That may be true if the speaker is feigning emotions as a means of manipulating an audience into accepting a claim that would not stand up to the test of reason. But there *are* other types of emotional approaches that you might find useful to consider that are generally regarded as being within the parameters of ethical behavior.

Feelings and Experiences

If the feelings you have about an issue are genuinely strong, you are not deceiving an audience by expressing them. In fact, if you fail to communicate sincere concern for the plight of people who deserve compassion, the audience might regard you as being a person who is cold and uncaring. In order to engage the emotions of the audience, you must begin with your own emotional involvement. You can't expect the audience to be moved unless you are willing to speak from the heart and convey the depth of your own feelings.

Selecting a topic in which you have had personal experience is an excellent way to help establish for yourself the credibility that you want the audience to perceive. If you are able to say "I know because I was there . . . ," your listeners are more likley to pay attention than they would be if you were making a secondhand report. There are a few caveats, however, to this approach. First of all, you don't want to come across as a braggart. If the listeners get the idea that you are telling about your experiences in order to extoll your own virtues, they may reject your claim, regardless of the merit it may have. Second, make sure you are able to keep your emotions from getting out of control. If your topic is child abuse, for example, and you yourself were an abused child, you may be able to make your point in a very powerful way. But if you can't talk about the subject without breaking down, you might find that the public speaking mode of communication makes the experience too painful for you to handle.

Language of Emotion

Effective arguments may influence the way people think, but it's the emotional appeals that are built into a speech that inspire listeners to act. As a speaker, you can move people to action if your timing is good and conditions are right. Listeners must have a concern for the cause that is being addressed, they must be willing to take personal responsibility, and they must believe that their efforts will make a difference. What the speaker can do is reinforce those

"The glow from that fire can truly light the world."

beliefs with motivating language and provide an opportunity for the energies of the audience to be directed and released. During times of crisis, a key phrase can be a powerful force. In 1941, for example, tens of thousands of young men enlisted in the military forces after hearing the call, "Remember Pearl Harbor."

There are many examples we could cite of times when the words of the speaker were clearly the inspiration for action. We know that people were profoundly affected by the language that John F. Kennedy used in his inaugural address. He might have made a simple request for people to volunteer for government service; instead, he reached out in a much more dramatic way:

> The energy, the faith, the devotion which we bring to this endeavor will light our country and all who serve it—and the glow from that fire can truly light the world. And so, my fellow Americans, ask not what your country can do for you; ask what you can do for your country.

The thought, the phrasing, and the quality of the language make this a great speech, but even more important is that people were challenged and *acted* on the words. A follow-up to this speech was the formation of the Peace Corps, and thousands of young people from all over the country answered the call to serve their country in the cause of peace.

Credibility of the Speaker

Having gone to all the trouble of gathering the information, organizing it, and practicing the delivery, can you be sure that the audience is going to believe what you say? If you are known in the community and have acquired a reputation for being honest and well-informed, your words will carry considerable weight. But what if people are hearing you for the first time? How will they know if your information is accurate and if you are telling the truth? The capacity to establish your credibility when you are unknown to the audience is one of the most important variables in determining success in public speaking.

If people are going to trust that you know what you are talking about, you have to speak as though you do. Make sure you are familiar with your own evidence. If you appear to be seeing it for the first time on your note cards, your credibility is going to take a nosedive. Cite your sources whenever you need to so that your listeners know that you are not making things up out of your own head. And, above all, make sure that you let them know that what you are saying is what you yourself believe.

Don't make the mistake of assuming that your sincerity will be self-evident. Even though there are people who proclaim they can tell whether or not someone is telling the truth, the evidence indicates the contrary. Those who declare they can perceive the sincerity of a speaker are just guessing and are wrong half the time. What people in the audience do is observe and evaluate characteristics of delivery—the posture, the gestures, the facial expressions, the eye contact, and the vocal inflection—all the features that appear to be the indicators of integrity. However, the effective application of these speaking techniques is available to any speaker—honest or not. It's clear that just *being* sincere isn't enough; you have to know how to *project* sincerity if you want people to believe what you say. Whether you like the notion or not, the audience members are going to apply subjective criteria in making their determination of whether or not they are going to believe you.

Truth is not self-evident. The only way it can prevail is if it is advocated by honest and just men and women who are effective in their communication. Sixteen hundred years ago St. Augustine wrote:

> Who would dare to say that truth should stand in the person of its defenders, unarmed against lying, so that they who wish to urge falsehoods may know how to make their listeners benevolent, or attentive, or docile in their presentation, while the defenders of truth are ignorant of that art? Should they speak briefly, clearly, and plausibly while the defenders of truth speak so that they tire their listeners, make themselves difficult to understand and what they have to say dubious? . . . Who is so foolish as to think this to be wisdom?[2]

EXERCISE

Develop a speech on gun control using the information cited below. Remember that evidence does not speak for itself. You will have to select the data you want to use and combine each fact with a claim that supports your point of

---

[2]Saint Augustine, *On Christian Doctrine*, Book Four, trans. D. W. Robertson, Jr. Copyright © 1958 by Macmillan Publishing Company. Reprinted by permission of the publisher.

view. The thesis you establish and the recommendation you make can be of your own invention. You do not need to use all of the information in your speech, but you should be able to respond to questions that members of the audience might ask. The statements below are listed at random. Arrange them in a logical sequence, and combine them in outline form with your thesis, main headings, and conclusion.

- The Bureau of Alcohol, Tobacco and Firearms reported that 86 percent of the firearms traced to crime in 1995 were junk guns called "Saturday Night Specials."
- Firearms are involved in more than 30,000 deaths each year in the United States.
- There are 70 million gun owners in the United States.
- Violent crimes continued to rise in New York and Washington, D.C., after passage of strict firearm control measures.
- 87 percent of the U.S. population say they would support a federal law to require a seven-day waiting period and background check for the purchase of a handgun.
- The National Rifle Association has certified 26,000 instructors and trains 750,000 students each year in the use of firearms.
- Twenty-two people were killed in Killeen, Texas, on October 16, 1991, by a berserk gunman firing a 9-mm pistol that holds a clip of seventeen rounds.
- About 3 percent of the members of the National Rifle Association are women.
- The Second Amendment to the Constitution says, "A well regulated militia, being necessary to the security of a free State, the right of the people to keep and bear arms shall not be infringed."

QUESTIONS FOR REVIEW

1. How do you define *coercion, manipulation, bribery,* and *deception?* In what way do they all differ from persuasion? Why do we say that free choice is an important element of persuasion?
2. What did Aristotle mean by the "modes of proof"—the logos, the pathos, and the ethos?
3. What is meant by the term *status quo?* Which way do you vote on a ballot measure when you favor the status quo? Explain.
4. What is meant by the term *cognitive dissonance?* What do people tend to do in order to avoid experiencing cognitive dissonance?
5. Why do we say that information in its raw form is not persuasive? What do you have to add to the information to make it persuasive?
6. In the theory of argumentation, what is meant by a *claim?* What is meant by *evidence,* and how does evidence affect the claim?
7. What is the difference between physical and rhetorical evidence?
8. What is a warrant for a claim? Why is a warrant sometimes necessary in order for an argumentative statement to be clear?
9. What is a thesis statement? What role does it play in a speech to convince?

10. What is the most important personal quality needed to make the emotional appeals of a speaker effective? Why is it not a good idea to apply lofty values to trivial issues?
11. What are three approaches a speaker might use as a means of appealing to the emotions of an audience?
12. What is meant by the *credibility* of the speaker?
13. What did St. Augustine have to say about the defenders of truth learning effective methods of persuasion?

THE SPEAKER

THE SPEAKER'S FRAME OF MIND

**AFTER READING THIS CHAPTER, YOU SHOULD
BE ABLE TO DO THE FOLLOWING:**

Think to yourself that you really want to have people hear what
you have to say; understand that preparing thoroughly before
giving your speech is the best way to overcome anxiety.

Create a self-image that serves you well by giving yourself positive
messages; know how to set the self-adjusting mechanism in your brain
to the point where you are able to achieve your highest potential;
understand what is meant by *comfort zones*; know how you can expand
your comfort zones by changing the picture you have in your
mind of what is possible for you; make adjustments in your
self-perception through a six-step process.

Imprint the new image you have of yourself by writing down and
reviewing the assets you have that make you an effective public
speaker; convince yourself that you are a capable speaker by
going through the process of desensitizing yourself to the
anxieties of public speaking.

If you can honestly say that you do not suffer from speech anxiety, you may not need to read this chapter. I certainly don't want to call your attention to something that is not a problem for you in the first place. But if you do feel the proverbial butterflies in your stomach when you have to speak in public, you can be assured that you have a great deal of company, and there are steps you can take to relieve the condition. It is quite understandable to have an aversion for giving a speech, and there is nothing unusual about wanting to shy away from it. Public speaking generally ranks close to the top of the list of experiences that people say they fear the most. The fact that you are nervous simply means that you regard the situation as being important, and that you want to do your best. If your concern makes you put more effort into your preparation, speech anxiety can actually work in your favor. I have heard some excellent speeches given by people who were highly stressed but well-prepared, and very poor ones given by those who were completely relaxed but had nothing to say. My conclusion is that anxiety itself need not be an inhibiting factor. However, if the fear disrupts your thought process while you are speaking, you need a plan to prevent that from happening. Taking a speech course will help, but there are also other things you can do.

DESIRE TO BE HEARD

Sometimes I hear a student in my class say, "Let me give my speech first so that I can get it over with." If you have ever had this feeling, it probably means that you are not motivated to give the speech because you want the message to be heard; you are viewing the experience only as something to be endured. If you really want to overcome speech fright, direct your attention to the importance of what it is that you are going to say.

Thorough Preparation

Almost all of the literature pertaining to stress reduction in oral communication emphasizes that making thorough preparations is the best way to deal with public speaking anxiety. But in the years I have been teaching speech I have found that it is often the least prepared students who have the most anxiety. It seems that anxiety often begins not at the moment speakers step onto the podium, but at the very beginning stage when they are planning what they are going to say. Think about that and see if it applies to you. You might be going through the motions of preparation when you really don't want to give the speech at all. Sometimes students will manage to begin the speech, but their volume is so low they can't be heard. What's happening is that subconsciously they don't really *want* to be heard. The reason for this may be that they lack confidence in the quality of the message and fear that it may not be adequate. Often, speech anxiety is used as an excuse by people who really mean that they are not prepared. There is a certain logic to that thinking: If you don't prepare a speech, you can't be expected to give one. That rationale is called *creative avoidance.* It may get you out of having to give speeches, but it doesn't help you cope with the problem, and it tends to reinforce the anxieties. A better procedure is to confront the fears and deal with them.

Techniques to Relieve Anxiety

Most of the evidence we have pertaining to techniques for overcoming speech anxiety is anecdotal. Some people have reported success by taking a walk just before speaking or doing breathing exercises. These methods can't hurt, and you should try anything that works. However, if you begin to feel anxiety even as you are preparing the speech, it is important that you take remedial measures early. Experts who teach public speaking in the business world list preparation, positive thinking, visualization, relaxation, and confidence in yourself as the key elements in reducing anxiety.[1] But the process begins with forming a positive attitude.

CREATING A NEW SELF-IMAGE

A great deal of your anxiety is related to the attitude you have toward public speaking. The word *attitude* simply means "the way you lean." If you have a positive attitude, you lean *toward* something; if you have a negative attitude, you lean *away* from it. Attitudes develop over a long period of time, and we never know when they start. Your attitude toward public speaking may have begun when you were very young and your parents had you stand up to recite a poem for company. Later on, you probably had to do "show and tell" in school, and your attitude was reinforced. If those were good experiences for you, the attitude you have toward public speaking may be positive; if they were bad experiences, you probably have a negative attitude. The point is that you did not *choose* the attitude intentionally; it just happened.

Attitudes are formed out of your experiences—not the way they really happened, but the way you *perceived* they happened. If someone laughed when you were doing "show and tell," you may have thought the laughter was directed at you, and you probably became embarrassed by it. The laughter may actually have been totally unrelated to anything you did, but if you thought at the time that the other students were laughing at you, that's the way the experience was recorded in your subconscious mind. What's more, every time you recall the experience, the memory of it is reinforced, until it becomes a permanent part of your mental data bank.

It's that kind of data that makes us feel the way we do. In later life, when we are confronted by new situations, such as an opportunity to give a speech, we automatically search the memory banks in our subconscious mind to recall occasions that might be similar. If the previous experiences were unpleasant ones, we might be inclined to say "No, thank you" and make up some

[1]Robert Edward Burns, "Combating Speech Anxiety," *Public Relations Journal,* March 1991, p. 28.

excuse for not doing it, without ever giving our conscious mind a chance to review the decision.

Self-Esteem

The attitudes we hold constitute a significant part of our self-concept—the image we have in our minds as to who we are and what is or is not appropriate behavior for us. Self-esteem is how we feel about that image.[2] A positive self-concept means we have high self-esteem. If we feel confident that we are able to deal with a wide variety of challenges that life hands to us, we will be willing to take risks and explore opportunities that lead us into new experiences. If our self-esteem is low, we might be reluctant to do anything that would jeopardize our security or expose us to criticism.

[2]Em Griffin, *A First Look at Communication Theory,* McGraw-Hill, New York, 1991, p. 70.

We all have an image in our minds of who we are, but how did that image get there?

Messages to Ourselves

Our self-concept is reinforced by the messages we give to ourselves in the form of thoughts or even words spoken out loud. Have you ever heard yourself saying, "Boy, am I dumb!" Listen sometime to what is being said by students when they come into the classroom on the day they are to give their speeches. You will hear a great deal of disparaging language that can result only in creating a negative self-concept. Some students will say, "I wish I didn't have to do this," or "I'm not ready," or "My topic is going to be really boring." This is called *self-talk,* and it has a profound effect on the way we think about ourselves. The negative self-talk affects our attitudes, and our attitudes in turn affect our self-talk. The result is a downward spiral of our self-esteem that often leads to poor performance. What we do is talk ourselves into falling below our true potential—not because of low ability, but because of the image we create of ourselves. The unfortunate thing is that it all happens without our even being aware of it.

But the spiral effect can work the other way, too. Positive messages can lead to successful performance, successful performance leads to high self-esteem, and high self-esteem means we give ourselves more positive messages. It all gets back to that self-concept, or self-image. How do we change the picture of ourselves from something we don't like and don't want, to an image that more accurately portrays what we can do and really want to do?

Changing Our Self-Perception

If you find that any part of your self-image is not serving you well, you can change it. We call the process *cognitive restructuring*—that means you can re-design the way you think about yourself so that your self-image becomes more like what you *want* it to be. This process serves as more than just a pill to calm your nerves; it is a "refined, systematic technique that alters the cognitive dimension of anxiety."[3] The idea is not a new one, nor does it always go by the same name. Maxwell Maltz calls it *psychocybernetics,* and he describes it in the following way:

> Whether we realize it or not, each of us carries about with us a mental blueprint or picture of ourselves. It may be vague and ill-defined to our conscious gaze. In fact, it may not be consciously recognizable at all. But it is there, complete down to the last detail. This self-image is our own conception of the "sort of person I am." It has been built up from our own beliefs about ourselves. But most of these beliefs have unconsciously been formed from our past experiences, our successes and failures, our humiliations, our triumphs, and the way other people have reacted to us, especially in early childhood. From all these we mentally construct a "self" (or a picture of a self). Once an idea or a belief about ourselves goes into this picture it becomes "true" as far as we personally are concerned. We do not question its validity, but proceed to act upon it just as if it were true.[4]

[3]William J. Fremouw and Michael D. Scott, "Cognitive Restructuring: An Alternative Method for the Treatment of Communication Apprehension," *Communication Education,* May 1979, p. 130.
[4]Maxwell Maltz, *Psycho-Cybernetics,* copyright © 1974 by Dr. Maxwell Maltz. Reprinted by permission of Pocket Books, a division of Simon & Schuster, Inc.

Self-Regulating Mechanism

You may have all the potential in the world to give excellent speeches, but if you have somehow acquired the notion that you stumble over words and forget what you want to say when you are in front of an audience, that's probably what will happen. You have a self-regulating device that will go to work to see that the image you have of yourself becomes reality.

Your self-regulating device is what Maxwell Maltz calls a *psychocybernetic mechanism*. A good example of such a device is a *thermostat*—a mechanism that will allow the temperature of the room to rise and fall within a limited margin. If the room gets too hot or too cold, the thermostat cuts in and makes an adjustment. You have a similar kind of mechanism in your mind that tends to confine your behavior to a range that your self-image has said is appropriate for you. If you begin to deviate too much from that central zone, you start to feel uncomfortable, and you adjust your behavior to bring yourself more in line with your picture. The interesting thing about the mechanism is that it will regulate your behavior whether you're doing better or worse than you think you should be. You may have observed this phenomenon if you play sports—let's say, tennis. Maybe you are playing someone who always beats you, but in this set you are ahead 5 to 4; you are serving, and the score is 30 to 15. Suddenly you start thinking, "I'm playing a better game than I have ever played before!" What happens? Your psychocybernetic mechanism goes to work and tells you to get back where you belong. So, you start blowing shots, you lose the next three games, and your opponent beats you 7 to 5.

Why does this not happen to champions? Because they have adjusted their psychocybernetic mechanisms to the high end of the scale, where they have to win in order to feel comfortable. That seems to be a good way to become a winner, and it is. However, be sure to heed a word of warning: When you do that, you place yourself under a great deal of stress, and the discomfort of losing can be quite severe.

Comfort Zones

What our self-image does is to establish for us behavior patterns that make us feel comfortable. If we find ourselves forced to do something that is in conflict with our self-image, we become stressed and start resisting in any way we can. Attending a lecture may be well within your comfort zone, but *giving* a lecture perhaps is not. People who have rich and fulfilling lives are those who have a broad comfort zone—one that permits them to feel okay about themselves in a variety of situations. If you perceive that your comfort zone is too narrow and restrictive, can you change it? Yes, you can, by cognitive restructuring.

Sometimes people try to make changes in their behavior patterns by writing resolutions for themselves; often this is a ritual that takes place on New Year's Day. But generally people who sit down on January First and list all the things they intend to do in the coming year wind up forgetting what they wrote even before the ink is dry. Often they include on their list what they believe they *ought* to do rather than what they really *want* to do. What's more, change in their behavior fails to come about because the *picture* they have of themselves is still the same as it was before. When you try to do something that is in conflict with your self-image, you make yourself uncomfortable. So, in order to bring about change in your *behavior*, you have to change your *picture*. The question is, Which one should you change first? If you have a strong resolve you might try changing the behavior first—that is, just grit your teeth and do it, regardless of how uncomfortable it makes you feel. Eventually, if you have successful experiences, your self-image might also change. But if the stress level is very high and you get no satisfaction from your efforts, you will ultimately abandon that behavior. That's why we may need to make a different approach.

Making Adjustments

The key to all of this is your internal self-adjusting mechanism—you need to know how to set it to a challenging, but realistic, point. If you decide you want to embark upon this program, what you will be doing is restructuring the way you picture your communication behavior and your attitude toward being a public speaker. But this time, instead of letting it all happen at random, you will be selecting intentionally the skill level that you want. To begin the process, you must decide that you really have the desire to be a person who is able and willing to speak to groups. The choice must be made freely—without pressure from your parents, teachers, or anyone else. This process is not going to work if you are merely trying to comply with goals that someone else has set for you. If you can honestly say that you want to make some changes, you are ready for the next phase of the process. Start by taking out a notebook and making the following entries:

1. *Goals.* First, decide specifically what you want to be able to do. You don't have to set a goal of having the ability to address large audiences on high-minded topics. You may want to begin by saying you would like to be able to talk to small groups of fifteen or twenty people on subjects pertaining to your business or hobby. Or, you may simply want to be able to speak up during class discussion. Whatever your goal is, get a picture of it in your mind as you write it down.
2. *Limitations.* Identify any real limitations that you will have to deal with in order to attain your goal. For example, if you are a recent immigrant from another country, you may be struggling with English as a second language, or you may have a speech impediment or a learning disability. These are real obstacles that will not go away just by reconstructing your self-image. You may have to enter into a specialized program to bring about the change you want. What your self-regulating mechanism can do, however, is to make it possible for you to confront those obstacles and not allow them to defeat you.

3. *Assets.* Your next entry will be a list of characteristics and abilities you have that will assist you in achieving your goals. You may say, for example, that you really enjoy relating to people, that you listen well and remember what you hear, that you read a lot and have a good vocabulary, that you are interested in a variety of topics, or that you have some expertise in a particular subject. Put down on your list anything you think will contribute to your ability to give a good speech.

4. *Previous experiences.* Even if you have never made a speech before, there are occasions in the past when you have communicated effectively to someone. Think back and recall times when you have been able to say something just the way you wanted to say it. It may have been in conversation with a small group of friends or in a class discussion; perhaps it was at a meeting or on a radio talk show. Try to remember what the subject was and what point you were making. Re-create the episode in your mind, and as you write it down, reinforce the good feeling you had about speaking on that occasion.

5. *Topics for speeches.* Make a list of topics that you would be able to address after you have had some time for preparation. You could list things you know about already, or you could include subjects you would be interested in researching. What this list will do is help you relieve the anxiety of feeling that you don't have anything to talk about. It will also help you to focus on the subject matter of the speech rather than on your nervousness in delivering it.

6. *Affirmations.* Select three or four items from your list of assets and previous experiences, and write them on a separate piece of paper in the form of *affirmations.* An affirmation is a positive and realistic statement you can honestly make about yourself that will reinforce the best characteristics that you have at the present time. The statement should be phrased in such a way as to replace your negative self-talk with assertions that are designed to improve your self-concept and raise your self-esteem. They need to be fairly specific so that you can get a clear picutre of what you do or have done that substantiates the positive messages you are giving to yourself. For example, a list of affirmations might look like this:

   - I am well-acquainted with environmental problems and have an appreciation for wilderness areas. I have given thought to conservation measures, and I can elaborate on my opinions with sound and concrete evidence.
   - I have good conviction in my voice, and people take me seriously when I speak. In social conversations my ideas are heard and respected.
   - The nervousness I sometimes feel when I am speaking to groups does not inhibit my ability to say what I want to say.

These are *suggested* affirmations. The ones you write for yourself must be your own. Be sure you don't exaggerate or make false claims. You have to believe with all sincerity that what you are saying is realistic and that you want these qualities to be the prominent features of your personality. It is important that

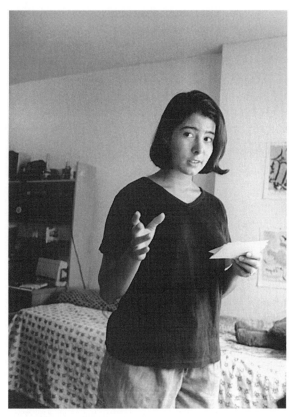

An affirmation is a positive statement you can make about yourself.

you phrase them in the *first person, present tense* ("I am . . . not "I will be . . ."), because the idea is to reinforce the positive characteristics that you have now, not vague speculation of what you think you could be in the future. People who continually say to themselves, "Someday I will become . . . ," usually put off indefinitely making any constructive changes.

IMPRINTING THE NEW IMAGE

Once you have written your list of affirmations in this form, carry the paper around with you and read the statements to yourself several times a day for about two weeks. Soon you will find that when you change your self-talk, the image you have of yourself will also begin to change. And as your image changes, so will your feelings and your behavior.

Richard Weaver, professor of speech communication at Bowling Green State University, defines *imaging* as the process of creating mental pictures that substitute for the real thing.[5] In a speech delivered to the Golden Key National Honor Society at Ann Arbor, Michigan, he described how he got through college by creating in his mind an image of himself as a university student. You must understand, however, that it is not the image alone that does the trick. What makes this method work is your accepting responsibility for behaving in a way that is commensurate with the image you have created. Just picturing yourself as a student is not enough. You must be able to see yourself doing what a student does—going to class, spending time in the library, staying up late at night studying for an exam. If those pictures do not appeal to you, a little voice inside your head is going to say, "Whom do you think you're kidding?"

Convincing Yourself

If you can really convince yourself that you are a person who fits the image of a public speaker, there are a number of ways to imprint your new self-concept. Take some time when you are alone to relax in a comfortable chair and create an image in your mind of yourself going through the process of preparing and delivering a speech. Picture yourself writing the outline and thinking about what you are going to say. Then get a picture of yourself as you come into the room on the day you are going to give your speech. Get the feeling of waiting until you are introduced; then going to the front of the room, stepping up to the podium, and turning to face your audience. As you create all these mental images, keep thinking to yourself that you are well-prepared, you have sound ideas, and your supporting evidence is interesting as well as factual. Now picture yourself as you deliver the speech. Try to get a clear image of what you are doing and how the audience is responding. See yourself making good eye contact, gesturing, and maintaining a relaxed and composed posture. Imagine as much detail as you can—the way you are dressed, the pacing of your speech, the energy you are projecting, and the reaction of the audience. In other words, picture it just the way you want it to be.

The value of this exercise is that you desensitize yourself to the real experience. When the time comes to actually give the speech, you will already have been through it and will know what it is like.

Rewards of Speaking

To become an effective speaker, it is essential to develop and maintain a positive attitude toward what you are doing. If you simply endure the experience with reluctance and distaste, you will not have a good feeling before, during, or after the presentation. Consequently, the next time you do it, you will suffer the same anxiety, and it may be even worse. On the other hand, if you project to the listeners that you like being there and believe that your message is

---

[5]Richard L. Weaver II, "Self-Fulfillment Through Imaging," from the keynote address delivered at the induction ceremony, Golden Key National Honor Society, Ann Arbor, Mich., November 8, 1990, *Vital Speeches*, January 15, 1991, p. 217.

important, they will respond in a positive way and reinforce your good feelings. Some of the rewards of speaking come in the form of applause and affirming statements that people make to you afterward. But you will find that the approval that makes the most difference is that which you give to yourself. Preparing and delivering public statements provides you with the opportunity to clarify your thoughts and values—and having the confidence of knowing that what you believe is clear in your mind contributes significantly to the upward spiral of your self-esteem. The method of cognitive restructuring makes it possible for you to communicate effectively with the most important person of all—yourself.

EXERCISE

Make arrangements to have one of your speeches videotaped; then watch the playback with your instructor or with someone who is able to give you constructive feedback. First, write down on a sheet of paper all the things you liked about the speech—the qualities of delivery, content, and organizational structure that you want your other speeches to contain. Next, make a list of the characteristics you can change and you would like to improve upon. (Don't worry if your voice sounds strange to you; you are probably just not used to hearing it on a recording device.) Keep the two lists, and review them when you prepare your next speech. Mentally reinforce the qualities you like, and work on at least one item that you want to improve.

QUESTIONS FOR REVIEW

1. What is meant by the word *attitude?* How are attitudes formed, and how do they affect behavior?
2. How do you explain the fact that attitudes are generally not chosen intentionally?
3. What is meant by the term *self-concept?* How does self-talk affect self-concept?
4. What is meant by *self-esteem?* Why is a person with high self-esteem generally willing to take more risks?
5. What is meant by the *spiral effect?* What determines whether the self-esteem spiral goes up or down?
6. What is meant by the *process of cognitive restructuring?* How can it affect one's attitude toward public speaking?
7. What does Maxwell Maltz mean by the term *psychocybernetics?* What would be an example of a psychocybernetic mechanism?
8. How do psychocybernetic mechanisms affect a player's performance in sports? What do champions do to make themselves winners? What is the disadvantage of doing what they do?
9. How does a narrow "comfort zone" reduce the richness of a person's life?
10. Why is it that New Year's resolutions are generally not successful in changing behavior?
11. What's wrong with having someone else set goals for you?

12. What advantage is there in recognizing your limitations as well as your assets while you are in the process of goal setting?
13. How might your previous experiences in communication situations affect your self-concept?
14. What is meant by an *affirmation?* Why should affirmations be written in the first person, present tense?
15. What are some ways to imprint affirmations? What is the value of imagining yourself going through the process of preparing and delivering a speech?

DELIVERING THE MESSAGE

**AFTER READING THIS CHAPTER, YOU SHOULD
BE ABLE TO DO THE FOLLOWING:**

Practice using standard English when speaking to an audience for the sake of making your ideas clear and comprehensible; recognize that words have denotative and connotative meaning; use connecting phrases to tell how one thought is related to another; avoid offensive language.

Know how to make a short, impromptu speech by responding directly to a question, developing your answer, and moving toward your conclusion; know the advantages and disadvantages of a fully scripted speech and a memorized speech; know how to prepare for an extemporaneous speech.

Recognize the primary, auxiliary, and secondary dimensions of a message; be aware of what can and cannot be communicated nonverbally; enhance your articulation through volume, projection, pitch, vocal emphasis, and rate of delivery.

Draw attention to key points in your speech by using the right amount of repetition, pointer phrases, oratorical emphasis, and visual reinforcement.

Respond to questions from the audience.

Henry Higgins, a character created by George Bernard Shaw and who appears in the play *My Fair Lady*, admonishes the linguistic characteristics of the people in his own country when he says, "Why can't the English teach their children how to speak?" He is critical of another character, a young woman named Liza Doolittle, who he claims will never be anything more than a miserable street peddler as long as she continues to corrupt the language with her cockney accent. Higgins says to his friend, "If you spoke as she does, sir, instead of the way you do, you might be selling flowers, too."

Almost everyone has an accent of one kind or another. Yours may be one that identifies you as a person who comes from a particular section of the country, such as New England or the deep south, or it may be that English is your second language and you reveal your national origin when you speak. The accent itself does not need to be a problem as long as your diction is clear. But if you run words together, leave out syllables that need to be sounded, mispronounce words, and use careless grammar, your audience will be as critical of you as Henry Higgins was of Liza Doolittle.

THE USE OF LANGUAGE

I recommend to my students that they learn to speak standard English. Although this may not be necessary on every occasion, some audiences will expect you to use proper grammar and correct syntax, and you will lose credibility if you are unable to do so. E. D. Hirsch makes the following observation in his book, *Cultural Literacy:*

> Linguists have used the term "standard written English" to describe both our written and spoken language, because they want to remind us that standard spoken English is based on forms that have been fixed in dictionaries and grammars and are adhered to in books, magazines, and newspapers. Although standard written English has no intrinsic superiority to other languages and dialects, its stable written forms have now standardized the oral forms of the language spoken by educated Americans. The chief function of literacy is to make us masters of this standard instrument of knowledge and communication, thereby enabling us to give and receive complex information orally and in writing over time and space.[1]

You probably never think about the grammatical construction of your sentences when you speak. If you had good models in your early childhood years, you perhaps learned correct usage just by example. Later, when you went to school, you were taught how to diagram a sentence and how to identify the nouns, verbs, adverbs, and adjectives. You learned that a sentence must have a subject and a predicate and must express a complete thought, and that you use a semicolon or conjunction to connect two clauses and place a period at the end of a sentence. You were also taught that the verb in the

---

[1] E. D. Hirsch, Jr., *Cultural Literacy,* Houghton Mifflin, Boston, Mass., 1987, p. 3.

sentence must agree in person (I am . . . you are . . . he or she is . . .) and in number (he doesn't . . . they don't . . .) with its subject. You can probably recognize by sound that it is incorrect to say "I is . . ." or "he don't . . . ." You may also remember that it is redundant, and therefore ungrammatical, to use double negatives when you are speaking English. (This is not the case in all languages.) People who say, "We didn't do nothin' . . . " reveal that there are gaps in their education and should make an effort to learn the basic rules of grammar in order to communicate in a style that does not detract from their message and credibility.

Words and Their Meaning

Your primary vehicle for communication is verbal language. If you have ever played the game of charades, you know how difficult and frustrating it is to try to convey an idea without being able to use words. For everyday interaction with people, we rely very heavily on language for communication, but we often develop careless speech habits. We frequently take verbal shortcuts when we speak, assuming that the listener will be able to fill in the blanks. For example, we may say, "You know what I mean." The other person might nod in the affirmative but not really know what we mean at all. In public speaking, we need to break our careless speech habits because the people we are talking to don't know us well enough to guess accurately at what we mean. We need to use the right word or phrase to express what we want to say, and we must arrange our words in a sequence that people can follow.

Making Meaning Clear

Words have both *denotative* and *connotative* meaning. The denotative meaning is the one we find in the dictionary and forms the basis for our understanding. The word *forceful,* for example, is defined in the *American Heritage Dictionary* as, "effective; persuasive." But there is also a connotative meaning, which is a subjective interpretation that is attached to the word. I might say that a speaker was very *forceful* in his delivery, meaning that his arguments were convincing and he was confident in what he was saying. But to you the word *forceful* might connote arrogance and abrasiveness. If you had to rely on a one-word description, you might misconstrue my meaning. For that reason, I build on my message by using other words for clarification. Perhaps you have had conversations with people who do not elaborate on what they are saying, such as the following example:

"How was the movie?" you ask.

"It was good," your friend replies.

"What do you mean, 'good?' Was it funny? Was it exciting?"

"No, it was good."

The point is that words are not absolutes. By themselves, they have limited ability to convey precise meaning. Expanding your vocabulary will open up possibilities for expressing more thought in greater depth.

Connecting Phrases

In an earlier chapter we looked at phrases called *transitions* that are used to help the audience follow our progression of thought leading to our conclusion. A similar kind of rhetorical device is a *connecting phrase,* which points out the relationship of one thought to another. A connecting phrase is commonly used when you want to tell the audience how a specific instance relates to a generalization. Throughout this book I have frequently used the phrase *for example* in order to tell you that what follows is an illustration of the thought that I want to convey. Here are few other commonly used connecting phrases:

- What this means is . . .
- This shows that . . .
- As evidence for this we can see that . . .
- This indicates . . .
- As one suggestion . . .

Just as transitions help the audience to know that it's time to move on to the next point, the connecting phrase provides a link between the abstract statement and concrete example.

Offensive Language

Comedians who entertain at "roasts" for prominent actors, politicians, and sports figures generally try to avoid "stepping over the line." That expression has come to mean the use of offensive language and crude references that are more embarrassing than they are funny. Once in a while entertainers will violate this code for the sake of gaining headlines, but when they do so, they alienate themselves from audiences that have a regard for good taste.

Obscenity

In many social circles obscenity seems to be a common part of everyday conversation. Because it is so, we may have come to believe that it is equally acceptable in public address. We need to understand, however, that obscene words and references that are often merely tolerated in discussions with our friends sound coarse and degrading when spoken from the podium. For example, in the Senate confirmation hearings of Supreme Court Justice Clarence Thomas we heard a great deal of graphic language and vulgar references, and we learned how unacceptable and repugnant such talk was deemed—even when it was simply being quoted. Obscenity is not only crude, it is also generally sexist and racist, characteristics that make it even more offensive. People who rely heavily on the use of vulgarity identify themselves as being callous and insensitive, and consequently suffer a loss of credibility. Those who are offended by it may become distracted and may fail to comprehend any legitimate point that the speaker might be making. Certainly, there are some audiences who will find such remarks to be humorous and colorful, but seldom if ever does the use of obscenity in rhetorical dialogue contribute to the clarification of an issue.

Slang

What about the use of slang expressions? If they are used in moderation and are part of your own speaking style, they might keep a speech from sounding too "stuffy," but they do also tend to lower the intellectual tone of the speech. However, sometimes a slang expression has more impact than the standard English equivalent. For example, saying "I was blown away" has greater intensity than "I was very surprised." Given the right circumstances, the authentic use of slang can bring you closer to people who are comfortable with that kind of language and who appreciate your ability to speak it correctly. The danger is that a slang term used in the wrong way can make you sound rather foolish. The primary criterion is that the expressions you use must be understandable to the audience. Another drawback is that slang is often spoken as a means of excluding outsiders, and that's not what you want to do when you are on the podium. Yet another problem with slang is that it tends to oversimplify complex concepts. To say that a particular event was "awesome" does not tell a great deal about the specific characteristics of what is being described. People who rely heavily upon slang often neglect standard English terms that would be more precise and frequently wind up saying such things as, "you know" and "you really had to be there."

MODES OF DELIVERY

Sometimes we watch experienced orators at work on the podium as they express themselves with power and clarity, and we tend to think that it looks easy. It seem as though the words are simply flowing with complete spontaneity. When Daniel Webster made his famous "Reply to Hayne" on the floor of Congress in 1830, he was asked how he could have made such as eloquent speech on the spur of the moment. His answer was, "I've been preparing that speech all my life."

Fortunately, you do not have to spend your whole life in preparation, and no one expects you to give an eloquent presentation on the spur of the moment. You generally will have a reasonable amount of time to prepare for a speech, and you'll be able to practice before you deliver it.

Impromptu Speaking

On some occasions you may be asked to speak without preparation; this kind of speech is called *impromptu*. People who give the best impromptu speeches are those, like Daniel Webster, who have anticipated the opportunity to speak and have made their preparation in advance. An impromptu speech should be given only by a person who has some understanding of the issue under discussion; it is pointless to take up the time of an audience when you have

On some occasions you may have to speak without preparation.

nothing of significance to say. It may be better to decline politely than to make a valiant, but meaningless, effort. But if you do anticipate that you might be called on to speak, here are a few things to keep in mind:

Pay attention. Whenever you attend a meeting or gathering of any kind, stay alert and pay attention to what is being said. Think in terms of how you would respond if you were asked to comment on something the speaker had just said.

Give a direct response. Often, the impromptu speech will be a response to a question. Begin by answering the question as directly as you can; then qualify and develop your answer. Don't leave your listeners wondering what your position is, so that they have to ask the question a second time.

Keep it short. No one expects a full-length speech on the spur of the moment. If the chairperson had wanted you to give a major address, you would have been included on the program. Keep your remarks short and to the point, and don't deviate from the central idea.

Move toward a conclusion. The hardest thing about giving an impromptu speech is ending it. Remember that all speeches, whether they are prepared or not, must have conclusions. In order to make sure your speech doesn't just wither away and trail off into silence, plan your concluding statement as soon as you begin talking, and start phrasing it in your mind before you come to it.

Impromptu speaking is not easy. The people who do it well are the ones who do it often and have a large fund of ideas and information to draw upon. In this respect, good impromptu speeches are not really spontaneous. They reflect ideas that have been given considerable thought and have probably been expressed before in less structured communication settings.

The Fully Scripted Speech

Don't feel defeated if you are not comfortable in giving impromptu speeches. You might be the kind of person who has a lot to say but needs to spend time in preparation before expressing it. That's quite understandable, and there are alternatives for you. You can, of course, write the speech out word for word and then either read it or deliver it from memory. There are advantages and disadvantages to each of those two choices, as we shall see.

Speaking from a Manuscript

This kind of speech is difficult to prepare but easy to deliver. The advantage is that you can include as much detail as you want and not have to worry about forgetting something. You can polish each phrase with just the right words, and if you read well, you can make yourself appear to be an eloquent orator. Political speakers like to use this mode of delivery because it reduces the danger of their saying the wrong thing. The delivery, with practice, can be made smooth and articulate, and an advance copy can be made available to the press.

The manuscript speech does have disadvantages, however. It tends to diminish audience contact, because speakers have to direct their attention to the script rather than to the listeners. If a speaker does not read well, the speech can sound stilted, and it often becomes boring. Furthermore, there is a loss of credibility when the speech is read from manuscript. The audience may wonder whether the speech was actually written by the person reading it.

Memorizing

Committing a speech to memory can be a worthwhile method if you plan to give the same speech on a number of different occasions. You can make sure the language is precise, the content is detailed, and the organizational structure is flawless without losing audience contact, which happens when you read a speech from manuscript. The problem is that if the speech is a long one, you may have a hard time memorizing the whole thing. Even if you can do so, you often find yourself thinking in terms of the sequence of the words rather than the meaning of the ideas, and if you forget a word, you may lose your composure. Another problem with the memorized speech is that it often *sounds* memorized, and the audience may wonder if you are really giving thought to what you are saying.

Speaking Extemporaneously

The best alternative for making a prepared presentation is to deliver the speech *extemporaneously.* Make sure you understand what that term means and how it

Have an outline in front of you, but express the ideas in your own words.

differs from the impromptu speech or the fully scripted speech. An extemporaneous speech is one that is *prepared* but not written out word for word. As the speaker, you would work from an outline—getting the main ideas and specific information from the printed page, but choosing the actual words from your own vocabulary in order to express what you want to say. There is a very important difference between extemporizing from an outline and reading from a manuscript. A person can read a speech word for word and make it sound eloquent, yet have no idea of what the words mean. When you deliver a speech extemporaneously, it is necessary that you engage your brain as well as your voice. Having the outline in front of you to provide the structure makes it possible for you to utilize your time efficiently, while your expressing the ideas in your own words conveys sincerity and enhances your credibility. The audience is more likely to believe that the ideas are your own and that you have an understanding of what you are saying.

The extemporized speech is the kind most frequently emphasized in public speaking courses because it provides students with the best learning experience. Preparing for the speech helps you to develop skills of research and critical thinking, and knowing that you are prepared builds your confidence. The most important thing is that you *feel* prepared. A great many of the anxieties people have about public speaking can be significantly reduced by thorough preparation. If you are confident that you have gathered the information you need, have organized it in a way that makes sense to you, and have practiced out loud what you want to say, you will begin to feel much more comfortable.

Using Note Cards

A common source of anxiety about public speaking is the fear of forgetting what you are going to say. Don't feel that you have to rely on your memory—provide for yourself materials that will assist you in remembering what you want to include in the speech. Note cards are perhaps the most reliable memory aids. You can carry them with you and use them wherever you happen to be. They are inconspicuous and do not create a distraction, because listeners are generally accustomed to speakers' using notes. You can keep them in one hand and not have to put them down when you move around or gesture. If you are working without a lectern, you can hold them at a comfortable level (for example, eye level) without having to lower your head and break eye contact with the audience. Another advantage is that cards don't rattle the way a sheet of paper does if your hand happens to shake a bit. When you are preparing note cards, there are a few things you should remember:

1. Type or write legibly. The print should be dark enough so that you will be able to see the words clearly at a glance. Underline or highlight important words. It's also a good idea to put quotation marks around direct quotes and to include the source of the quotation.
2. Write on only one side of the card. If you have to turn the card over, you may forget whether or not you have already covered the material on the other side. End each card with a completed thought; don't carry a sentence or a phrase over to another card. You may also find it advisable to number each card.
3. Include only necessary words and phrases. If you write the whole speech on the note cards, you will be tempted to read rather than extemporize. Don't make your notes so detailed that the speech becomes one that is read from manuscript.

Practicing the Delivery

The hours you spend gathering material and organizing it into a workable pattern will pay off when the time comes for you to deliver the speech. Confidence results from knowing that you have done your "homework." The delivery of the speech is the part of public address that you will probably find the most gratifying, because you will have a sense of really having accomplished something. When you write an article for a magazine or newspaper, you seldom know whether or not anyone reads it. But when you give a speech, you can see the response of the people who are hearing your ideas.

An important part of the preparation for a speech is practicing the delivery. This does not mean that you have to memorize every word and every gesture. What it does mean is that you should try out the speech on someone else before you deliver it to the audience. Hearing the sound of your voice expressing your ideas will help you become familiar with them.

Try to anticipate as much as you can about the situation before you step into it. If it's possible to do so, visit the room where you will be speaking. Note the size and decor of the room, the seating arrangement, the ventilation, and anything that might create a distraction. Walk up to the front of the room and see what the perspective is from the place where you will give the speech.

When all your preparation is completed, the time will come when you will see what the audience looks like from the speaker's platform. It's then that you have a chance to apply all that you have learned and see if the theory really works for you. If it does, remember what it is that you did. If what you do falls short of your expectations, don't be disheartened; learn from the experience, and do better next time.

THE DIMENSIONS OF THE MESSAGE

You can improve your chances for success if you try to anticipate how the audience is going to receive you. From the moment you step up to the podium, your listeners will be forming in their minds an impression of the kind of person you are, how well they like you, and whether or not they are inclined to believe and accept what you have to say. The impression they receive is important, because it will affect the way they react to what they see and hear. One way to analyze an audience's perception of a speaker is to look at the three dimensions that every speech contains: (1) the primary message, (2) the auxiliary message, and (3) the secondary message.

Primary Message

The term *primary message* refers to the verbal content of the speech—the words that the speaker uses to express the ideas, the information, and the opinions that form the substance of the message. This is the meaning the audience would get if the channel of communication were the printed page rather than the spoken word.

Auxiliary Messages

By *auxiliary messages* we mean the dimensions to communication that can be added when the message is delivered orally. We refer here to what the speaker can do deliberately to enhance the reception of the primary message. Auxiliary messages include tone of voice, vocal inflection, posture, gesture, rate of delivery, eye contact, style of dress, and other delivery techniques that the speaker can employ to reinforce what he or she is saying.

Secondary Messages

Messages that are projected to the audience but are not part of the speaker's plan are called *secondary messages*. They are impressions created by characteristics over which the speaker has no control, such as age, sex, race, nationality, or physical appearance. They could also come about as a result of unconscious behavior patterns. Secondary messages can work to the advantage or to the disadvantage of the speaker. If they are mannerisms that indicate nervousness, uncertainty, or insincerity, they can be quite detrimental. For example, the speaker might have a distracting twitch or may be toying with a pencil. These are secondary messages that would interfere with the audience's receiving the message that the speaker wants heard. On the other hand, secondary messages can have a positive effect. The speaker may have attractive facial features, natural poise, or an empathic expression. Qualities such as these would contribute to the audience's willingness to accept and believe what the speaker is saying.

Nonverbal Communication

The visual impressions that we call *nonverbal communication* could be in the form of auxiliary or secondary messages. Whether such communication is intentional or unintentional, it has a lot to do with the establishment of the speaker's credibility. Consider your own perceptions: What is it that you, as a member of the audience, like to see when you are listening to a speaker? Generally, people say they like to observe a posture that conveys a feeling of confidence, gestures that seem natural and at ease, direct eye contact, and friendly facial expressions. Although these characteristics are by no means proof of sincerity, audiences do tend to make judgments based on them. We no longer teach students to rehearse gestures in front of a mirror, as teachers of elocution used to do in previous generations. Today, we believe that what you do on the podium should develop naturally out of your own style and personality. There are, however, some conventional behavior patterns that might be appropriate for you to consider.

Posture

The basic posture for the speaker is to stand. When you stand, you are in a better position to gain and hold the attention of the audience—which is, of course, what you want to do. Keep your weight on both feet. Don't slouch, and don't lean heavily on the desk or lectern. Avoid shifting your weight from one foot to another or pacing back and forth across the room. Try not to look as if you are tired; your audience wants to see you awake, alert, and displaying a reasonable amount of vitality.

You probably will want to establish yourself behind a lectern, if there is one. But remember that this piece of equipment is designed to rest your notes or manuscript upon—not your body. Don't grip the sides of the lectern too tightly. A speaker with white knuckles tends to lose the confidence of the audience.

Gesture

If you are motivated to gesture, do so. Allow your hands and arms to help you communicate your ideas. It is probably better to stick with conventional speech gestures rather than to try to transmit elaborate descriptions in the air with your hands. There are several simple gestures that are easy to use and will look natural to the audience: Holding up fingers to indicate a number of items, drawing the hands toward the body in a welcoming motion, turning the palm out toward the audience to suggest *enough,* using a rolling motion with the hands to indicate an idea in process, and pointing to a chart or visual aid. All of these are referred to as *motivated* gestures. They are not to be inserted artificially or at random; rather, they should contribute naturally to the emphasis of the thought.

Movement

Feel free to move around if there is a reason to do so. You may want to walk to the chalkboard or to a flip chart. You might wish to change your position in order to have better visual contact with your audience. Another reason to move is to communicate intensity in the thought you want to convey. Closing the distance between you and the audience is a nonverbal way of saying that the next point is very important.

Eye Contact

Maintaining eye contact with members of the audience is the speaker's way of saying, "I am aware of your presence, and I want to establish communication with you." Looking at faces is important for the sake of establishing rapport with the audience. Don't look over the top of the listeners' heads or stare at your notes; let people know that you are interested in the feedback they give you, as you deliver the speech. Eye contact is one of the factors people use to determine the sincerity of a speaker. You are less likely to be trusted if the audience members believe you are not willing to look them in the eye. Your eye contact is also perceived by the audience to be an indicator of your confidence level. Looking at people's faces tells them that you are sure of what you are saying.

Vocal Communication

Although a great deal of communication occurs at the nonverbal level in public speaking, the voice is the primary instrument for conveying messages. How well you are understood depends on your ability to verbalize what you want to say. You will find that using your voice for public speaking is somewhat different from using it in ordinary conversation, particularly in terms of volume.

Volume

Beginning speakers sometimes have difficulty in determining the volume level that is required when they are speaking to a large group. Probably you are used to talking to two or three people at a time; if you use that same volume level for twenty or thirty people, you will probably not be heard. If speaking up is hard for you, you will need to practice. Before you make the speech, have a friend stand 30 or 40 feet away from you. Deliver the speech to your friend, increasing the volume until he or she is able to hear you easily. Make note of the way your voice sounds at that volume level. When the time comes for you to give the speech, you will know how loud you have to talk. Adequate volume is one of the most fundamental requirements in public speaking. Unless people can hear what you say, your message will not be communicated.

Projection

Volume is not the only factor responsible for audibility. The extent to which you *project* your voice will also determine whether or not you can be heard. Projecting the voice means aiming the words directly at the people who are the targets of your message. The best way of doing this is to *extend* the sound of your voice to reach the people farthest away. That works much better than talking loud to the people in the front row.

Pitch

The word *pitch* refers to a speaker's tone of voice. What you want to achieve is a *modulated* pitch—one in which the vocal tones rise and fall, giving emphasis to your meaning. If you are not modulating your voice, you are said to be talking in a *monotone*. Although this problem can be difficult to overcome, you want to work on it—a monotone can make a speech sound dull and tedious. Practice by speaking into a tape recorder; then play back the tape and hear how your voice sounds. If you perceive that you are speaking in a monotone, go back over the written material of your speech and *underline* key words and phrases. Now, record the speech again, placing vocal emphasis on the items you underlined.

A related voice problem is that of a *patterned pitch.* This means that your voice is modulated, but the highs and lows are coming at regular intervals without regard for the points you want to emphasize. This problem is most likely to occur when you are *reading* from a book or manuscript. An audience can generally tell when you have stopped extemporizing the speech and have begun reading—the rise-and-fall patterned pitch is a dead giveaway. If you have to read portions of your speech, try to maintain the same modulated vocal inflection that you use when you extemporize.

Vocal Emphasis

Vocal emphasis is important, not just for the sake of making what you say sound interesting, but also for the sake of making your meaning clear. It is possible to modify the way your audience perceives your meaning without changing any of your words. For example, the following sentence could convey several different meanings, depending on the words that are emphasized:

I didn't say he stole my book.

Try saying this sentence seven times, emphasizing a different word each time. You will find that there are seven different meanings:

1. *Someone else* said he stole my book.
2. I *deny* that I said he stole my book.
3. I might have implied it, but I didn't *say* he stole it.
4. Someone stole it, but it wasn't *he.*

5. He might have borrowed it, but he didn't *steal* it.
6. He stole someone else's book, not *mine.*
7. He stole something else, not my *book.*

From this illustration, we can see that it is not the word that conveys the meaning but the way the speaker uses the word. Words are tools that a speaker uses to communicate, just as a hammer is a tool that a carpenter uses to drive nails. The hammer does not drive the nail; it's the way the hammer is used that drives the nail.

Rate of Delivery

How fast should you talk? That's a question that is hard to answer. A lot depends on your own personal style. The best thing to do is to speak at a rate that is comfortable for you; however, a brisk pace works better than a slow one. By *brisk* we mean a rate that is rapid enough to hold the attention of the audience but not so fast that your words are running together. If you can speak rapidly and still enunciate clearly, do it. But don't sacrifice clarity for speed.

Here is some quantitative evidence you might consider: The average conversational speaking rate is about 150 words per minute; a disk jockey on a rock station will probably clip along at about 170 words per minute; a fast-talking announcer doing a commercial for a used-car company may hit 200 or 210 words per minute. Even if you could talk that fast, you probably would not want to. At that rate, words begin to become indistinguishable, and listeners are unable to comprehend what is being said. Speaking too fast also results in loss of both vocal inflection and emphasis on key words and phrases. Therefore, deliver your speech at a rate that allows you to modulate your voice, and pause for the sake of emphasis.

EMPHASIZING KEY POINTS

Speakers sometimes seem to have the idea that everything they say will be remembered. Classroom lecturers would certainly like to think that is so, but the results of final examinations do not always confirm that notion. Gaps in listening are also evident in the business world. A study conducted for the Unisys Corporation revealed that adults listen at only a 25 percent efficiency level.[2] There are, of course, a number of variables: The importance of the information to the listeners, the extent to which they will be held responsible for the information, whether or not they are taking notes, the time of day, the temperature of the room, the attentiveness of other people in the audience, and so on. But as a speaker, you must be realistic about how much people are able to assimilate.

If your listeners are only going to retain a small percentage of what you say, you have to ask yourself two questions: (1) "What are the important points of

---

[2]Roy Berko, Andrew Wolvin, and Darlyn Wolvin, *Communication: A Social and Career Focus,* 6th ed., Houghton Mifflin, Boston, Mass., 1995, p. 81.

my message?" and (2) "How can I emphasize those points so that they will be remembered?"

Repetition

Repeating key words and important points appears to be the most effective mode of emphasis. Instructors know that this is absolutely necessary when they have reason to believe that the word or the information is being heard by students for the first time. For example, as we noted in Chapter 9, an expression that is used in the theory of argumentation and persuasion is *cognitive dissonance.* This is a term that appears frequently in professional journals, but it probably does not come up very often in everyday conversation. The two component words are not really difficult to understand; *cognitive* means "knowing" and *dissonance* means "out of harmony." So, *cognitive dissonance* refers to the condition that may develop when you learn something that seriously conflicts with what you had believed to be true. As a teacher, I would not expect students to be able to remember that term unless I first explained what it meant, and then used it several times in my lecture. Let's look at another example and see how we might use repetition in emphasizing a key piece of information:

> The population of the world will double in the next thirty years. There will be twice as many people on our planet in the year 2028.

This form is called *concentrated repetition.* The information is reinforced immediately after it is said the first time. In this case, different words were used when the data was expressed the second time, but that's not always necessary; the information could be repeated in exactly the same words. Repeating a phrase in the same words is a rhetorical device that skilled orators use to create a strong impact. Recall the words of Winston Churchill:

> We shall defend our island, whatever the cost may be. We shall fight on the beaches. We shall fight on the landing grounds. We shall fight in the fields and in the streets; we shall fight in the hills. We shall never surrender.

Pointer Phrases

Try to make it as easy as you can for your listeners to recognize what you want them to remember. One way to do this is simply to say to them, "Now here is an important fact . . . ." We call this a *pointer phrase;* it's a device instructors often use to call attention to something that they want students to remember. In class sometime you might have heard your instructor say, "Now this information is going to be included on the final examination." That's a pointer phrase, and it's designed to get your attention. Let's go back to the previous example regarding population. If you wanted to use a pointer phrase, you could preface your information in this way:

> One point stands out, and this is something that will affect us all within our own lifetime. Unless we can change the present trend, the population of the world will double in the next thirty years.

Always be sure, however, that the statement you are pointing to is truly significant and that it is stated in a way that is easily remembered.

Oratorical Emphasis

The methods we have discussed so far apply to written statements as well as to spoken ones. However, there are some modes of emphasis that are available only to speakers. They include such things as dramatic pauses, vocal inflection, changes in volume, and the use of gestures. As a speaker, you have access not only to verbal communication, but to all the methods of nonverbal communication.

Visual Reinforcement

Human beings probably first learned to talk by using visual aids. When you are shown an object and hear a sound, you establish a connection between the word and the thing. Once that connection is made, it's no longer necessary to show the object. Children learn to talk in the same way. As their vocabularies grow, children are able to communicate more of what they mean through language. But visual reinforcement is still a powerful teaching tool at any age. If you want something to stick in your listeners' minds, give them a picture as well as a verbal description. Modern learning theories tell us that people store events in two ways—through visual images and through verbal codes.[3] The more vivid you can make the visual image, the more likely it is that the idea will be remembered. Not every point you want to make can be projected pictorially, but when you have access to visuals that illustrate your words, use them. Here again, the principle you want to remember is that your chances for success in public speaking have a lot to do with your ability to make it as easy as you can for the audience members to comprehend the message and then retain it after they have heard it.

RESPONDING TO QUESTIONS

Most of the time, your communication with the audience does not end with the conclusion of your speech; it's very likely that there will be a question period afterward. This is a time you should welcome as a speaker, because when the audience members ask questions, you can learn what they were thinking while you were talking. The interaction that takes place at this time provides an opportunity for you to clarify any misunderstandings and to elaborate on points of interest. If the topic is controversial, you will get some insight into the objections people have to your thesis or to your arguments. Be sure to communicate to your listeners that you are interested in their reactions and welcome their comments. Regard their questions as evidence that they were involved in what you were saying and want to extend the dialogue. For the most part, the

[3]Albert Bandura, *Social Learning Theory,* Prentice-Hall, Englewood Cliffs, N.J., 1977, p. 59.

responses you make to questions will have to be spontaneous, but there are some things you can do to prepare:

Know Your Subject

It is at this time that your audience will not only have a chance to clarify any points of confusion but will also be able to find out if you really know what you are talking about. You should be able to add new information and use different examples in your replies, so that you aren't simply restating what you have already said.

Anticipate Questions

If you are well-prepared, there should be few questions that take you by surprise. If your subject matter is controversial, try to think of what objections there might be to the claims you are making. Don't let the audience believe you have been caught off guard by a challenging question. Make the listeners think that you welcome the opportunity to clarify your point.

Direct Your Answers to the Whole Audience

First of all, make sure everyone has heard the question; if you have any doubt about this, repeat the question so that the whole audience can hear it, and have the questioner confirm your paraphrase. By doing this, you make sure you understand what the questioner is asking, and you also buy a little time that you can use for thinking about how you are going to respond. When you give your answer, make sure that everyone knows you are addressing the whole audience. Remember, your response to the questions is part of the speech.

Be Succinct

Don't make the mistake of launching into another speech in response to the first question; that has the effect of discouraging others from participating. Answer the question directly, but make it brief. If the question calls for a more detailed answer, or if it is off the topic of the speech, invite the person to speak to you at the end of the presentation so that you can discuss the issue further.

Encourage Involvement

The question period should move rapidly and involve as many people as time allows. There will always be those who will try to make speeches of their own from the floor or who will ask you one question after another. Don't let that happen. If a question starts getting too lengthy or has too many parts to it, you may have to interrupt. Do it politely, give the best answer you can, and then move on to someone else. If you get caught in a dialogue with one person, you will lose the attention of the rest.

Maintain Control

The question period is part of your presentation; it is not a group discussion. You should try to get lots of people involved, but be sure they don't take the floor away from you and start addressing questions to each other. This can easily happen if you allow long questions or fail to reply to each one. Sometimes a person will make a comment that is not in the form of a question. Treat it as a question and make some sort of response to acknowledge that you have heard.

Know When to Stop

Because the question period is an important part of your speech, be sure you allow enough time for it. The length of a question period depends entirely on the circumstances. Often, there are time limitations—other speakers may be scheduled, or your listeners may be on their lunch hour. If your time is not restricted, you will have to judge for yourself how long to allow questions to continue. Probably there will be a moderator who will let the audience know that the time is up. When that happens, have a final comment in mind that you can use to bring closure to the presentation.

After you have made your first speech, you are in a position to assess your progress. This is a good time to stop and reflect on what you have learned so far from the text, from the lecture material you have had in class, and from your actual experience of speaking. Review the criteria that were suggested in the first chapter and see how well you think you have observed them. You may have received some feedback on your speech from the other students in the class, and you probably also got a grade from your instructor. All of that is very helpful, but the important thing is for you to be satisfied with your own progress. Don't let a speaking opportunity go by without learning something from the experience.

EXERCISE

Public speaking is a lot less difficult when you know what information your audience is interested in hearing. A good way to practice is to provide your listeners with a set of questions that you know you can answer. As a preparatory exercise, write three or four questions on small slips of paper and give them to several members of the class. Have those people sit in the back of the room while you stand at the front. The questions should be open-ended so that you have an opportunity to elaborate rather than giving just a simple yes or no answer. Number the questions so that they are asked in a logical sequence. This exercise will give you practice in phrasing questions, organizing material, speaking extemporaneously, and talking loud enough to be heard. In responding to a question, give a complete answer, but don't ramble. When you have finished your thought, drop your voice so that another person can ask the next question. Here are examples of questions you might want people to ask on the subject of family counseling:

1. What are the requirements in this state for becoming a marriage and family counselor?
2. How does a person receive the kind of experience needed to obtain a counseling certificate?
3. What career opportunities are there for a person who has the certificate?
4. What are some of the problems people have when they come to a marriage and family counselor?
5. How successful can a counselor expect to be in helping families to deal with their problems?

You might notice that the questions above appear to be similar to what you might find as the main headings in the outline of a speech. You are right; they are. The only difference is that they are phrased in the form of questions. When you prepare your next outline, you might consider using this technique. There is nothing wrong with writing your main headings as questions.

QUESTIONS FOR REVIEW

1. What do we mean by *standard English?* Why is it recommended for most public speaking situations? What are the disadvantages of using slang expressions?
2. What effect might the use of obscenity have on an audience?
3. Who made the "Reply to Hayne" on the floor of Congress in 1830?
4. What do we mean by *impromptu speaking?* What are some ways you can "prepare" for an impromptu speech?
5. What are the advantages and disadvantages of memorizing a speech or reading it from manuscript?
6. How does an extemporaneous speech differ from an impromptu speech? Why is the extemporaneous speech generally the mode of delivery that is emphasized in most public speaking classes?
7. Explain the meaning of *primary, auxiliary,* and *secondary* messages.
8. What do we mean by *motivated gestures?*
9. Why is it important for a speaker to maintain eye contact with the audience?
10. Besides making the speech more interesting to listen to, what else is accomplished by vocal inflection?
11. How fast does the average person speak? About how fast can a really rapid talker speak?
12. What do we mean by *connecting phrases?* How do they differ from transitional phrases?
13. What are four ways to put emphasis on a word or a phrase?
14. How does concentrated repetition differ from distributed repetition?
15. What is meant by a *pointer phrase?*
16. What kinds of devices fall under the heading of *oratorical emphasis?*
17. How can you prepare for the question period of a speech?

SPEAKING WITH VISUALS

AFTER READING THIS CHAPTER, YOU SHOULD BE ABLE TO DO THE FOLLOWING:

Know that a specific audience that may have more background in a given field than a general audience will expect speakers to develop their subject matter in greater depth; be prepared to use physical objects or two-dimensional illustrations for visual aids; know how to generate graphics by using a computer; recognize what visual aids are able to accomplish.

Be familiar with the use of a computer to display graphics; be able to use visual aid equipment to project slides and transparencies; be able to use a chalkboard and flip chart while you are making a presentation.

Know how to speak into a public-address microphone; know how to conduct yourself when you are giving a talk on radio or television.

Confucius was probably right when he said that a picture is worth a thousand words. Advertisers who invest heavily in pictorial displays on television, billboards, magazines, and Web pages believe that it's true, and people involved in making business presentations would do well to follow their example. The fact is that there are many things that cannot be communicated in words. How could a fashion designer describe to an audience of buyers the latest Paris styles, without using pictures or models? How could an architect convey to a group of contractors what a building was supposed to look like, without showing them drawings and blueprints? Words alone are just not adequate for important presentations that require the audience members to reproduce in their own minds the same picture that you have in yours.

HIGH-STAKES PRESENTATIONS

With so much emphasis being placed on giving speeches in the classroom, you might begin to think that the purpose of learning the skills of public address is entirely academic. The fact is that your most important speeches probably will be given after you leave college. You might find yourself in the position of having to make a presentation to an influential group such as a city council. Possibly your opportunity to speak will come on the job, when a proposal needs to be made to a senior management–level committee. The stakes after college are likely to be much higher than they are now, and the success of your presentation may have a significant effect on your career.

Everything that has been said so far in this text applies to real-life situations as well as those that occur in the classroom. There is, however, a difference that should be taken into consideration in regard to the way you will be evaluated. In the classroom, your instructor is going to give you a grade based on how well you fulfill the assignment, prepare the outline, develop the topic, and deliver the speech. In a real-life situation, the people in the audience are the ones who will be making the evaluation, and they are going to base their assessments on how useful the information is to them and how clear you are able to make it. Let's look at effective ways to proceed when it's really important that your listeners get the full impact of your message.

Speaking to a Specific Audience

We have already discussed the importance of learning as much as we can about a *general* audience, but when you prepare a speech for a *specific* audience, it is necessary for you to sharpen the focus of the topic even more. In a classroom, you have a general audience composed of people with many different interests and levels of comprehension. The material you present to them cannot be highly technical, because they would not have the background to understand it. But an audience of people that have assembled because of a specific interest will expect you to go beyond their common knowledge and present material in greater depth and detail. If the speech is to be useful to them, they must be able to connect what you tell them to what they already know, and they must be able to *remember* what they hear. It may be that the purpose of your presentation is to get the audience to approve your recommendation, to buy what you are selling, or to take action based on your information. That's a real challenge, particularly when you may be limited to only twenty or thirty minutes. What we're talking about here is a speech that looks and sounds like a professional presentation.

The purpose of a speech to a general audience—one that would be appropriate for the classroom—might be to describe how a network of computers can perform a variety of tasks in a business office. But if you were speaking to a group of people who already use computers in their places of business, you would have to go into more depth and detail. For example, you might make a presentation on a particular program application that is designed for a specific accounting function, or recommend a way to provide security for confidential information that is stored in a computer. Before you make this kind of speech, there are several matters you have to consider:

- Does the audience have the technical background to understand the new information that you plan to present?
- Is it enough for the audience members to merely understand the information, or must they be able to retain it and apply it?
- Do you have all of the facilities you need in order to make it possible for the audience to visualize the object of your explanation? And will the listeners be able to keep the picture in their minds?
- Will your explanation be a sufficient teaching tool for the audience members, or will they need to have "hands-on experience?"
- Are materials available for the audience to review after the presentation is over?
- Is it necessary for you to know whether or not the audience members have retained what you have told them?

The Tools of the Trade

There are times when you may have to be more than just a speaker; you might need to be a teacher. Under those circumstances, you must anticipate what your listeners require in order for them to be able to learn. Holding an audience's attention is one thing, but now we are adding a new and much more difficult dimension to public speaking—getting people to fully comprehend and *integrate* what they have heard. To do this, it is necessary that you learn to use all the "tools of the trade." Language will still be your principal means of communication, but often you will find that it is not enough.

Physical Objects

Of all the visual aids you can use, the physical object itself is perhaps the best. To teach a person to swim requires that you have a body of water; to help someone play the guitar, you must let him or her hold the instrument; to provide instruction on how to use a piece of software, you will need to demonstrate on a computer. In all of these cases, verbal description alone is not sufficient, and there is no point in going through the motions of teaching unless the listener is able to learn. There may be occasions when it is not possible to produce the physical object itself, and the speaker may have to rely on a model. This is a technique that might be used by an engineer who is describing a plan for a new suspension bridge or a dentist who is explaining how to do a root canal. The model helps the listener to *visualize* what the speaker is saying, and we know that visualization is an important key to learning.

Two-Dimensional Pictures

If you can't get the object itself and are not able to obtain a model of it, you can use two-dimensional visuals in the form of photographs, drawings, sketches, paintings, cartoons, exploded or cutaway diagrams, bar charts (Figure 12-1), line graphs (Figure 12-2), pie charts (Figure 12-3), blueprints, maps, key words (Figure 12-4), or any combination of these. Illustrations in color are best, but black and white will do. They can be displayed by means of computer projection, overhead transparencies, slide projection, opaque projection, movie projection, or video screen. And, of course, a method that does not require electronic equipment is simply to mount the visuals on the wall or on an easel. The important thing is that they be big enough and clear enough for the audience to see.

Computer-Generated Graphics

No longer do you need to be a talented artist or excel in calligraphy in order to produce professional-looking visuals for your presentation. Computer presentation programs designed for this purpose are readily available and easy to use.

FIGURE 12–1. Bar chart.
(Source: Commerce Department—estimate.)

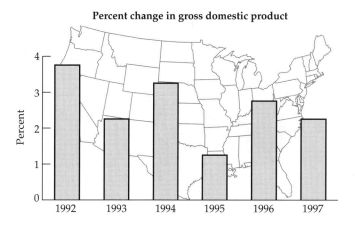

Percent change in gross domestic product

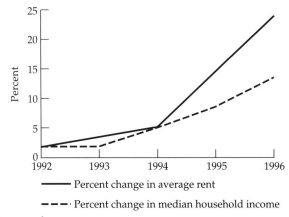

FIGURE 12–2. Line graph.

Once you have your lettering and graphics laid out on the screen, you can print your work or have it converted to slides or transparencies.

In *Windows Internet Magazine,* Robert Lindstrom writes,

> The proliferation of presentation software, coupled with graphics cards and color monitors, has opened a vast color spectrum to presentation creators, making misuse a constant threat. Aware of this, presentation software makers routinely build design templates and recommended color palettes into their applications. As with other elements of design, it is wise to follow these suggestions and recommendations.[1]

[1]Robert Lindstrom, "Slide Rules," *Windows Internet Magazine,* June 1995, www.winmag.com.

FIGURE 12–3. Pie chart.
(Source: Internal Revenue Service.)

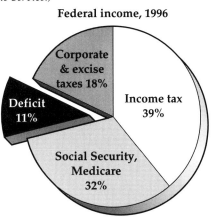

```
BILL OF RIGHTS

 1. Speech, press, religion, assembly
 2. Right to bear arms
 3. No soldiers quartered
 4. Search and seizure
 5. Right to remain silent
 6. Speedy and public trial
 7. Right to trial by jury
 8. No cruel or unusual punishment
 9. No denial of other rights
10. States' rights
```

FIGURE 12–4. Key word chart.

Lindstrom advised that you stick with the standard fonts and not use the ones that are "gimmicky" and hard to read. Here are a few of his other tips for preparing slides and transparencies:

- Use uppercase and lowercase letters. Avoid excessive use of all caps, except for emphasis.
- Keep type large and legible.
- Use no more than two typefaces.
- Limit the number of text lines to six, with a maximum of ten words per line.
- Do not center long lines of text.
- Proofread, and proofread again. Misspellings are unacceptable.

The size of the print is critical, because the words can have no impact if they can't be seen. Lindstrom has guidelines for determining the size of print on slides and transparencies:

- Hold your side up to the light at arm's length. If you can read the text easily, the contents are big enough for the audience to read when the slide is projected.
- Place the overhead slide or transparency on the floor, stand over it, and look down at it. If it is readable when you're at that distance, it will be readable when projected.

What Visuals Can Accomplish

Using visuals for important presentations will help you transform a casual speech into one that has a professional appearance. Consider the visuals you need for your speech in the same way you regard information and evidence. If there were a particular fact that you had to have for the support of your position, you would need to find it. By the same token, if there is a visual you need in order to make your point understandable, you will need to create it. Not every speech requires visuals, but if you try to do without them when they are needed, you will leave gaping holes in your presentation. Let's look at some of the ways that visuals can contribute to your talk:

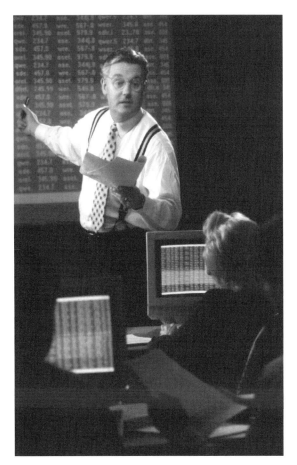

Projecting computer-generated visuals gives your
presentation a professional appearance.

- *Picturing what can't be described in words.* This is the most obvious contribution and one that has already been mentioned. But even when your thought is describable, keep in mind that visuals are more *succinct* than words; they reduce the amount of time you have to spend in elaborate explanations. People can see for themselves what you would otherwise have to spend considerable time explaining to them.
- *Giving the speech a professional tone.* Quality visuals convey the message that you know what you are doing and that you care enough to make an extra effort in helping the audience to understand. They set the speech apart from others and let people know that you have "done your homework."
- *Gaining and maintaining attention.* Your verbal facts and assertions may go unheard if your audience is not paying attention. Visuals keep the audience awake and focused on what you are saying.

- *Creating the "Ah ha" experience.* Every teacher will tell you that the best learning takes place when a light goes on inside the student's head and elicits the expression, "Ah ha." That's when the listener literally "gets the picture."
- *Producing an emotional impact.* An audience can understand an issue in the intellectual sense, but still not feel the full impact at the emotional level. If the success of your presentation depends on your listeners' being able to internalize the feelings you want to convey, visuals will help to achieve that effect.
- *Appealing to the aesthetic senses.* If you were to rely on words alone to express pure beauty, you would have to speak in poetry. That may not be something you do easily, nor is it an appropriate vehicle for business presentations. You can gain a similar advantage, however, with visuals. For some kinds of speeches, such as travelogues and talks on architectural design, pictures are essential.
- *Imprinting an image for future recall.* Our hope is always that the material we present in the speech will be remembered. It doesn't need to be recalled word for word. What probably will happen is that images will be stored in the memory cells of the listener's brain. We can, of course, rely on people's creating their own images, as they used to do when they listened to drama programs on radio. That may work for the person with a good imagination; the problem is that everyone creates a different image, and some get no picture at all. If you want people to recall a specific scene or a complex idea, you need to provide for them a detailed illustration of what you have in mind. Explanations and descriptions may accomplish that, but well-prepared visuals often make a clearer impression and stay with the listener longer.
- *Providing an organizational structure for the speaker.* Visuals provide an advantage to the *presenter* of the material, as well as to the audience. When you speak, you can use visuals to help you recall what you want to say. Often, speakers find that they can dispense with notes altogether when they do this, allowing the visuals to give cues for both the substance and the sequence of the ideas. For example, the photographs you take of your vacation provide you with a means of recalling what you did and what you saw. If you were going to tell friends about your trip and show your photos, you would have no problem; the pictures themselves would provide all the recollection you would need. You would probably arrange the snapshots in a sequence that would give continuity to your story. This is precisely what you do when you use visuals in making a presentation.

MAKING IT HAPPEN WITH VISUAL AIDS

At the same time that you study the possibilities in using visual aids, you need also to recognize their limitations. No visual is going to tell the whole story by itself. It is not advisable simply to run a film or a videotape. The fact is that there is no adequate substitute for personal contact, and in the final analysis, the persona of the speaker is the best of all visual aids. There is no chart, screen, or cathode-ray tube that will make people feel welcome, generate trust, or answer specific questions. The personality that you as the speaker project to your audience is the factor that will determine whether or not the message will be accepted. Visuals are simply tools that you can use to help make it happen. Let's start by talking about the ones that are the most effective:

Computer Displays

The use of computer displays requires some computer expertise, and even if you are a whiz on a keyboard, you will need to practice before you try this. It will take a good deal of time to familiarize yourself with the equipment and make the necessary preparation for a smooth presentation. The unit you need is a liquid crystal display (LCD). Placed on an overhead projector and connected to the video port of your computer, it can show on a large screen what you see on your computer monitor. The effect is quite impressive, because you are able to create your visual aid right before the eyes of the audience. Line graphs, pie charts, and histograms can be projected, and then the shapes and numbers can be changed as the viewers watch. This technique is especially useful when you are making a presentation on a complex topic such as budgetary expenditures. For example, if you are working with variables on a spreadsheet that must add up to a fixed figure on the bottom line, you'll be able to alter the priority rating for one item at a time and all the other numbers will automatically adjust. You could compare best-case and worst-case scenarios with a variety of alternatives in between.

The possibilities for using computer display panels are constantly changing with each new technological development. Right now, you can make a presentation using a memory panel that you can operate with a wireless, infrared remote control unit. Your preparation would consist of creating a series of screen displays, arranging them in the sequence you want, and then projecting them as you would when running a slide show. A handheld device allows you to preview the next visual before you display it and get a palm-size image of your notes. You can also set the timing between images and have the program run by itself while you make the commentary.

A less complicated method of displaying computer-generated visuals is to have your audience watch the monitor screen directly. However, this works only for a small group, because a twenty-five-inch screen, for example, can accommodate not more than twelve or thirteen people. Figure on one person being able to view a monitor comfortably for every two diagonal inches of the screen.

Projecting Images

Projecting slides and transparencies against a screen still works as well as it ever did. This method of displaying visuals is effective in gaining and holding attention, and contributes significantly to the impact of the message.

The content of the slide or transparency can be just about anything you want it to be. The slide projector is probably a better piece of equipment to use for displaying color photographs, although transparencies can also be used for that purpose. The overhead projector lends itself effectively to the display of charts, graphs, lists, diagrams, and key words, but slides can be made to do those things as well. Here are the generic functions of slides and transparencies:

- They can project an image on a screen so that it is large enough to allow all members of the audience to see the picture at the same time.
- They work equally well for large or small audiences.
- The pictures can be changed easily and quickly either by an operator or by the person who is giving the speech.
- The speaker can call attention to items on the screen with a pointer.
- The speaker can be facing the audience while describing the image or changing the picture.

Speaking with Transparencies

Always make sure that the visuals you work with in making a presentation are set out in a way that facilitates the logistics of their use; you don't want to have to hunt for something when you are under pressure. The transparencies should have cardboard borders for easy handling, they should be titled, and they should be stacked in order. Here are some other suggestions for using transparencies:

- Have the first transparency lined up on the projector and in focus so that when you turn the machine on, it will appear without delay.
- Cover with cardboard any part you don't want displayed immediately. During the presentation, slide the cardboard down to reveal the figures or diagrams you want the audience to see. This technique will give focus to the audience's attention.
- Display the transparency long enough for the audience to assimilate the information, but don't leave it there when you have gone on to another point.
- Have some comment about every transparency you display so that the audience will know what you have in mind. Don't expect the visual aid to speak for itself; your responsibility as the presenter is to help the audience understand the significance of each illustration.
- Be familiar enough with the material on the transparency so that you can direct your attention to the audience rather than to the screen.

Transparencies and slides each have characteristics of their own that may cause you to select one medium over the other: Transparencies have the advantage of being flexible. You can change the sequence more easily than you can when you are using slides; the room does not have to be totally darkened in order to get clear resolution on the screen; you can call attention to items in the picture by pointing on the transparency itself; you can write on the transparency with a marking pencil; you can conceal part of the material on the transparency with a blank card or sheet of paper until you are ready to have the audience view it.

Speaking with Slides

Slides have the advantage of producing high-quality images. Photographs can be projected with a realistic, three-dimensional look; the color in slides gives the presentation a highly professional appearance; the projected images can be changed quickly and easily, moving forward or backward with the press of a button. Be sure you know how the equipment works. Familiarize yourself with the kind of projector you will be using in the presentation. The best equipment would consist of a carousel projector with remote controls. Load the carousel yourself (slides go upside down and backwards) and run through them to make sure they are in the right sequence. Experiment with the switches on your remote control unit. You will be able to go backward and forward; you may have to focus manually, unless that function is automatic on the projector. Here are some other suggestions for using slides:

- Position the projector to accommodate the audience. Make sure the slides will be displayed so that everyone will be able to see. Try to avoid the "key-stone" effect by keeping the projector on a straight line with the screen. Select a place where you can stand so that you are not blocking anyone's view. And be sure to bring a cord long enough to reach the electrical outlet.
- Practice using a pointer. There may be occasions when you want to call attention to a particular item on the display. The conventional speaker's pointer may work well enough, but if you are some distance from the screen, a light-beam pointer might be necessary. If you have never used one before, try it out before you confront your audience.
- Consider how you will use your notes. Remember that the lights are going to be out when you show the slides. In a darkened room, you may not be able to see your note cards. It may be that you will not have to use them at all, because the slides themselves will help you recall what you want to say. But if you do have to use notes, provide for yourself a small light at the speaker's lectern.
- Designate a person to turn the lights on and off, and another person to start the slide projector. Remember that you are going to be in the front of the room facing the audience, and you don't want to leave your listeners in darkness with nothing to see or hear.
- Pace your presentation. There are too many variables to make a recommendation on how long to show each slide; you will have more to say about some than about others. But keep in mind the attention span of your audiences and the number of slides you intend to include. Averaging 4 slides a minute, you'll be able to show 120 slides in a half-hour presentation. Remember that the audience members are sitting in a darkened room. After the first twenty minutes, their attention may begin to decline. Don't let them fall asleep.
- Begin by establishing your own personal contact with the audience members. Use some introductory material to get their attention and provide for them enough orientation information so that they will know what you are going to talk about and what you will be showing them.

- When you are ready for the slides, signal the people who have previously been designated to control the light switch and start the projector. Don't try to do those things yourself.
- Control the changing of the slide by using your remote switching device. You can do that easily with your thumb. (Make sure you have the right button so that it goes forward instead of backward.) Have something to say about each slide that is projected.
- When the last slide has been shown, have the lights turned back on and the projector turned off. Don't finish the speech in darkness. Let the audience see you as you are delivering your conclusion.

As you can see, there are some logistical complications in making a slide presentation and more things to think about than there are in the unaided speech. You will need to do some planning and make advance preparation, but the impact on your audience will be significantly greater.

Plain and Simple Visuals

An oral explanation, in my opinion, is more effective than a written one. There are, however, some advantages to information that appears on the printed page. Complex material, particularly that which contains a great many names and numbers, may require some study on the part of the receiver. Sometimes oral presentations do not allow enough time for the listener to assimilate the material, and the message does not get thoroughly imprinted. When you

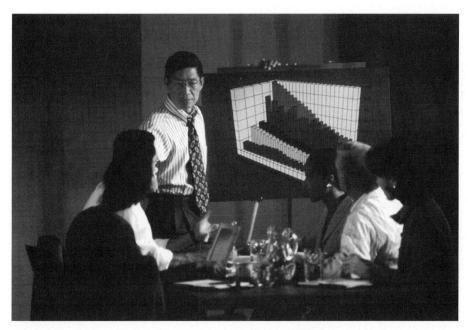

Words and graphics projected on a screen help people remember what you say.

believe that your listeners may need to review what you have told them after the presentation, you can provide a handout sheet for them. If you want them to follow along while you are providing the explanation, give it to them in advance. But most teachers will tell you that it's a better idea to give your information orally first; then, distribute the handout sheets.

Not all visuals need to be prepared in advance. There are times when you may want to create the visuals as you deliver the speech. The best example of such an occasion is when you are conducting a brainstorming session. You have several choices in selecting your equipment:

- *The chalkboard.* This is the old standby—possibly the world's first visual aid. It works well enough if you don't mind chalk dust on your clothes. I'm not fond of it for professional presentations, because it looks a bit funky and old-fashioned and tends to create a classroom atmosphere. It is also restrictive in terms of space, and your material cannot be saved.
- *The whiteboard.* This is a better choice. It eliminates the chalk dust factor and gives a more professional appearance to the presentation. However, there is still the restriction of space and the necessity of having to erase your material.
- *The flip chart.* This is perhaps the best choice. You have enough pages so that you are not going to run out of space, and you don't have to erase the material. The pages can be torn off and turned over to a secretary to be recorded, or possibly pinned up around the room so that the participants have a visual record of the ideas that have been generated.

The flip chart has other advantages as well as those just mentioned. I like to use this piece of equipment as a substitute for note cards. What I do ahead of time is to put my key words and main ideas on the pages in the sequence that I want to follow. As I move through the speech, I simply turn the pages— just as though I am revealing my notes to the audience as I go through the speech. The advantage of this technique is that I can give my full attention to the listeners without the need to be looking at something that they can't see. When I look at the page on the flip chart, they can see it too. Then, with my felt-tip pen, I can highlight items that I want to emphasize.

Desktop Visuals

As we observed earlier, there are times when the best visual aid is the object itself or a representative model. Small pieces of equipment or artifacts can be held up or passed around if your audience is not too big. There are a number of ways you can display small, lightweight objects. The important thing is that they be visible to the audience while you are talking.

- Pin items to a corkboard.
- Hang objects from overhead clips.
- Place felt cutouts on a flannel board.
- Prop posters on an easel.

Don't put yourself in the awkward position of having to hold a large visual aid in front of you for a long period of time; either prop it up or have someone else hold it. For a small audience, a desktop easel can be used in the same way as a flip chart. A loose-leaf binder that can be mounted on a stand is also very convenient. It can also be carried easily and set up quickly.

Whenever you use visual aids, you need to take into consideration the particular circumstances of the speaking occasion. What works for a small audience may not work for a large one. The same is true in regard to your own voice and appearance. Let's consider what equipment is needed in order to extend your speech to a larger audience.

MICROPHONES AND CAMERAS

The presentation you give to a small group should work well enough without amplification, but when you are speaking to a large audience, you may need a public-address (PA) system. As the speaker, the only thing you should have to be concerned about is the way you use the microphone, because the technicians will monitor the volume control.

Public-Address Systems

There's no need to be intimidated by a PA system; all it will do is amplify the sound so that you can be heard without your having to raise your voice to an uncomfortable level. Use enough volume so that you can be heard twenty or thirty feet away, and the amplifier will do the rest. Just remember a few techniques:

- Speak into the microphone from about four to six inches away and at a slight angle. Try to keep the distance as constant as possible. You will know that the system is working when you hear the sound reverberation that is created by the amplifier.
- While the microphone is turned on, don't make any muttering or whispering sounds to yourself or to anyone else that you don't want the audience to hear. Microphones are sensitive and will pick up even low-volume noises.
- Handling the microphone will cause it to rattle. If it needs to be adjusted, let someone else do it for you. If you have to adjust it yourself, grasp it firmly, move it, let go, and then start talking. Never tap on the microphone or blow into it.

Radio Microphones

If your speech is being carried on a radio broadcasting station, apply the same microphone techniques that were described for the use of public-address systems. The only difference is that you will not hear the sound of your voice amplified. There are two other very important things to remember when your speech is being broadcast:

- Don't start talking until you are given the *cue*. That will come in the form of a red light going on or a director's hand pointing at you. Once you have been given the cue, start right off with your first word, not a nonverbal sound such as "uh." And *never* begin by saying "Are we on?"
- As you get to the end of the speech, the director will give you a "wind-it-up" signal by making a circular hand motion in the air. This signal doesn't mean that you are to stop abruptly in the middle of a sentence; it means you are to finish what you are saying and drop your voice to indicate that you are through. Don't ignore the signal; there is hardly any point in continuing to speak when the mike is turned off.

Television Cameras

Being televised is not so much of a novelty as it used to be. Local cable channels and broadcasting stations are able to take portable cameras almost anywhere to provide news coverage. Using a camcorder to capture the action of people and events is a common practice in schools, colleges, industry, and the home. It is quite likely that you will find yourself sometime facing a television camera and having a professional or amateur director point a finger at you to start. Here are some hints to keep you from getting completely flustered:

- If you are alone in the picture, talk to the camera. If there are other people with you, talk to them. Never look at the monitor screen, regardless of how tempting it may be to see yourself.
- Avoid sudden or unpredictable movements. If you stand up quickly or walk off to one side, you will move right out of the picture. If you move suddenly toward or away from the camera, you will go out of focus.
- Pay attention to your posture, whether you are standing or sitting. Avoid slouching, scratching your head, tapping your foot, and other ungainly and unnecessary movements that distract the viewer. Remember that those mannerisms will be amplified, because the television screen is able to bring you up close to the audience.

PUTTING IT ALL TOGETHER

Modern technology has made public speaking a great deal more complex than it was in Aristotle's time—or in the time of Confucius. You can still give speeches the old-fashioned way, relying completely on your unaided voice and your personal image. In fact, that may be what you will be doing most of the time when you have the opportunity to speak. But be sure you know that audio and visual aids are available to you. Don't feel that you are restricted to any one particular kind; you can use a combination of those that have been mentioned. Think in terms of the effect that you want to create and what it is that you want to have stand out in the minds of the audience. Then select the object or the equipment that will do the job most effectively for you. Actually, it may be that Confucius underestimated—a picture could be worth a good deal more than a thousand words.

EXERCISE

Prepare a visual of one of the kinds listed below. You can create it on a computer or simply print it by hand. It could be in the form of a poster, an overhead transparency, a slide, or a handout sheet. Stand in front of the class. Take three minutes to display the visual and make a short presentation telling what it represents and its significance. Be sure you plan the logistics: Figure out how you are going to display the visual and where you are going to stand.

- A printed list of key words to indicate steps in a process
- A bar chart, a pie chart, or a line graph showing percentages
- A map of a geographic area that you can describe
- A painting, diagram, poster, or large photograph

Make sure that the visual is large enough to be seen. If you use a poster, the paper should be stiff enough to stand upright on an easel or chalk tray. Use a dark-colored felt-tip pen for printing and drawing. If you plan to use an overhead or slide projector, be sure to order the equipment in advance and come into the classroom early enough to set it up.

QUESTIONS FOR REVIEW

1. In a real-life situation (as opposed to a classroom), what will probably be the audience's main criteria for evaluating a speaker?
2. When your speech is being given for a specific audience rather than for a general audience, what changes might you have to make in the purpose and in the content?
3. What new challenge is added to a presentation on the occasions when you have to be a teacher, rather than just a speaker?
4. What are some of the ways visuals can be displayed? In terms of the audience's perception, what are the most important criteria for the display of visuals?
5. How have computer presentation programs helped speakers to make professional-looking visuals?
6. Why would you want to use visuals in a speech? What are some things they can accomplish?
7. What do we mean when we say that visuals communicate more *succinctly* than words?
8. What do we mean by *appealing to aesthetic senses?*
9. In addition to helping the audience understand and retain the message, how do visuals help the speaker in making the presentation?
10. Why is the persona of the speaker still the most important element in speechmaking? What can the speaker do that visuals cannot do?
11. What kind of visuals can you display using computer projection? What advantage does a computer-projected image have over a standard transparency?
12. What piece of equipment is probably best for displaying color photographs?

13. What piece of equipment would you probably want to use if you had several graphs, charts, and lists to display, but you did not want to be confined to arranging them in a particular order?
14. What advantages does a flip chart have over a chalkboard?
15. What is the value of handouts? At what point in the presentation should they be distributed?
16. What are some things you should not do when talking into a PA system?
17. What are some things you should not do while talking in front of a television camera?

MEETING ETHICAL STANDARDS

**AFTER READING THIS CHAPTER, YOU SHOULD
BE ABLE TO DO THE FOLLOWING:**

Understand what Aristotle meant by "ethos" as one of the modes of
proof; be able to apply the criteria of *practical wisdom, virtue,* and
goodwill in your speeches; know what Quintilian said
about the ethical speaker.

Recognize the pressure that has to be resisted by politicians who try to
maintain high ethical standards; know what is meant by *sophistry* and
what Socrates said about those who practice it; understand
the term *caveat emptor* and other ethical fallacies.

Be able to distinguish between utilitarianism and categorical
imperatives; understand the qualifications that are
attached to civil disobedience.

Know what is meant by *social contracts* and the way John Rawls says
they should be established; understand the *practical, intrinsic,* and
social value of maintaining high ethical standards; be able and
willing to apply the speaker's code of ethics; give
thought to moral questions.

In the 1996 presidential campaign, Republican advisors urged their candidate, Bob Dole, to raise the "character issue" in his debates with Bill Clinton. Attacking an opponent's ethical standards and behavior has been used by politicians for as long as there have been elections. It is a strategy that must be implemented with caution, because it can backfire if the voters think that the attacker has gone too far or has made unfair charges. And, of course, it can work only if the public believes that the person accused is guilty of flagrant moral turpitude. The standards to which Americans hold their elected representatives are subject to continual change, and a politician who raises the "character issue" needs to know what voters regard as a serious infraction and what they perceive as a mere casual indiscretion. In a survey conducted by the Knight-Ridder Washington bureau, 65 percent or more of the people polled said that they would not vote for a candidate who had used illegal drugs, had not told the truth about what policies would be, had friends suspected of being in organized crime, had failed to pay income taxes, or had been a member of a white supremacist group. On the other hand, there were several pardonable offenses: More than 50 percent said they *could* vote for a candidate who had avoided the draft, broken a promise not to raise taxes, or cheated on his wife.[1] This evidence may be of more concern to people running for public office than it is to the rest of us on the lower levels of the celebrity scale; nevertheless, it behooves us to give serious thought to maintaining constancy in what we say and what we do.

ETHICAL STANDARDS FOR PUBLIC SPEAKERS

Any criteria for evaluation in public address, as mentioned in Chapter Nine, must include the ethical qualities of the speaker consistent with the "mode of proof" that Aristotle calls the *ethos*. The very essence of persuasion has its roots in the ethos, because the other two modes of proof, the logos and the pathos, fail to persuade unless the audience perceives the speaker to be a person of good character. When the integrity of the speaker is in doubt, listeners will question the validity of the evidence and will resist being moved by any attempted emotional appeal.

The Roman philosopher Quintilian (A.D. 40–118) regarded the speaker's moral integrity as an essential element in rhetorical evaluation. A speech of lofty purpose, he maintained, must be delivered by a "good man speaking well." Setting aside the obvious sexism of this declaration, we note that the character of the speaker in the classical view is inextricably tied to the quality of the speech itself. The same observation had been made four centuries earlier by Aristotle:

> There are three reasons why speakers themselves are persuasive; these are *practical wisdom* . . . *virtue* and *goodwill*. . . . Speakers make mistakes in what they say or advise through failure to exhibit either all or one of these. . . . For either

[1]Knight-Ridder Washington bureau poll by Princeton Survey Research of 1,002 registered voters, conducted September 3–15, 1996; reported in the *San Jose Mercury News*, October 24, 1996, p. 25A.

through lack of practical sense they do not form opinions rightly; they do not say what they think because of a bad character; or they are prudent and fair-minded but lack goodwill.[2]

Here, Aristotle is saying that the speaker's code of ethics is violated when he or she makes a "mistake" in one of the three categories. If we are to utilize these standards, we might want to make a distinction between "honest mistakes" and those that are made out of carelessness or malice. One might argue that speakers who acknowledge their mistakes and who offer an apology or redress demonstrate their sincerity sufficiently to restore their integrity.

Let's look more closely at Aristotle's three criteria: (1) *Practical wisdom and sense* means that the speaker is knowledgeable and can reason clearly, consider supporting evidence, and use good judgment in arriving at conclusions. (2) *Virtue* means that the speaker is honest and will not knowingly lie to listeners or withhold information that they need to know. (3) *Goodwill* means that the speaker will advocate only that which is in the best interest of those whom he or she has the responsibility to serve.

Being Knowledgeable and Having Good Sense

If speakers were required to be knowledgeable and have good sense, many would not be allowed on the podium at all. But who is to make that determination? There will always be those who will applaud and be influenced by even the most poorly reasoned speech. All we can say is that good sense can be judged only by "sensible critics"—those in the audience who are listening with a critical ear and are able to perceive whether or not the message of the speaker conforms to sensible standards. If the speaker succeeds in reaching only the uncritical members of the audience—those who are willing to accept bogus claims lacking evidence or reason—we would say that the speech has failed to inspire confidence in the orator's character.

Speakers who fail to meet the criterion of having practical wisdom might attain a temporary measure of success, but they can very quickly fall from grace when the audience catches on to what they are doing. One such figure was Senator Joseph McCarthy, who enjoyed considerable praise from his supporters for many years as he carried on his campaign to weed "communists" out of government. He was finally stopped by a resolution of censure when a majority of senators recognized that he was making irresponsible charges against innocent people without having evidence for his accusations.

Telling the Truth

Perhaps the clearest standard of good character is honesty. We want to know that when people make public statements, they are telling the truth. Failing to measure up to this criterion can be costly, as it was when Mark Fuhrman lied

---

[2]Aristotle, *On Rhetoric*, trans. George A. Kennedy, Oxford University Press, New York, 1991, pp. 120–121.

Richard Nixon's involvement in the Watergate scandal was serious enough to drive him from office.

about his not having used racial epithets at any time in the five years before he appeared in court during the O. J. Simpson trial. Many analysts say that his false testimony resulted in the acquittal of Simpson for double murder. Another example of prevarication under oath was revealed in 1986 when Colonel Oliver North was called to testify in the Iran-Contra investigation. He openly acknowledged that on a previous occasion he had lied to Congress about a deal to sell arms to Iran and use the money to aid the Contra rebels fighting in Nicaragua. Colonel North tried to justify his lie by declaring that he believed the falsehood was in the best interest of the country; however, Aristotle's criterion does not accommodate that kind of exception.

In regard to Ronald Reagan's role in the Iran-Contra affair, there are other pertinent questions: Did the President know about the deal? And if so, when did he know it? Did he lie to the press when he said that no arms were being sold to Iran? Again, in this case we can see how Aristotle's criteria can be applied. If President Reagan knew of the transaction, he would be guilty of making a false statement. If he did not know, he would be in violation of the "good sense" criterion, because a President should certainly have knowledge of the activities of his own staff.

Speaking and Acting in the Best Interest of the Audience

Often, we think of unethical behavior as being acts that are in violation of the law. Perjury, for example, is a punishable crime, and a person found guilty of this can go to jail. But the law must not be our sole basis for determining moral infractions. Surely we can hold people to a higher standard than that which is mandated by judicial decree. In particular, we might cite the examples of wealthy individuals who make large financial contributions to a politician's election campaign and admit openly that they hope to receive favorable treatment in return. The givers may be acting within the law, but the gifts put the integrity of the receiver in question. How can the politician speak and act in the best interest of the general audience when he or she is beholden to those who give large sums of money?

What do we mean by *the goodwill of the audience?* Which audience? For example, when tobacco executives advocate the sale and consumption of cigarettes, they are not acting in the interest of those who will contract lung cancer and heart disease. But when those same executives address the people who work in the tobacco fields and warehouses, their words do gain the goodwill of the listeners, who know they will benefit from continued employment. The question is, "Does the advantage to one group compensate for the damage done to the other?" We cannot always legislate matters of this kind, and for that reason we need standards of ethics.

ETHICAL STANDARDS AT RISK

The issue of ethics in public life is most conspicuous in the political arena. Many voters feel that the term *political ethics* is an oxymoron. Is it possible for anyone to hold an elected position and still be able to maintain high ethical standards? Politicians sometimes refer to the "rule of survival," which means that they have to save their seats before they can save the world. There are many intelligent, highly qualified people in this country who would make excellent legislators but do not wish to serve because of the compromises they believe they would have to make in their principles in order to get elected. Members of the U.S. House of Representatives must run for office every two years; that means a person in Congress needs to be campaigning almost all the time. Political campaigns cost a great deal of money, and politicians must gain the favor of large contributors in order to build up what they call their "war chests." This certainly does not justify making exaggerated promises or accepting fees for favors, but it helps us to understand the pressure that is placed on a person who makes politics a career.

One former U.S. representative, Paul "Pete" McCloskey from California, who served for twenty years in Congress, speaks frequently on the subject of ethics in politics. His advice to young people who are considering running for office is to wait until they have established their careers in the private sector before they subject themselves to the rigors of an elected position. By doing this, he says, representatives do not become dependent on the political office for their livelihood and are free to say "no" to those who try to buy their vote. Then if they lose an election, they have a career to fall back on.

The pressure on a politician to get reelected can be illustrated in the example of Richard Nixon's involvement in the Watergate scandal. Overzealous supporters of the Republican party hired burglars to break into Democratic headquarters to learn about the political strategies of the opposition. It was a clumsy and unnecessary act, because the polls showed Nixon leading his opponent, George McGovern, by a comfortable margin. The discovery that the President and his advisors had authorized the break-in had devastating consequences. Political writers frequently compare this issue with the Iran-Contra affair and observe that the transgressions that occurred in Ronald Reagan's administration were far more serious than the one that led to the resignation of Richard Nixon. Why is it that Congress and the general public were as upset as they were over the relatively mild offense that was committed by the staff of Richard Nixon? It's true that the President lied about his involvement in the matter and the subsequent cover-up, but no lasting harm was done either to the nation or to the Democratic party, so why the big fuss? It appears that the American public is offended to a greater extent by the act of lying than by the damage that is done by the lie. It also seems that the lie is much worse when it is told by a person who is in a high position of public trust.

Sophistry

The philosophers in ancient Greece had a term for speakers who ignored the principles of logic, reasoning, good sense, and sound ethical practices. The word was *sophistry.* Originally, it applied to a person of great wisdom—a teacher of rhetoric. But, as those who taught the art began to instruct their students in ways to deceive the audience and to make, as Socrates said, "the worse appear to be the better reason," the reputation of the sophists became severely tarnished. Today, the word is used in an accusatory fashion in reference to someone who attempts to manipulate an audience into accepting superficially plausible, but specious, reasoning. Unfortunately, such manipulation is frequently successful. When the audience is not diligent, speakers are able to base their claims on flimsy evidence without being challenged.

Ethical Fallacies

It has been said that human beings are not so much rational animals as they are *rationalizing* animals. We tend to invent reasons that we should go on believing what we want to believe, even though there may be no logical or moral justification for the belief. If these rationalizations are not recognized for what they are, they begin to take on the appearance of having validity; actually, they are merely manipulative devices that we could call *ethical fallacies.* There are many such fallacies, and a list follows. The first listed below, "let the buyer beware," goes by a commonly used Latin expression, *caveat emptor.* I have taken the liberty of giving Latin names to the others.

Let the buyer beware (caveat emptor). This fallacy claims that it is the responsibility of the receiver, not the presenter, to discover flaws in the merchandise. In the context of public speaking, it suggests that if the listeners are foolish enough to accept a spurious argument, they deserve what they get.

Everyone is doing it (omnes hoc faciunt). This is a favorite ploy of teenagers who want to get parents to believe that a particular behavior is perfectly acceptable. The term *everyone* is generally a hyperbole and may include only a few close friends. But it's equally important to recognize the fallacy of believing that conformity is a valid criterion for acceptable behavior.

The only crime is getting caught (scelus solum est prehendi). This fallacy says that if you are smart, you deserve to get away with anything you want to do. It suggests that self-interest is the only moral imperative and that there is no intrinsic value in doing the right thing. It is, of course, a blatant violation of any ethical standard, but it is all too frequently used as a basis to justify unprincipled behavior.

If I didn't do it, someone else would (si non ego, alius quis). This claim might be made by someone wishing to justify his or her being engaged in an illegal or immoral activity, such as selling narcotics or taking bribes. It could never be a defensible position for any responsible speaker, because it ignores the fact that if nobody did it, the deed would not be done.

You can steal from the rich, because they can afford it (furamini abdivitibus). Many people erroneously believe that nobody gets hurt when a big company is the victim. In reality, however, industry loses billions of dollars every year from the theft of tools and office supplies, for example. Insurance companies are frequently targets of this fallacious reasoning when people who are otherwise fair and law-abiding citizens see nothing wrong with filing exaggerated claims for losses and suing for amounts far in excess of their pain and suffering. Unfortunately, the more people do this, the more it seems to be acceptable, and the result is higher consumer costs for everyone.

It doesn't matter, because nothing will change anyway (non potestis cum decurionibus pugnare). This moral fallacy allows people to avoid their responsibilities out of a feeling of futility and fatalism. For example, it is a reason given by those who don't vote in elections and who pay no attention to current events. When this becomes a pervasive attitude in a democratic society, the groundwork is laid for abuse of power, corruption, and the erosion of human rights.

A high ethical standard is not something you can turn on when you step onto the podium and turn off when you step down. It is a quality that must be consistent in the personality and character of anyone who intends to engage in public address. Whenever you face an audience, you reveal not only your point of view, but also your moral integrity. If there are flaws in your character that you are trying to hide, your public speaking experiences will begin to feel uncomfortable.

MORAL PHILOSOPHIES

We cannot legislate against ethical fallacies—and certainly we would not want to do so. Any moral standards that we establish must be founded on principles of reason and accepted on their own merit, rather than being prescribed by law. As an individual, you may have your own code of ethics that perhaps is working well for you. But as you begin to extend yourself to others, as you do when you speak in public, you may need to expand upon your code so that it includes a broader range of situations and takes into consideration your community responsibilities. Fortunately, we do not have to embark upon that task alone and unassisted; there is a great deal of philosophical groundwork that has already been laid.

Utilitarian Ethics

The philosophy of *utilitarian ethics* has a great deal of appeal because it is flexible and permits adjustment on the basis of changing social mores. It states that actions should be judged in terms of the good that results, compared to the harm that is done. That is, if there is more benefit than there is injury, the action would be regarded as ethical. This philosophy was espoused by John Stuart Mill, who published his thesis *Utilitarianism* in 1861. He maintained that pleasure or happiness is a basic good and there is no reason why it should not be pursued if nobody gets hurt in so doing. What he means is that we ought to pursue the general happiness—the happiness of everyone, including ourselves. But we must be cognizant of the effects of our actions and be able to perceive whether or not we are inflicting pain of any kind on someone else. The idea is similar to that which Thomas Jefferson expressed in the Declaration of Independence: "We hold these truths to be self evident, that all men are created equal, that they are endowed by their Creator with certain unalienable Rights, that among these are Life, Liberty, and the pursuit of Happiness." Both Mill and Jefferson started with the premise that happiness is intrinsically good and that there is no virtue in depriving others or yourself of it. Jefferson took the principle a step further and made it part of a social system, saying that the right was "endowed by the Creator." It's hard to argue with a mandate like that! The problem with Mill's philosophy is that it assumes that whatever brings happiness to you will also bring happiness to others.

As a governing philosophy, the ethics of utilitarianism work well as a means of filling the needs of the majority. However, the philosophy sometimes treads on the interests of the minority. It relies heavily on contemporary cultural mores and often permits social injustices. In the years before the Civil War, for example, advocates of slavery were able to maintain their position because, in their local regions, they had popular support. They could argue that a greater good was being served by the institution of slavery because slaves on the southern plantations were helping to assure economic stability and provide prosperity for the whole population. Furthermore, they could assert that slaves in the south were generally treated better than the free workers in the northern factories. The reasoning of those who are guided by the code of utilitarianism is that there can be no universally accepted standard for moral behavior.

Categorical Imperatives

In the eighteenth century Immanuel Kant argued in support of what he called *categorical imperatives*—principles that are constant and not affected by changing social circumstances. We see this philosophy at work in some elements of our culture today. In the traditional family, parents may attempt to instill certain values in their children, teaching them to be honest and self-reliant, regardless of the behavior of their peers. The Boy Scout and Girl Scout Law has served a valuable purpose for many generations, teaching young people to be trustworthy, loyal, helpful, friendly, courteous, kind, obedient, cheerful, thrifty, brave, clean, and reverent. Actually, that's not a bad list, and one that would be difficult to criticize. We would have to look at the fine print to see what is really meant by those pronouncements, but we could do that. In fact, the Scout Law includes several sentences under each one of those words that express the concept in more detail. For example, the text says that a scout is "loyal to all to whom loyalty is due." Now, that is still a bit vague, but at least it puts the scout on the path that embraces that value. Skeptics may say there are no universally accepted categorical imperatives, but when we examine the moral codes of social and religious institutions, we may see that there are several principles to which people of goodwill in almost all cultures could probably agree.

The Kantian philosophy does not have the flexibility of Mill's utilitarianism, because it requires maintaining the constancy of a principle, regardless of the consequences. For example, a categorical imperative might be that slavery is a violation of human rights and that there is no economic or social value that could give it redemption. In reference to this analysis, it is interesting to note that Jefferson used phrases that sounded like categorical imperatives: "All men are created equal . . . and are endowed by their Creator with certain unalienable rights." Yet, in 1776 those rights belonged only to white, male property owners, and not to women or to slaves. In this respect, his edict was utilitarian.

In more recent times, we can see what an important difference there is between the utilitarian philosophy and categorical imperatives. On March 16, 1968, U.S. soldiers killed several hundred civilians, many of them women and children, in the town of My Lai in Vietnam. Can such an act have any justification? The utilitarian could argue that although the event was a terrible tragedy, it was necessary given the circumstances of the war: American soldiers never knew when a civilian, even a child, would have a concealed hand grenade, ready to explode; therefore, our troops did what they needed to do in order to survive.

On the other hand, the Kantian philosophy would assert that the killing of civilians, even in wartime, is a violation of a basic categorical imperative and is not justifiable under any circumstances. This was, in fact, the ruling of a military court that tried and convicted Lieutenant William Calley for the responsibility of commanding and participating in the act.

Civil Disobedience

What about civil disobedience? Can a speaker ethically advocate the breaking of a rule in a society that is committed to creating an environment that makes the pursuit of happiness a God-given right? Henry David Thoreau wrote, "If the law is of such a nature that it requires you to be an agent of injustice to another, then I say, break the law. Let your life be a counter friction to stop the machine."

The consideration that civil disobedience could be included in the ethical criteria for public speakers is certain to draw objection from those who subscribe to law and order. Yet, the issue must be raised because of the integrity and prestige of the people who have espoused their right to protest legal statutes that violated their personal moral codes. The fact that Martin Luther King is a national hero and is honored with a day that commemorates his birth is testimony to the ethical status of protesting a law by breaking it.

Civil disobedience does not mean that you have a right to break any law you don't like without paying a price. Thoreau, King, and others who were principal players in civil protests took the action they did with full knowledge of the consequences and with the willingness to accept the penalties of the law. Furthermore, they were prepared to defend their actions in open forum, with reason and evidence.

When the civil rights movement is measured by the standards of utilitarian ethics, we see that the benefits did finally come to outweigh the disruption of the society. The fact that the laws restricting racial equality were eventually struck down vindicated those who brought about the change through their physical actions and rhetorical protests.

SOCIAL CONTRACTS

Civilization depends on social contracts. Society cannot allow all people to follow their own interests at the expense of others; therefore, we establish laws, customs, and codes to govern and regulate individual behavior. But on what basis do we make those rules?

Harvard University professor and philosopher John Rawls suggests that, ideally, the rules of a society should be established by reasonable people who are acting in their own self-interest, but who do not know in advance what their position in the society will be. In his hypothetical scenario, the people chosen to set the rules do not know, for example, if they will be male or female, black or white, young or old, rich or poor. Being reasonable and acting in their own self-interest, they would not pass laws that would discriminate against any particular sex, race, age group, or social class, because such discrimination might ultimately infringe on their own welfare. Rawls says, "The intuitive idea is that since everyone's well-being depends on a scheme of cooperation without which no one could have a satisfactory life, the division of advantages should be such as to draw forth the willing cooperation of everyone taking part in it."[3]

This perspective may help us to establish a basis for our moral values because, as speakers, we do make contributions to social contracts. It is not enough for us to think in terms limited to our own conduct; we need to look for a philosophy that pertains to *policy*. We know that when we step onto the speaker's platform, we are extending our values to others, and even if we declare that we are speaking for ourselves, we are at the same time modeling what we would prescribe for those we address.

The Value of Ethical Conduct

But what is the real value of ethical conduct? If the audience likes the speech, why should we, as speakers, be concerned about whether or not it conforms to ethical standards? That's an important question for us to address, because altruism may not be sufficient motivation for those whose actions are normally governed primarily by self-interest.

1. *The practical value.* The speaker whose position is based on sound ethical standards will be perceived by an audience as someone who can be believed and trusted. Therefore, the speech has a better chance to succeed.
2. *The intrinsic value.* This is value for its own sake. It is not measurable in terms of rewards, but it generates confidence and self-esteem within the speaker, who can say, "In my heart I know I'm right."
3. *The social value.* Any society will work better if its people subscribe to and behave according to rules and principles that are just. Those who speak in public have an added responsibility, because they influence the thought and behavior of others.

All of this may sound as though demands are being placed on public speakers to be perfect in all respects. Not so. We all make mistakes and fail from time to time to abide by even those moral principles we have established for ourselves. But the fact that we commit indiscretions does not mean that we should advocate them. If a man is unfaithful to his wife, he need not feel that he must stand on the podium and advocate infidelity. In public speaking, we profess what we believe *should* prevail. If we acknowledge transgressions in our own behavior, it would be only to illustrate the point that there is need for vigilance against future misconduct.

Public speaking differs from other forms of discourse in a very important way. In private conversations or in closed meetings, we can explore problems

---

[3]John Rawls, *A Theory of Justice,* The Belknap Press of Harvard University Press, Cambridge, Mass., 1971.

The issue of ethics in public life is most conspicuous in the political arena.

and perhaps try out ideas by expressing them tentatively, without having them become open declarations. But, in public address, we are standing on what we profess to be our considered and reasoned values and opinions.

The Speaker's Code of Ethics

Almost every profession has its code of ethics; doctors, lawyers, broadcasters, journalists—all have established standards of ethical conduct. That is not to say that everyone in each of those professions abides by the standards to the letter. There is no force of law that compels them to do so, only their own sense of moral obligation and regard for their professional reputation. Schools, colleges, and universities require that graduates have an understanding of ethical standards in their field of study in order to maintain the historical tradition and the integrity of the profession.

In 1972 the Speech Communication Association adopted a Credo for Free and Responsible Communication in a Democratic Society. It condemns physical and coercive interference in the free speech of others; it urges respect for accuracy in communication and for reasoning based on evidence. Although the ability to speak in public is not something that requires a license or a degree, it is a recognized academic discipline, and students who choose to study the art at the college or university level should have the same appreciation for a code of ethics that people who pursue professional careers have. Those of us who teach public address certainly have a professional responsibility to see that ethical standards are observed in the classroom. As someone who is beginning to practice the art of public speaking, you will have to work out your own code for yourself. Some considerations to take into account are as follows:

1. The claims of the speaker must be based on accurate information, and no false or misleading evidence must be presented to the audience.
2. No information that would have a significant bearing on the speaker's case must knowingly be withheld from the audience.
3. Recommendations made by the speaker must be in the best interest of the audience, and any personal gain for the speaker must be clearly understood by the audience.
4. The message must clarify what the probable consequences would be, and who, if anyone, would be adversely affected if the postulates of the speaker were to be accepted.
5. The speaker must be prepared to take responsibility for claims made and be willing to speak in their support if called upon to do so.
6. The information of the speaker must be presented with the intent to clarify the issue rather than obscure or confuse it.

The conditions of this code do not provide any guidance for positions taken on particular issues, nor do they specify what moral principles should be followed. The implementation of the code is the responsibility of the speaker, and the interpretation must be that of the critic. Furthermore, the code is by no means comprehensive; there are a number of significant questions that are left unanswered:

Moral Questions

1. *Does the end justify the means?* Students of philosophy continue to wrestle with this question. Is it ethical to set aside a moral principle if a greater good is the result of the action? Would you, for example, condone torture as a means of obtaining information from a terrorist in order to save the lives of hostages? If you subscribe to the philosophy of categorical imperatives, you would have to say "no." If you apply the principles of utilitarianism, however, you would need to weigh the harmful consequences against the benefits of the end results.
2. *Is omission as bad as commission?* Certainly, if you lie to an audience you are violating a basic ethical standard. But what if you are in a position to give needed information and you fail to do so? Is it a breach of ethics for the victim of a crime or misconduct to abstain from pressing charges? Is a woman who has been sexually abused or harassed guilty of an ethical omission if she fails to come forward with information that would identify the offending party? How does such omission compare to a false accusation?
3. *What is the best response to make to charges of misconduct?* Making a public statement to defend yourself against charges of misconduct is probably not something you will be called upon to do, unless you are a celebrity. But

what would you do if you were guilty and in this position? Would you be open and candid, even if it meant jeopardizing the reputation of another party? If a person refuses to answer the charges, is he or she committing an ethical violation? Is honesty always the best policy? We can see from the past experience of high officials in government that attempts to cover up transgressions can sometimes be more damaging to a cause than the mistake itself.

Reason Is the Ultimate Ethic

In the final analysis, reason must be the basis for any ethical code. We strive to do the right thing, not for the sake of demonstrating altruism, but because we know that it is ultimately in our own interest and that of the society to do so. Oliver Wendell Holmes said, "Reason means truth and those who are not governed by it take the chance that some day the sunken fact will rip the bottom out of their boat."

EXERCISE

Discuss in a small group how you would handle each of the following hypothetical cases:

1. You have a good job working for a large, prestigious company that manufactures silicon chips. Your job description includes making presentations to community organizations about the work your company is doing. Recently, you have heard rumors that your company has been violating EPA (Environmental Protection Agency) regulations pertaining to the dumping of toxic wastes. You contact your supervisor and ask her if the rumors are true. She is evasive and says it doesn't affect your department and you shouldn't be concerned about it. Furthermore, she suggests that your job might be in jeopardy if you continue to pursue the matter. In the next presentation you make, a member of the audience asks you about the rumors. How do you respond?

2. A close friend of yours is applying for a job at the company where you work. Your friend asks you if you would make a personal recommendation on his behalf to the human resources manager. You go in to see the manager, and she shows you your friend's résumé and letters of application. You notice that the résumé says your friend graduated from a university that you know he never attended. The manager says if you would like to make a recommendation you should speak to the hiring committee. What do you do?

3. You are about to make a major presentation to a top management group regarding the safety tests that have been made on a new windshield design for automobiles. If this management group accepts your proposal, your company will be awarded a major contract, and you stand to get a large bonus. You have studied this design for months and are thoroughly familiar with it. You have rehearsed the presentation a dozen times, and you are armed with a battery of handout materials and visual aids. Ten minutes before you go into the meeting, your assistant informs you that there appear to have been some mistakes in analyzing the test results. You know that a delay would mean that the order would go to another company. Your assistant tells you

that the flaws are not very bad, and would probably go undetected, even if the car were in an accident. What do you do?

4. You are an instructor in a college speech class. A student shows you an outline for a persuasive speech he plans to give to the class the following day. The speech advocates white supremacy and calls for the organization of an Aryan club on campus that would have as its goal discouraging black, Asian, and Mexican American students from attending the college. You are not able to persuade the student to change the thesis in any way. Do you allow the student to give the speech? If so, what kind of evaluation do you make?

QUESTIONS FOR REVIEW

1. What was the point made by Quintilian regarding the "good man" theory?
2. What were Aristotle's three criteria for inspiring confidence in the orator's character?
3. Why was Joseph McCarthy censured by the U.S. Senate? Which of Aristotle's ethical criteria did he violate?
4. What ethical infraction did Oliver North commit? What arguments did he use in his defense?
5. What is meant by the term *sophistry?* Why are sophists often able to get away with specious reasoning and unsupported claims?
6. What is the Latin phrase for "let the buyer beware"?
7. What are other arguments cited in the text that are commonly used to justify questionable ethical behavior?
8. What is meant by *utilitarian ethics?* Who was the philosopher who espoused it?
9. Who was the American author who wrote the essay "Civil Disobedience?" Who was the civil rights leader who practiced the principles described in the essay? What do we have to understand about civil disobedience before we go out and break a law we don't like?
10. What did Immanuel Kant mean by *categorical imperatives?* How does Kant's philosophy differ from that of John Stuart Mill?
11. When Thomas Jefferson wrote, "All men are created equal . . . and are endowed . . . with certain unalienable rights," to whom was he referring?
12. What happened in the town of My Lai on March 16, 1968? Explain how utilitarian ethics and categorical imperatives relate to this event.
13. Describe how John Rawls of Harvard University believes that the rules of society ideally should be created.
14. What are three reasons in the text that give value to having a code of ethics? What are the principal responsibilities that might be included in a speaker's code of ethics?

S P E A K I N G
O P P O R T U N I T I E S

SHORT SPEECHES FOR SPECIAL OCCASIONS

The expression *giving a speech* has an ominous sound to it. It suggests the need to spend hours in the library researching a topic, writing an outline, making notes, and practicing the delivery. A long speech certainly may require all of that. But many times, a talk you are called on to give will be short and need very little preparation. The principles that have been described so far in this text are still going to apply; the only difference will be that what you say can be compacted into what we might call a "minispeech." Although that term sounds easier and a lot less demanding, there are still a great many people who make contorted efforts to avoid making even the shortest announcements if there are more than a dozen people listening. Having a willingness to speak to groups makes it possible for you to provide a valuable service to others, and at the same time contribute to your own personal growth, self-esteem, and professional advancement. Let's look at a few of the opportunities you might have to make a minispeech.

Introducing a Speaker

When you are called on to introduce a speaker, you need to consider that you are performing two functions: You are giving a brief speech of your own, but you are also part of the presentation that is to be made by the major speaker. Your own speech must have an introduction, a main idea, specific details, and a conclusion. At the same time, you must remember that what you say is designed primarily to help the person you are introducing gain the attention of the audience. Your most important purpose is to pave the way for the main event by generating interest in the topic and establishing the credentials and expertise of the speaker. Here are some ways you can accomplish that:

- Begin by welcoming the audience. Let the listeners know you are glad they could come.
- Relieve the speaker of any mundane responsibilities such as asking the audience members not to smoke and telling them where the bathrooms are.

- When you start your introduction, use the speaker's full name and title; make sure your pronunciation is correct.
- Tell what position the speaker currently holds and what recent accomplishments he or she has made that pertain to the subject matter of the speech.
- Relate a bit of the speaker's personal history and perhaps an anecdote that conveys some of his or her endearing qualities. You want to portray the speaker as being a likable person.
- Don't say, "Our speaker today needs no introduction." It's trite, and it may not be true.
- Don't exaggerate the speaker's wisdom or capabilities; it will embarrass the person and may cause the audience to become disappointed.
- Conclude your introduction with a cue for the audience to applaud. You can say simply, "Please welcome Mr. So-and-so," and then yield the podium.

Always remember when you are giving a speech of introduction that it's not you who are the featured attraction. You may be very interested in the topic and perhaps even know a lot about it. But be sure you don't preempt the speaker's remarks by making your own editorial comments about the subject matter. Doing that is intrusive and may, in fact, conflict with the speaker's message.

Expressing a Word of Thanks

Special occasions such as large dinner parties, business conventions, class reunions, weekend workshops, or daylong seminars require a great deal of planning and preparation on the part of the people who organize them. Often that work is done on a volunteer basis, and the individuals who put in their time need to be recognized for their efforts. At some point during the occasion, either at the beginning or at the end, take the initiative to give a word of thanks to those who made the event possible. When you do this, make sure you get the attention of everyone, have the people who are receiving acknowledgement stand, know all of them by name, if possible, and make sure you don't leave out anyone. After you have said the words to express your thanks, start the applause so that others in the audience will follow suit. The main thing is that you want the ones being honored to feel affirmed.

Making an Award

An award presentation is a short occasional speech that you might need to give when someone achieves something special, such as winning a tournament, receiving a scholarship, or graduating with honors. Again, start by getting the attention of the group; then call up the one who is to receive the award and have the person stand beside you. Next, describe the reason the person is being honored and what he or she was required to accomplish. You might want to give a bit of the history of the award itself so that people will appreciate the significance of the achievement. After that, tell the audience about the qualifications of the person receiving the award. Make the presentation short, and be sure that the focus is on the recipient rather than on yourself.

Announcing a Coming Event

If you are a member of a club or an organization, you know that there are many occasions when announcements have to be made about coming events. You may wonder why such an effort is necessary. It seems as though we should simply be able to post a notice on the bulletin board and let people read it for themselves. The fact of the matter is that flyers or written memos do not have the same impact as the oral message. A speaker can generate interest and communicate a sense of importance that cannot be conveyed effectively by the printed word. To announce a coming event, make sure you have in your mind everything the audience needs to know. If you have any concern about forgetting, write the details down on a note card before you begin. Use the same methodology that the journalist uses: Tell *what* the event is, *who* is invited, *why* it is important, *how much* it will cost, *where* it is to be held, *when* it will start, and *how long* it will last. The audience members might also want to know whether it's a benefit for a cause, how often it will be repeated, and if they need to get tickets in advance. Try to be as well-informed as you can, and be sure to convey enthusiasm. After you have made the announcement, you can provide reinforcement by posting a written notice or giving handout sheets to people who are interested.

Calling for Volunteers

Public speaking is an important part of leadership, because it's a skill that makes it possible for you to mobilize other people to support a cause. You may be a creative and hardworking person, but if you can't recruit others to help, you will be limited in the amount you are able to accomplish. Getting people involved has multiple benefits. You as the initiator receive the help you need, the project gets completed, the burden of the task is distributed so that no one person is overloaded, and the persons recruited receive the satisfaction of being part of a team effort. A mistake you want to avoid when you are asking for volunteers is to be apologetic about it. You are, of course, requesting that people take time away from their busy schedules, but you have to be sure in your mind that what you are having them do is worthwhile. Begin by describing the task that needs to be done and what results you expect to achieve; let the group know that skills are needed and how much time and effort is going to be involved. Be sure you are realistic. Don't say it's going to be easy if it's not. Don't minimize the skill level that is required if what you want is quality work. Let the people know how firm a commitment they are making and the extent to which you are counting on them. When you get your volunteers, write down names and phone numbers, and make a follow-up call to each without delay.

Giving a Toast

Making a toast at a wedding or any special occasion is a long-standing tradition. To do this well you must have a close connection to the people being toasted and be familiar with the values of those who are to share in the toast. The most important element at this kind of speaking occasion is sincerity. The toast may have a humorous twist to it, but it also needs to be seriously affirming, with perhaps a touch of sentimentality. It does not have to be elaborately developed; it can be a single thought. However, you still need to gain the attention of the audience, identify the subject, express the main idea, and end with a concluding statement, just as you do in any other speech. For example:

> May I offer a toast—to my readers! They have mastered all the prerequisites to this course; they have endured discussions on the theory of oral communication; they have tolerated my occasional verbosity; they have placed themselves in harm's way as speakers at the lectern. May they receive the applause of their fellow students for their efforts.

FORMATS FOR SPEAKING OCCASIONS

On some occasion, you may be the organizer of a public speaking event and will need to handle the logistics, such as setting up the chairs, placing the microphones, and so on. You may also be the one to establish the format for the program. There are a number of different ways you can arrange to have information communicated orally to an audience.

Interview

A two-person interview is the simplest and most basic unit of interpersonal communication. It can be private, of course, but when we add an audience to the model, we have a format for public address. There are several reasons that it is valuable for us to examine the dynamics of an interview: It is a prominent format for newscasts and public affairs programs on radio and television, and it's an effective way to help knowledgeable people structure their comments when they have not had public speaking training. What you are doing when you interview someone is drawing out the information that interests you (and the audience) without letting the person go off on tangents that are not relevant to the main idea. In other words, the interviewer provides the organizational structure whereas the person being interviewed relates the information.

You as the Person Interviewed

The interview format is a good place to begin your own public speaking training. Select a topic that is familiar to you. Then, sit down in private with the person who will be conducting the interview and work out a set of questions that pertain to the subject matter. The interviewer will do the audience analysis and will guide you into presenting the most pertinent information. You, of course, will also be able to suggest questions that lead into aspects of the subject you think are interesting. When you have your list of questions, arrange them in a logical sequence and think about how you are going to respond to each one. Now you are ready to do the interview in front of a real audience. In its entirety, the interview contains all the elements of a conventional speech. However, the only responsibility you have is to provide the substance in the body of the presentation; the interviewer will do the introduction and the conclusion.

You as the Interviewer

When you are to be the interviewer for a public presentation, take time before you meet the audience to find out what questions the person to be interviewed wishes you to ask. During the interview, you can extemporize around your list of questions if he or she is reasonably experienced, but it would be discourteous of you to ask something that is going to cause the person embarrassment. The interview format is designed to allow people an opportunity to make the best case they can for the idea they want to express. Your job is to help them do that. Don't turn the interview into a debate, and don't start making a speech of your own.

Symposium

One of the more structured formats is an arrangement called a *symposium.* In setting up a speaking occasion of this kind you would first decide on a topic— one that is clearly stated but fairly broad. Suppose you are considering "Alternative Energy Sources in a Petroleum-Based Society." A topic such as this gives speakers a general direction but enough latitude to pursue their own interests. Usually, a symposium consists of five or six people who prepare their remarks independently of one another and speak in turn on a given topic for a specific length of time. The topic may be either of an informative or a controversial nature, and the participants may or may not agree with one another's points of view. After all the speakers have made their presentations, they may be given the opportunity to respond to questions from the audience or perhaps interact in a less formally structured exchange of ideas. The symposium is not competitive; it is designed to offer information and, perhaps, arguments that members of an audience can consider and evaluate.

Panel Discussion

A typical format frequently used on television is the *panel discussion.* This arrangement can also accommodate five or six speakers but is less structured than the symposium. Generally, the panel discussion will have a moderator who will introduce the topic and pose questions to the panelists. There is no set order in which the participants speak and no specified time limit for each one.

They react to the questions as they are moved to do so, and they direct their attention to each other as well as to the audience. In many respects, the panel discussion is similar to a conversation; the difference is that the panelists know that an audience is listening and that they need to project their voices with enough volume so that they can be heard beyond their immediate circle. Panel members may prepare for a discussion and may even bring notes, but they know that they are not going to express all of their comments from start to finish without interruption. They need to be flexible, to listen to what other panelists say, and to be able to respond in an impromptu fashion. The moderator is responsible for getting the discussion started and providing some closure at the end.

INDEX